EVIL
BESIDE HER

The True Story of a Texas Woman's Marriage to a Dangerous Psycopath

KATHRYN CASEY

(Originally published as *The Rapist's Wife*)

HARPER

An Imprint of HarperCollins*Publishers*

EVIL BESIDE HER is a journalistic account of the 1992 investigation and conviction of James Edward Bergstrom on five counts of rape in Houston, Texas. The events recounted in this book are true, although some of the names have been changed and identifying characteristics altered to safeguard the privacy of certain individuals. The personalities, events, actions, and conversations in this book have been constructed using court documents, including public transcripts, extensive interviews, letters, personal papers, research, and press accounts.

Originally published as *The Rapist's Wife*

HARPER

An Imprint of HarperCollins*Publishers*
10 East 53rd Street
New York, New York 10022-5299

Copyright © 1995 by Kathryn Casey
Afterword copyright © 2008 by Kathryn Casey
ISBN 978-0-06-158201-1

First Harper paperback printing: November 2008

HarperCollins® and Harper® are trademarks of HarperCollins Publishers.

Printed in the United States of America

Visit Harper paperbacks on the World Wide Web at
www.harpercollins.com

10 9 8 7 6 5 4 3 2

To Linda Bergstrom for her courage and her willingness to tell her story so those who follow may be believed. And to Ashley Bergstrom—may she always remember that children are not responsible for the sins of their fathers.

Author's Notes

Chris, Tina, James C., Irene, and Maria Bergstrom refused requests for interviews. Accounts of events and conversations involving them were principally reconstructed from interviews with Linda, James, and Adelaide Bergstrom, and public records. James Bergstrom has neither confessed to nor been convicted of any rapes or attempted sexual assaults in Washington State. The account of his confession to such crimes is as recounted by Linda Bergstrom.

In addition, some physical descriptions and names have been changed throughout this book, including Linda's maiden name, those of all James Bergstrom's victims, and some who played minor roles in his story: Caesar, Mack, John, Sam McDonald, Eddie Smith, Sally and Bill Rogers, Jane Richards, Penny Jacobs, Gayle Thomas, Diane Siler, and Colt Hargraves.

Acknowledgments

As with any project of this scope, there are many people to thank: my parents for raising an inquisitive child; my husband and children for their patience with my frequent absences while I was off chasing a hot story; my editors at *Ladies' Home Journal:* Myrna Blyth, Jane Farrell, Pamela Guthrie O'Brien, and Shana Aborn for the opportunities and support they've given me throughout my long association with the magazine. In fact, I first sought Linda Bergstrom out for an article for the *Journal,* an article that ran in July 1993.

Then there are those directly involved in the task of shaping *Evil Beside Her.* Thanks to: Sandy Sheehy and Claire Cassidy, who critiqued, guided, and encouraged my original proposal; my agent, Philip Spitzer, who took a chance on a Houston magazine writer who wanted to write her first book; Lisa Wager, my initial editor at Avon Books, for believing in Linda's story; Tom Colgan, who took over the project after Lisa's departure, for his enthusiasm while steering the book through to publication; Jim Loosen at JAL Data Research Services in Olympia, Washington, and his magic computer for helping to track down sources; Shari Hall for many, many hours of transcribing taped interviews.

Special thanks are deserved by Jane Farrell and Claire Cassidy, my two dedicated readers. I know there were many times, especially weekends and evenings, when projects of their own were put on hold while they dissected my latest chapters. I am grateful for their counsel. They are truly cherished friends.

Finally, I would like to thank the many people who shared their hospitality and their stories with me, some named in the book, others not. I am especially grateful to Linda Bergstrom and the other women victimized by James Bergstrom who agreed to be interviewed. They are members of a painful sisterhood, and I appreciate their courage, their honesty, and their friendship.

—Kathryn Casey
1994

Prologue

September 30, 1992

The wait, like September's typically hot Texas weather, was stifling. Inside the courtroom, witnesses, victims, and reporters clustered together. Their strained murmurs reminded Linda Bergstrom of mourners at a wake. In fact, much of the scene felt funereal. Scanning the courtroom, she noticed her mother-in-law, petite, fiftyish, with salt-and-pepper hair and a heart-shaped face, huddled with her husband in a center pew. Like his son, James C. Bergstrom was slight in stature, a spare, angular man, but with a roof of white hair and rheumy-eyed behind thick-lensed glasses. Although he usually had a ramrod-straight, military bearing, this day James C. appeared stooped and tired. Linda wondered fleetingly if she was supposed to feel sorry for the Bergstroms. She didn't.

Then Linda glanced toward the judge's imposing bench and the narrow defense table where her ex-husband sat eerily still. Ex-husband. A reassuring designation, she mused. As she knew he would—he had throughout much of the two-day hearing—James Edward Bergstrom assessed her icily, his dark hair cut short, his hazel eyes hollows in a face ashen from six months in a sunless Houston jail cell. As she watched, a bailiff approached James, took him by the arm, and pulled him to his feet to take him to a holding cell while the jury deliberated. As he sauntered off, James grinned at

Linda, catlike. She spun away, but not before her skin chilled. It's almost over, she thought, *almost over.*

One hour passed, then another. She sat alone, shunning the television, magazine, and newspaper reporters scattered throughout the room. There had been no actual trial; James Bergstrom had pleaded guilty on five counts. What the jury deliberated was his sentence. It seemed preposterous, but the court-appointed defense attorney was asking for probation, arguing these were his first convictions and that a Texas prison would only turn James Bergstrom into an even more brutal man. "You never know what a jury will do," the assistant district attorney prosecuting the case had cautioned Linda. Even in the guarded safety of the Harris County Criminal Courthouse, she was frightened. If James was released, she knew he would want revenge—against her.

What if they let him out? She shuddered. *They can't let him out.*

Seated in one of the courtroom's massive oak pews, Linda cut a diminutive figure. At twenty-nine, she had shoulder-length chestnut brown hair falling softly around large, almond-shaped eyes. She wasn't stop-traffic pretty, but lithe and appealing with an unmistakable aura of vulnerability, detectable in her slight frown, the shy downturn of her dark eyes.

But there was another side to Linda—a flinty determination, the strength she relied on throughout the seven torturous years she was married to James. Without it, she could never have endured the endless abuse, the physical battering and its emotional and psychological carnage. But the worst was learning something so repugnant, so vile, about her husband that acknowledging it always made her stomach roil—her husband, her daughter's father, was a rapist.

The thought of it filled her with such anger, such hatred, such confusion and humiliation, she felt her face flash hot. Once she discovered who she was married to, Linda had refused to remain silent. She would have shouted the truth from a street corner in downtown Houston, if that would have stopped him. Laughing, James told her to tell the world. He wasn't worried. "No one will listen to you," he taunted. For a long time, he was right.

James C. and Irene Bergstrom were two of those she confided in. In fact, she had once brought James's paraphernalia to their house—a rope and handcuffs, the tools of a rapist.

When the Bergstroms refused to help her, she called the Houston Police Department and warned them to be on the lookout for her husband. A dispatcher listened sympathetically, but it would be years before anyone at HPD followed up on her suspicions. *No one believed me,* Linda remembered. *No one.*

Still, she kept trying. How could she not? Every time her husband left their apartment, she feared he would attack again, another woman, someone's wife, mother, daughter, added to his roster of pain. In the end, it was Linda who endured. In December 1991, a Houston detective assigned to the sex crimes unit listened and believed. It was another three months before police had enough evidence to arrest James Bergstrom. By that time, Bergstrom himself admitted he'd raped or attempted to rape as many as thirty women.

When she finally looked at her watch, it was after four P.M. and the jury had been sequestered for more than two hours. Gathering her courage, Linda sought out four of her ex-husband's victims, banded together whispering just inside the courtroom door. She felt compelled to speak to them. The women's testimony had touched her deeply. One, a lithesome mother of two in her twenties, had the look of a cowgirl. James had raped her as her two-year-old daughter cowered in terror under a table. Another had been so traumatized the afternoon James Bergstrom hid in her apartment, tied her to her bed, and raped her that she'd spent five weeks in a psychiatric hospital. More than a year later, the frail woman in the flowered dress continued to sleep with a light on.

Once a rape victim herself, Linda recognized their pain. She hoped they could understand hers.

As if they expected Linda to join their circle, the women parted, making room for her. "I want y'all to know how sorry I am," she said, her voice hoarse with emotion. "I wished I could have stopped him sooner. I tried."

Just then, a buzzer sounded twice in the courtroom. The jury was in. The bailiff led a sullen and angry James back to the defense table as twelve jurors—ten women and two men—shuffled into place in the jury box. Linda searched their faces, but they were as blank as unused paper.

Hurrying back to her seat to await the verdict, Linda left the cluster of women at the door.

"Who's that?" she heard one query softly as she retreated.

"That's *his* wife," whispered another. "The rapist's wife."

Yet so love precedes hatred,
desire precedes aversion,
hope precedes despair,
fear precedes daring,
and joy precedes sadness.
>   —St. Thomas Aquinas
>   *Summa Theologica,* Part I

Evil flourishes far more in the shadows than in the light of day.

>   —Jawaharlal Nehru
>   *The Unity of India* (1937)

PART ONE

Chapter One

What attracts one person to another has long fascinated poets, perfumers, psychologists, astrologists, and biologists. Is it an emotional, spiritual, or physical link that binds a man and a woman? Unable to diagnose passion, experts have relegated the phenomenon to the territory of the unknown. "No human creature can give orders to love," dismissed George Sand. "Do you know how uncontrolled and unreliable the average human being is in all that concerns sexual life?" asked Sigmund Freud.

When a union turns violent, criminologists are left to ponder the dilemma of what first drew, and later bound, a woman to her lover/abuser. Why didn't she just get out? they ask. Such large numbers of those battered as adults were abused as children that decades ago experts reluctantly came to one conclusion: Somewhere—whether in DNA or day-to-day experience—there is a force at work that defies random coupling. Abusers and victims seek each other out.

After it was all over, with the acute perception of hindsight, Linda would conclude life had set her up for James Bergstrom. That she had been bred to accept violence. And that their union was a tragedy she was fated to live.

The neighborhood in which Linda Martinez, nicknamed Lily by her family, grew up is the type of uniquely Houston setting only possible because of the city's lack of zoning. Businesses and industries mix with homes in a patchwork of

unrestrained urban development. Tucked just outside the 610
Loop, the area is bounded by two thoroughfares on which
strips of prefabricated metal warehouses, stores, and factories are interrupted only by the occasional tavern or storefront church. Nearby is a heavily industrial district bordering
railroad tracks. Even on quiet side streets, like the one on
which Linda's parents, Santos and Jesse Martinez, bought a
modest frame house in 1963, the homes are interlaced with
small factories and businesses.

Despite strong Hispanic roots, both Santos and Jesse were
born in the United States, the children of Mexican and Span-
ish parents respectively who immigrated in search of opportunity. They met in Arcola, a small town southwest of
Houston where Santos's parents raised ten children surrounded by trees and rolling acres to run. In 1958 they married and moved to Houston to start a family. The children
came quickly: first Gino, then Mary, Linda on Halloween
day, October 31, 1963, Alice, and finally Daniel. Another
son died at the age of two, a victim of pneumonia.

The Martinez house, sitting firmly in the center of the
block, was proud if modest. Its white clapboard exterior
was faded but not unkempt. Its yard, like those of its neighbors, was encircled in a sturdy metal fence to ward off the
encroaching violence of the city. Inside, it was well maintained, decorated with framed religious prints depicting the
Virgin Mary and the Sacred Heart of Jesus amidst photographs of the couple's five children. Jesse had a good job
working days in the shipping department at Devoe & Raynolds, a regional plant for the national company which
manufactured paint for stores throughout the Southwest.
The factory was just a short walk over the railroad tracks
from the house. Each evening when Santos, a seamstress,
returned from work, the Martinez house filled with the pungent aroma of frying corn tortillas and simmering tomatoes.

Despite its peaceful facade, Linda's childhood home was
a terrifying place. "It was like a prison camp," she would
say, with a grimace. Of course, there were the happy times:

fishing trips, parties, weddings, *quinceañeras* (elaborate fifteenth-birthday celebrations in Hispanic cultures that mark a girl's entry to womanhood), picnics, and afternoons on the beach. Yet from the beginning, Jesse, a short, stocky man with dark brown hair and strong, thick hands, was a frightening presence. Though he worked all day and often drank with cronies at night, when he was home, the family trembled under his domination.

One of Linda's earliest memories was of an incident when she was five. "My father was angry with me because I got up off the couch. We were never allowed to walk around unless we got permission," she whispered. "He took a belt and began walloping me." Santos stepped in to save her middle daughter and shared in the flogging. Days later both were still marked with bruised reminders of the battering.

According to Linda, when she was nine the physical abuse turned sexual. It began one morning as she stood on a footstool washing dishes. Her brothers and sisters were relegated to the living room, where they silently watched Sunday morning church shows on television. Her mother was visiting a neighbor. Alone in the kitchen, Linda heard her father enter, so quickly she at first feared his intention was to punish her for some minor offense. Instead, he pulled her toward him, groping between her legs. To her surprise, he stroked and fondled her. Linda wasn't sure what he was doing or why, but something told her it wasn't right. "I was terrified," said Linda. "I cried so hard, I couldn't stop."

The scene, she maintains, repeated itself twice more. After the final incident, Linda cried so uncontrollably, despite her father's threats, that her mother, who was in another part of the house, came to investigate. Pressing her head against her mother's chest, Linda recounted amid sobs her accusations against her father. Jesse Martinez denied Linda's accusations, yet an angry Santos warned her husband, "If this is true, it better not ever happen again."

By the time she was ten, Linda had become a reclusive yet pragmatic child. Since the alleged sexual abuse took place when she was alone with her father, the solution was not to be alone with him. "She would follow me wherever I went," said Santos. "Lily became my quiet, little shadow." On Saturdays when her mother cleaned another house on the block, Linda would tag along silently behind.

Still there was the physical battering, usually administered with her father's belt. Here, too, in Linda's methodical, childlike calculations, there had to be a way to survive. At first she, like her brothers and sisters, hid in her bedroom terrified as her father patrolled the house, cursing and screaming. When hiding failed to spare her from his wrath, Linda reasoned there had to be another option. "I began crying even before he hit me," said Linda, explaining how she eventually escaped Jesse Martinez's rage. "And I'd pretend that he'd already damaged me, that when I got upset, my hands didn't work right. My mother would scream that he'd get arrested if he hit me and he'd better leave me alone. Usually he did."

Though she wanted to tell her siblings about her scheme, she knew she couldn't. If they all adopted her act, her father would realize it was nothing more than a child's ruse. Soon it would cease working for any of them. So although she was no longer a target, Linda was still subjected to watching her father exact punishment on her mother, brothers, and sisters. "Sometimes I just couldn't stand it," said Linda. "I thought if he hit them one more time, he'd kill them."

On occasions when the violence was so traumatic she simply couldn't bear it, Linda gathered the boldness to use her untouchable status to cool things down, wedging herself between her parents as they fought. "Down deep, Lily was always a tough little kid. She'd stand up for herself when the rest of us wouldn't," said Daniel, her youngest brother. Though she dared not do it often, at times her interference would surprise her father long enough for the situation to cool.

Still, Linda feared him. So much so that if she awoke at night in the bedroom she shared with her two sisters and needed to go to the bathroom, she would silently shiver, afraid of venturing the short distance through the house alone. She couldn't bear the prospect of a chance meeting with him. Often she would wet her bed before summoning the courage to hazard the darkened hallways of her own home.

As bad as things were, they only worsened one afternoon in 1972 when Jesse drove home after working the day shift at Devoe. Just as he passed over the railroad tracks, a dump truck hit him head-on. A family friend ran to the Martinez home to tell Santos her husband had been gravely injured. By the time Linda saw her father, he was in Ben Taub, Houston's publicly funded hospital and trauma center, his head was swathed in white bandages, and she soon realized that he didn't recognize her or any of her brothers and sisters. Linda, then nine, recalls feeling conflicted about whether she preferred her father to live or die. When he returned home, weeks later, she often concluded she would have been better off if he had died.

While his rages had plagued the family for years, the Jesse Martinez who returned to the small, white clapboard house was even more obsessively controlling than before. With a steel plate covering part of his skull and nerve damage to his legs making it impossible for him to work, Linda's father was a constant presence in the household. He was the invalid, his spells the reason ambulances were called in the middle of the night. With braces on his legs, his pride kept him from tolerating even his children's laughter. "Whenever we'd giggle or laugh, he always assumed we were laughing at him," explained Linda. "That he was a cripple and we were making fun of him."

After his return, the children were relegated below to-be-seen-and-not-heard status. He ordered them to sit quietly at all times, their hands folded on their laps. If they stood up or talked without permission, they were subject to his vengeance. Their every move was his concern. Even when they studied, he was not happy, sometimes turning off the electricity so they would have no light to read by. Day after day, they were barred from playing outside with friends, instead banished to their rooms. The happy times became those brief episodes when Santos and Jesse drove off together, leaving the children at home. They escaped, spilling over the street and yard. Bounding with pent-up energy, the Martinez brood ran the block. "Sometimes we played kick ball and made too much noise and we wouldn't hear them drive in," said Linda. "When that happened we all rushed inside and hid in our rooms. We knew he'd be coming and that he would be furious."

Santos Martinez, a handsome woman on whom the pain of the years, like the dark circles under her eyes, hung heavy and thick, understood her children were suffering. Finally she determined her husband's reign of terror had to end. With her brood urging her on, she ordered him out. "Jesse was acting crazy, he even waved a gun threatening to kill the whole family," she said. Still he came around, one night attempting to force his way into the house. Terrified, Linda and her brothers and sisters barricaded the door with a sofa. As Jesse's youngest daughter, Alice, watched through a window, in desperation he feigned a heart attack, throwing himself to the ground clutching his chest. When no one opened the door to investigate, he reluctantly left. Days later, Santos filed for divorce.

As the late seventies approached, Linda was developing into a vaguely troubled but beautiful teenager. She made average grades in school. Though the family had little money, the freedom afforded by her father's absence made her feel wealthy. Like her girlfriends, she craved rock 'n' roll and fast cars. She suffered the occasional crush, and sometimes her mother fretted, with a laugh, that she was becoming "boy-crazy."

By the time she turned fifteen, Linda was five feet tall and slender. She had an infectious laugh and a wide smile. Only those who looked closely would see that it often melted into a slight frown. That year, Linda was allowed to date for the first time. In school, her boyfriend was considered a real catch. He was not only handsome but played bass guitar in a neighborhood Latin band. With typical teenage enthusiasm, Linda felt her life was changing, that from here on out, nothing would ever hurt her again.

Of course, she was wrong.

One night when Santos was busy, she asked a close friend to watch over Linda. The older woman offered to take the teenager to a local club to hear a popular new group. Linda agreed. The club was a hot, smoky place filled with a Latin beat and the pungent odors of alcohol and sweat. There, Linda happened upon the manager of her boyfriend's band. He was a bossy, disagreeable man at least ten years her senior, who had never paid any attention to her in the past. This night, however, was different. As Santos's friend danced, he plied Linda—who had little experience with alcohol—with one drink after another. When she didn't drink fast enough, he playfully chided her for falling behind. Before long Linda felt fuzzy-headed and giddy. Then the older man whispered that he had something in his van for her, a copy of a new publicity photo just taken of her boyfriend and the other members of the band. "Would you like one?" he asked with a smile. Linda jumped at the chance and padded along behind him as he headed for the parking lot.

The moments after he opened the back of the baby blue van and motioned for her to go inside will live with Linda forever. Instantly he was on top of her, pushing her head against the corroded metal of the van's filthy floor. Pinning her arms above her head and pressing against her with one knee, he shoved up her dress, then yanked down her panty hose. She could hear the rhythmic beat of Latin music pounding in the distance and smell the stench of liquor on his breath. "I was crying, shouting, 'Stop it. Stop it,'" said Linda. "I couldn't believe what was happening."

It was over in minutes. She crouched in the corner of the van as he smiled down at her, zipped up his fly, and cinched his belt. When she asked why he had done it, he simply laughed.

Linda returned to the club in tears. Her mother's friend asked what happened, but she didn't answer. In her bed that night, she cried herself to sleep. By morning, she had decided not to tell anyone about the rape. Her mother had enough of her own problems keeping the family together, she reasoned; why burden her? In the glare of daylight she faced the sobering reality of how it had happened, and concluded it must have been—at least partly—her fault. Why had she followed him outside? Into the van? For a picture? Shouldn't she have known better? "Could I have stopped it?" she pondered. "I couldn't shake the feeling that somehow, I was to blame."

More than anything, Linda wanted to put it out of her mind, to bury it forever. But she couldn't. From that night on, the horror in her nights was no longer her father but the man who had raped her. The nightmares were terrifying. She could hear the music, smell the alcohol, and relive the pain in her loins when he forced himself inside her.

For months after the rape, Linda drifted, unable to concentrate or care about much of anything. In her junior year, she dropped out of school. Without a high school diploma or a car for transportation, she spent long hours at home, occasionally picking up a job baby-sitting. Later she applied at a nearby McDonald's and was hired to work the counter part-time. When it came to the preoccupations of most girls her age, Linda had little enthusiasm. Especially when it came to dating. "I pretty much stayed off boys completely," she said. "I stayed yards away from them."

The truth was that Linda was never quite the same after the rape. It seemed her natural enthusiasm would be evermore underlaid with cynicism. "I felt like men wanted one thing from any woman—sex," she said. "I felt like I couldn't trust them, any of them."

That didn't mean that men weren't attracted to her. Linda

had developed into a desirable woman, and there was always one man or another expressing interest in her.

Finally, as months and then years passed, Linda relented. She did enjoy men. She enjoyed their company. They couldn't all be bad. Assessing the situation with the same logical approach she employed to plot a way out of her family's violence, Linda concluded the solution was really quite simple—she needed a chaperone. Her choice was easy. Her older brother, Gino, had already married and left the house. From then on, Daniel, three years her junior, became her protector. Every time she agreed to a date, she insisted on bringing her little brother along. "She'd say, 'Come on with us. I don't want to go out with this guy alone,'" recalled Daniel. "She was real skittish around men. She was real particular about who she saw."

It was in January of 1984—when she was twenty—that Linda first heard the name James Bergstrom. A family friend who worked at Devoe—the same factory where her father once worked—said he wanted to introduce her to a shy co-worker. "He's quiet, real quiet and gentlemanly," Caesar told her. "You'll like James." One of Caesar's relatives was celebrating a *quinceañeras* the following weekend, and he suggested they make that their first date.

It had been almost four years since the rape, but the nightmares still haunted her sleep, so—despite her friend's confidence—Linda was worried. She decided to put off her decision until she had a chance to talk to her brother Gino, who had followed in his father's footsteps and also worked at Devoe. That night she called Gino's apartment and asked him, "Do you know James Bergstrom?"

"Sure," said Gino. "James works at the plant. I've played basketball with him and had a few beers. He's a nice guy. Quiet. But really a nice guy. You got nothin' to worry about with him."

The next time Caesar called, Linda said it was all right to give her telephone number to his friend.

A few days later, the phone rang. When her mother called her to answer it, Linda put the headset to her ear and said, "Hello."

"Hi," a soft-spoken man answered. "I'm James Bergstrom. Caesar said I should give you a call."

Chapter Two

That night on the phone, James told Linda a little about himself: that he was the oldest in a family of four children, that his father was once in the air force, that his mother was born in Greece, and that the Bergstroms were a staunchly Catholic family. He even mentioned that he was once an altar boy. "You're Catholic, aren't you?" he asked.

"Yes," she answered. "I am."

By the end of the conversation, they had agreed to a date the following Saturday night. Linda, however, preferred not to follow Caesar's suggestion and attend the *quinceañeras*. "They'll have Latin music, and I really like rock 'n' roll," she told him.

Instead, they decided, James would call for her at her home around seven and they would make plans then. "I like to be spontaneous," Linda laughed.

"Me too," said James, whose voice was quiet yet friendly.

After she hung up the phone, Linda realized she had forgotten to mention bringing Daniel along on the date. "Then I decided that was silly. I didn't need Daniel. I knew where James worked, knew people who knew him," she said. "As far as I could tell, I didn't have any reason to be afraid."

Of course, James Edward Bergstrom failed to mention many things that night, things that would have made Linda feel vastly less secure. For a young man—then, like Linda, just twenty—he already had many secrets.

* * *

As far as it went, all of what James said about himself and his family on the telephone that night was true. His father, James C., was born in Brooklyn, New York. He'd served in the air force from 1959 to 1971. His exploits were part of the family's folklore: In military security, he had once traveled with a briefcase chained to his wrist, and there were still classified incidents he referred to in the obliquest terms, barred—he swore—by an oath to secrecy and national security. It was when he was stationed in Greece that James C. met his future bride, Irene Emanuel Lagoudaki, a seamstress, one afternoon when he dropped off a buddy who dated her older sister. James's future parents kept company for about a year before they married.

Their first child, James Edward Bergstrom, was born in the 36th Tactical Hospital on the U.S. Air Force base in Bitburg, Germany, at four on a Saturday morning, April 6, 1963. A chubby infant, he was just eighteen inches long yet weighed nine pounds twelve ounces. Their second son, Christopher, came less than a year later, followed by their first daughter, Maria, in 1967, in Tripoli, Libya, where the family was then stationed. Five years later the Bergstroms moved back to the United States, where the baby of the family, Adelaide, was born.

Catholicism was the centerpiece of the Bergstrom household, but from the beginning they were far from a picture-perfect family. James C. had started drinking when he was a teenager, and when drunk, he had a blustering temper. "My father is an alcoholic. My mom was the only normal one," said Adelaide about their family life. "She never did anything crazy, except letting it all go on."

Unlike Linda's father, however, James would say that when it came to their mother, his father's rages were strictly verbal. Neither James nor Adelaide recalled an instance when their father physically abused his wife. Instead, according to James, he and his younger brother, Chris, were the prey of much of his father's anger. Years later, he would recount how his father, with his mother screaming in the background, would often strike him. "He hit me in the head a lot," said James. "I remember he picked me up one time when I was five or six and he threw me on the floor from over his head. I thought I was going to die."

When his father left the air force in 1971, the family settled in a small eastern Pennsylvania town. Handy with electronics, James C. secured a job with a local company. Later he hired on with a sign company in Peru, Indiana. One of his accounts was Notre Dame, where he was in charge of the football scoreboard. Because of his position, James C. was able to take the family to all the games. "It was great," said James. But it was only a brief respite. Looking back, James would say that their home life was never what he would consider "quite normal." "My father was an alcoholic, my mother is Greek, not Americanized," said James. "All the time we were being raised, they always seemed different than other kids' parents."

If the Bergstroms were an odd couple, they would later insist that in the beginning their firstborn son appeared very normal. He was a good student. He loved sports, especially basketball and tennis. "James wasn't a bad kid," his mother lamented in her deep, brooding voice. Then she dismissed the man he became as beyond reason. "I don't know what happened to him."

Whatever happened, it undoubtedly had its roots in James's early life. Looking back, he would remember it as a tumultuous and often painful time. His family moved often, never allowing him to form any long-term friendships. When he was seven he attended a parochial school in Pennsylvania where the nuns were strict and kept the girls and boys divided on opposite sides of the classrooms. That year he also became an altar boy, serving mass along with the parish's priest.

It was when he was living in Peru, Indiana, that James would say everything began changing for him. That year he left a Catholic elementary school and enrolled in a public middle school. Immediately he felt like an outsider, as if the other students were continually teasing and picking on him, just because he was new. "I never felt like I belonged," he said. "I just didn't fit in."

Of his time at home in the Bergstrom household, James painted a portrait of an increasingly dysfunctional family. Sometimes during the summers, he would accompany his father to work. They traveled to Indianapolis and small towns around Peru where James C. rewired and repaired electrical signs. On the long drive home late at night, the older man would make James recite prayers over and over until they finally pulled into the parking lot of a tavern and James C. disappeared inside, leaving his son alone in the locked car. The then ten-year-old would wait for what felt like hours until his father returned to continue the journey home.

Along with his father's alcoholism, many of the old-world traditions Irene Bergstrom brought with her from Greece made James feel his family was estranged from those of his friends. In their bedroom, James's parents erected a small altar to the Virgin Mary. Every night the entire family spent twenty minutes or more saying the rosary, a ritualized link of Hail Marys and Our Fathers. "The church was always real important in our house," said James. "And there were things you just didn't talk about with our parents."

In Indiana, about the time James was trying so desperately to fit in, he began sensing he was different, apart from those around him, for more personal reasons—reasons he could never discuss with his parents. There were the voices he heard in his head: "whispers, they called my name." He would turn and no one was there. The voices made him afraid there was something wrong with him. Something bad. That fear was only reinforced when at the age of twelve he had a hallucination of a giant bat descending on him, landing on his chest and picking at his chin. He hit at it and screamed.

Sex was the other subject James Bergstrom instinctively knew he could never broach with his parents. At home his mother would change the channel on the television if a scene became intimate. This censoring, however, only made her young son more curious. By the time he was eleven, James's imagination of things sexual was flourishing. He found himself daydreaming often of what he knew was forbidden, and scenes on television sparked his imagination, especially depictions of women bound and gagged. One he often used as fodder for his fantasies was an episode of "It Takes a Thief" in which a woman was tied to a chair during a robbery. James never forgot how it seized his imagination as he sat mesmerized in front of the television. "That's when I started thinking about things," said James. "About someday doing that myself."

At night alone in his bed, he would masturbate, envisioning images he watched on television or sometimes bra and panty models he studied on the slick pages of a Sears catalog. Each time he felt guilty, conflicted, when he thought of what his parents and the priest at church would say if they knew. While it isn't unusual for adolescent boys to masturbate, it was what most titillated James that set him apart—fantasies of women in bondage.

Years later, a psychologist would analyze James Bergstrom and theorize that by early adolescence he had a history not unlike that of many serial rapists. He'd grown up in a middle-class family and claimed early physical and emotional abuse. He felt alienated from his family and had developed a strong imaginary world. And he had learned to rely on masturbating to deviant fantasies as a way to relieve tension.

The doctor would also speculate that more may have happened to James around the age of ten or eleven. Based on his dramatic metamorphosis, he would suggest that James—like 76 percent of all serial rapists—may have been sexually abused. If it did happen, James would maintain he had no such recollections. "I can't remember anything," he said later. "I've tried. Sometimes I think maybe, but I just don't know." Of course, it would not be atypical for James, like so many other victims of abuse, to have blocked out such traumatic memories.

At the age of twelve, James Bergstrom had his first girlfriend, a pretty Catholic girl named Michelle. James threw himself into the relationship, doting on her every wish. Although they were both just children, the Bergstrom family saw it as an important relationship. "We thought he was going to marry her," said his mother, Irene. But the following year, James's father was laid off from his job and the family was again moving. This time to Houston. Michelle was left behind.

To James it must have felt that he had no roots: Yanked from school to school, he had no consistency; his father's alcoholism was beyond his ability to understand or cope with it. "When he was drunk, all I could do was avoid him," said James. "I'd hide." By the time the Bergstroms arrived in the Houston area, James had become a reclusive adolescent, driven by the need to dominate even the smallest details, including having everything precisely in place in his room. Perhaps it was a way of building a pristine barrier to hide behind or a way to wrench some measure of restraint over his life. Whatever the case, he gradually found himself increasingly drawn to a mirage world where he—James Bergstrom—had power over another person, a woman—like those he saw on television—bound and gagged.

Chapter Three

Pearland, Texas, where the Bergstroms settled, was founded in 1882, fifteen miles south of downtown Houston and twenty-five miles west of Galveston Bay on the original route of the Santa Fe railroad. The first streets were cut over flat ranch lands by six yoke of oxen on a grader in 1894. The first brick school was built in 1911. Like its big-city neighbor, the city is a product of aggressive land developers who advertised it as a "garden spot with Gulf breezes and no malaria."

From the beginning, Pearland never quite lived up to its billing. The Christenson Land Corporation gave the town its name in the late 1890s when it sold off acreage hyped as pear orchards. But disease and insects continually attacked crops, and the 1900 hurricane that nearly leveled nearby Galveston ramshackled the town and ruined the orchards. A second land rush spearheaded by the Allison Richey company brought orange orchards, but those, too, failed to flourish and finally froze out in the winter of 1918. The town languished, never really taking root until it was fed, like most of Texas, by the big oil strikes of the 1930s.

Even more important for Houston's southeast suburbs was space travel—the industry of the future—which mushroomed in the sixties when President Lyndon B. Johnson pushed through funding for the National Aeronautics and Space Administration's (NASA) mission control, south of

Houston on formerly barren acres bordering Clear Lake. Twenty-five miles in circumference, the lake empties into Galveston Bay and eventually feeds into the Gulf of Mexico. High-paying, high-tech industries blossomed, and Pearland, along with Friendswood, Clear Lake City, and the southern reaches of Houston, all profited. Prosperity brought strip shopping centers, subdivisions, honky-tonk bars, and fast-food restaurants.

In 1976 when the Bergstrom family arrived and bought a home on the west side of town, Pearland, like all of the Houston area, was entering the boom years. Oil prices were spiraling upward and the nearby Houston ship channel was thriving, annually importing and exporting millions of gallons of oil, gasoline, and petroleum-based chemicals. On brisk days when those advertised Gulf breezes did reach Pearland, they often brought with them the faint stench of the pipeline jungle of chemical plants that hug the coastline. Before long James C. had a slot at Texas Instruments in the burgeoning computer industry as a fabrication equipment engineer. Irene Bergstrom found a position as a seamstress with a chain of bridal-wear shops.

The one-story home the Bergstroms bought in August of that year was in a blue-collar yet prosperous subdivision called Corrigan. To their neighbors, the family was a quiet yet friendly addition. James's father, who loved to work with his hands, often puttered with old televisions, phones, or small electrical appliances in the garage. More sociable than her reclusive husband, Irene Bergstrom always seemed happy to chat with neighbors. The four Bergstrom children were, from all appearances, not unlike the gang of others that lived up and down the surrounding blocks. James and his younger brother, Chris, loved sports and played often. James C. even raised a basketball backboard and hoop on the driveway for his sons. The two daughters, Maria and Adelaide, were attractive children, still in elementary school.

Few would have guessed the secrets the family hid inside their modest ranch house of off-white brick and chocolate brown trim.

One big secret, of course, was James C.'s drinking and the ways it affected all their lives. James, who was already troubled and confused, felt it continued to make a muddle of everything. As he would later describe it, the house was in continual chaos, never knowing when his father's temper would throw everything into an uproar. Always, before bringing anyone home, he would ask his friends to wait outside while he went in to check out the current situation and to ask his mother for permission.

In the neighborhood, James developed a small clique of friends. Most were a year or two younger than he, closer to his brother, Chris's, age, and all loved sports. They shot baskets, played baseball, sometimes tennis. A friend who grew up across the street from the Bergstroms remembers James as quiet and shy but a good athlete. Usually he would go out of his way to avoid a confrontation and rarely talked about his family, school, or anything but sports. Still there were times when the rage James was already masking inside broke loose: "James would get all hyped up. If he had a bad shot or didn't like a call, he'd holler and get angry," his friend remembers. "Really angry. More than the other kids. The truth was, James was competitive. He liked to win."

At Pearland Junior High School that fall, James was a good student, yet a reserved, "kind of nerdy" teenager. He hung with a group considered out of the mainstream, and because he was so noticeably shy, he was often the target of practical jokes. One day, for instance, a group of twelve- and thirteen-year-old girls surrounded him in the hallway, offering candies. James took one, amazed that they had sought him out. After he had eaten a few of the chocolate squares, they all giggled wildly. One girl, giddy as the rest, choked out the reason. The "candies" were actually chocolate-flavored laxatives.

James blushed, conscious of everyone in the hallway watching. Years later, his voice would take on a hard edge whenever he recounted the incident.

The following year, James entered Pearland High School, but little else changed. He was still treated as an outsider and easy prey. Later he would maintain just ambling through the hall could elicit taunts from the other students, who nick-named him "Turtle" because a classmate announced he resembled one. Others dubbed him "Ichabod Crane" after the lanky and awkward character in "The Legend of Sleepy Hollow," because James was angular and thin, his acne-plagued face and neck so lean, his Adam's apple protruded as round as a golf ball.

Though years later his fellow students would remember little of the taunts and in fact not even be able to place Berg-strom's name, in his own mind James was notorious on the high school campus, the unpopular kid everyone made fun of. "When my name was mentioned at pep rallies, people laughed," James said years later, his anger very near the surface. "When I walked between the buildings on campus, I'd get hit with water balloons." There were times when he returned to his locker between classes and found his lock smeared with gum and ink.

Through all the real or imagined injustices, James Berg-strom maintained a surface of calm joviality. "He always acted real goofy and happy," remembered one schoolmate. "James was timid. He never wanted to make anybody mad," recalled another. Yet inside, James viewed the childish pranks as condemnation. It was as if the other students knew his secret, his belief there was something wrong with him. "They could sense I was different," he said.

James Bergstrom's saving grace was sports. In his sopho-more year he joined the basketball team. Though only five feet ten inches and 140 pounds, James was fast and agile on the court. His teammates called him "Magic," after Magic Johnson, because he made such improbable shots during prac-tices. Yet Bergstrom rarely played when it counted, in the games. Though he excelled in the seclusion of workouts, on center court with the bleachers packed, James Bergstrom was self-conscious and inhibited to the point of becoming bumbling.

"I was afraid people were watching me," said James. "I was afraid about what they would say if I missed a shot."

As in the past, in response to his self-doubts, James turned obsessively controlling. Everything he owned had to be precise and neat. If anything in his room or the blue 1974 Chevy Nova he bought by working part-time at Pizza Hut was out of place, he felt destined to a disappointing night on the court. "I got so superstitious that if anything wasn't just right," said James, "I'd just know that I wouldn't play well in the game."

Not unlike the other students in school, the members of the basketball team initially saw James as odd man out. With them, too, he was exceptionally quiet, never talking about anything remotely personal, like his family or what he hoped to someday do with his life. Instead, he spoke only of sports.

Still, James was eager to belong, and by his junior year, the others included him as a bona fide member of not only the team but the group of friends it encompassed. His best friends were two of the team's outstanding players: Sam McDonald and Eddie Smith. Popular and with a bent toward girls and parties, Sam, six feet two inches and 180 pounds, came from a prominent Pearland family who ran a small grocery store not far from James's house. Eddie, six feet five inches, had shaggy blond hair and friendly good looks. Both were sought after not only within the school but by the girls who flocked around the team. Although they were a year younger than James, they treated him like the little brother. In fact, years later Eddie would say that James was "more like the team's mascot than one of the players."

Despite his growing acceptance, the players, too, treated James as something of an amusement. Once Sam and a clique of others dangled him by a belt loop from a clothes hook in the locker room. It was common for other players to give James's watch the "Timex Stress Test," in which a team member did everything from dropping it in a toilet, to sitting on it, to pounding it with a tennis shoe. Sometimes James would return after a game to find his locker emptied, his street clothes hidden while he was out on the court.

When Sam or Eddie had no other plans for a night out, they would often invite James. It was always understood that James would drive and buy the biggest portion of the beer or pay for more than his share of whatever expenses they incurred. "It was like everybody had girlfriends," said Eddie. "If we weren't going out with our girlfriends, we'd call up James."

On the surface, Bergstrom took it all in good spirits. He never objected, never acted hurt no matter now hateful the practical joke or how humiliating the slight. "If it bothered him, he never let on," said Eddie. But it did bother James, eating away under his skin. Inside, he kept a tally of each incident, each betrayal, and saw himself increasingly in the role of the victim. "They were supposed to be my friends," he said, "but they never gave me any respect."

There were, of course, perks involved in being a member of the basketball team. Principally, the players had an edge with the girls in school. Most were considered big men on the small-town high school campus. Yet here, too, Bergstrom was an exception. He rarely dated, appearing awkward and fumbling whenever a girl was around. "I was attracted to girls," said James, sullenly. "But I never did anything. I was just such an unpopular person."

"I never even remember James talking to or even trying to come on to a girl," another member of the team would remark. "The thing about James was that he was just so timid," said Eddie. "It was like he was afraid of girls or wasn't interested in them."

The one relationship James did have in high school was a short-lived attraction to a ninth grader while he was in the eleventh grade. James fawned over her as he had Michelle in Indiana, buying her whatever she wanted and showering her with attention. When she dropped him, James was despondent. "She was just using me," he said, bitterly. "Because I was on the team." Later he would also blame his position in school as "the most unpopular guy in the class" for her defection. "She could see how everyone treated me."

In retrospect, James would later contend that there were many in the school who undoubtedly assumed he was gay. In fact, in the ninth grade he was approached by several boys who invited him to one of their homes. Once there, one tried to corner him inside a closet and attempted to fondle him. "I ran as fast as I could and I never talked to them again," Bergstrom would later maintain. For a fourteen-year- old boy, such an incident could provoke doubt about his masculinity. Though James maintained that didn't happen—"I knew I was attracted to girls"—it did, however, make him envision himself as even more unappealing. "I figured there was no way I could be attractive to women if I was attractive to men."

By the time James reached the end of his school years, he was a confused and angry teenager with many secrets: his father's drinking; the imaginary voices that taunted him; the pain he harbored behind a smile as the school's outcast; and the biggest secret of all—that he had already sexually molested his first victim.

The way Adelaide, his youngest sister, would recount events, it began when she was three and the youngster, a relation, was eight. It was then that James, who was thirteen, started frequent, sometimes nearly nightly, invasions of the bedroom the girls shared, right down the hall from the one in which James roomed with his brother, Chris.

"Nobody knows why we didn't just go and tell, but we didn't," said Adelaide. "We just didn't know how."

At night, James would creep through the darkness, afraid his mother or father asleep down the hall would hear something and come to investigate. Once inside the bedroom, he inched his way toward the eight-year-old. "It went on all the time for five years," said Adelaide, who describes James at home as so quiet and reclusive, he was nearly a ghostlike presence.

Adelaide would refuse to say just what she witnessed, but James would later tell a psychologist he had acted out his fantasies on the girl, tying her up, like the women he'd seen on television, and fondling her.

In the twisted dysfunction of her brother's behavior, Adelaide became the girl's guardian. It was her job to stay vigilant throughout the night, sleeping lightly and waking each time he came in. In the darkness, she moaned or rolled over, hoping James would skulk off to his own room.

"James would leave if I started to wake up," she said. "I don't think he wanted me to see that. I was the little sister, the one he played ball with. He was always fairly normal toward me. He never wanted me to see that side of him."

The intrusions continued for many years. When the girl was a teenager, she and Adelaide went to the Bergstroms and asked them to install a lock on her door. Irene Bergstrom asked why, and accepted it when the girls mumbled a vague answer about wanting more privacy. "I guess we should have known something was wrong with James even then," said Adelaide. "But you don't want to think that your own brother is a pervert."

In James's estimation his senior year in high school was his best. He wore his school jacket with two big letters, one for basketball, another for the year he spent on the tennis team, and for the first time felt as if he was gaining some respect. "I turned a few people's heads when they saw that," he said, proudly. "They didn't expect me to be so athletic."

Still, in the 1981 *Gusher*, the Pearland High School yearbook, James Bergstrom is a gawky teenager with long, dark hair swept across his forehead, a wary smile, and a tightly manicured mustache. Nowhere is there a sign of the James Bergstrom of the future, not even in the eyes. Brows arched, he stares off the page to the left, without a hint of the anger and rage that would damage so many lives.

Chapter Four

Of course, no one in the Martinez family knew of James Bergstrom's past when he rang their doorbell at seven on the Saturday evening following his phone call. Santos opened her front door and saw only a neatly dressed young man smiling at her. "I'm here to pick up Linda," he said.

Santos called her middle daughter, and a few minutes later, dressed in jeans and a new shirt she bought for the occasion, Linda walked toward the door to meet her blind date. It was, in fact, her first blind date. She was nervous. "I remember having butterflies in my stomach," she said. She'd actually had second thoughts about the arrangement just that afternoon, but decided she'd made a commitment.

In the doorway, James stood smiling at her. He, too, was dressed casually in a pair of jeans and a white shirt with one red stripe. Linda thought it would probably be all right when she realized he looked as nervous as she felt.

A few minutes later, they were driving toward the freeway in James's new midnight blue 1983 Custom Deluxe pickup truck, trying to decide where to go. One of them mentioned Bennigan's, the other agreed, and they were on their way.

In a booth at the restaurant, Linda had her first real look at James. At five ten, he was eight inches taller than she and gaunt, so much so that his clothes hung on him. But James was not unattractive. His dark hair was meticulously combed over his forehead, and his hazel eyes looked back at her warmly.

They were both too nervous to eat, so when the waitress arrived, they ordered only drinks: Linda a frosty frozen margarita, and James a Crown Royal. While they drank, James did most of the talking, much as he had on the telephone. This time the conversation centered around music, especially rock 'n' roll concerts he had gone to with Eddie and Sam: the Police, Rush, and a dozen others, all the hottest groups. Linda had only been able to afford to attend one such event, a Van Halen concert the year before.

When they finished their drinks they got back in the truck. As he was throughout the night, James was gentlemanly, opening Linda's door and waiting patiently until she climbed inside. They then drove to The Galleria, the pricey Houston shopping mall frequented by River Oaks socialites, upwardly mobile young professionals, and vacationing Mexican nationals. On one end it was anchored by Neiman Marcus, and on the other by Lord & Taylor and Marshall Field's. The cavernous atrium in the center was an acre of ice on which skaters twirled, surrounded by multiple levels of onlookers. Linda and James—continuing their conversation from the restaurant—joined a cluster of sightseers on the second floor and talked while a panorama of the faltering and the fluid skated by.

To Linda's surprise, James grew suddenly quiet, then asked, "Would it be all right if I held your hand?"

She looked over at him and realized he looked not unlike a small boy requesting an ice cream cone. "Sure," she answered. "I guess so."

Smiling, James linked his arm through hers and held her hand tightly.

After the skating rink, James suggested they drive around his hometown and stop at his parents' house. Linda agreed.

It had been dark for hours and the streets of Pearland were nearly deserted when they arrived. James pointed out the high school, the park where he played basketball with his friends, and the store Sam's family owned. "He acted as if he was showing me around San Francisco or New York," Linda said later. "I couldn't believe how hard he was working at trying to impress me." Although the small city with its "Welcome from the Lion's Club" sign didn't sway her, James's eagerness to please her did. He was ungainly and overly solicitous, yet she felt touched by him.

Before long, they were weaving through the streets of Corrigan, the Pearland subdivision where James and his family lived. As they neared the Bergstrom house, James pointed it out. "The front light is on. That means my mom is still up," he said. "I'll go inside and see if it's okay if we come in."

They pulled up in front of the modest ranch-style house and James hurriedly ran inside. A minute later he came for her and, holding her hand, walked her through the front door. Inside the darkened living room with its wood paneling, Irene Bergstrom sat on the couch watching an old black-and-white movie and smoking a cigarette. She looked up and said, "Hi," but then stared immediately back at the television, barely shooting Linda a hazy gaze. James had already told her that his mother, just like her own, worked long hours as a seamstress. Linda couldn't help noting that she appeared to have had a very hard day.

As if he sensed how uncomfortable Linda was in the living room, James suggested they turn on the television in his room. Moments later, James was seated on a chair and Linda on his bed while they watched a movie, *Smoky and the Bandit*, on a small color television. While James laughed at Burt Reynolds leading a convoy of eighteen-wheelers at breakneck speeds, Linda studied his room. It was immaculate, everything precisely arranged. A Rush poster decorated one wall and a crucifix hung on another. On the dresser there was a photograph of a young couple holding a baby.

"Who's that?" Linda asked, pointing at it.

"My brother, Chris, and his family," James said proudly. "He's in the navy, stationed on a nuclear submarine in Washington State."

Suddenly James jumped up as if he had forgotten something, and a few minutes later he returned with a glass of ice water.

"This is for you," he said, handing it to Linda.

They sat quietly for a while, until James looked at her and said, "You're even prettier than Caesar said." Then he edged forward and kissed her softly. Leaning toward him, Linda fell into the well in the center of James's old mattress and tumbled over. She giggled nervously as she righted herself on the mattress.

"I better go home," she said, suddenly very self-conscious.

At her mother's doorstep, James kissed her again and said, "I'll call." Then he turned and left. She watched as he drove away.

Lying on her side in bed that night, Linda thought back over the evening. James Bergstrom had seemed so nervous and he was obviously trying so hard to impress her. *But I don't really feel attracted to him,* she thought. Though tired and eager for sleep, she kept remembering the way he had kissed her. There was something disquieting about it. The only word that came to mind was *desperate.* Linda was nodding off to sleep when the phone rang.

"I just wanted you to know how much I enjoyed our date," James Bergstrom said when she answered it. "Why don't we do it again, real soon."

Chapter Five

When James arrived at Devoe & Raynolds on the following Monday afternoon to start his evening shift, a crush of co-workers spearheaded by Caesar gathered around to inquire about his weekend. Usually James talked about playing basketball or tennis, or going out with friends from high school, most often his old teammates Sam and Eddie. But this week, everyone knew that on Saturday night James had had a date with Gino's pretty younger sister, Linda.

"Well, how'd it go?" asked Caesar. "You two have a good time?"

"Yeah," said James, who excitedly recounted his evening with Linda for his friends. Then, to all their surprise, he added, "I'm going to ask Linda to go out steady."

Allen Gibson, one of the plant's union stewards, shook his head at James. "You don't go doing that after a first date, young'un," he laughed. "You hardly know this girl."

Though just a few years older than James, Gibson, like much of the crew, had grown used to treating Bergstrom like an adolescent brother, just as the other players had on his high school basketball team. Because they worked together in the filling department, the two men had developed a friendship, and Gibson was pleased when Caesar suggested he introduce James to Gino's sister, hoping James might learn to be more comfortable around women. Now he was wondering if it had been a mistake.

"Give it a chance, little buddy, and see if you even like her or she likes you," cautioned the heavyset and levelheaded Gibson. "James, don't go overboard on this thing, huh?"

As he always did when Gibson or any of the others offered advice, James nodded agreement. "She's really beautiful," he said. "I think she might be the one."

With that the group disbanded as many chuckled and joined Gibson by shrugging and shaking their heads. Everyone at Devoe was used to James Bergstrom. "James was this quiet, timid little guy," one co-worker later said. "There weren't no way anybody ever thought that boy could hurt a fly."

Years later they would discover how wrong they had all been.

James had hired on at Devoe & Raynolds right out of high school in 1981. He'd worked there for nearly three years that January when he and Linda began dating, and he had a reputation for being generally "a nice guy." He'd gotten the job on the recommendation of the father of one of his friends from the basketball team, a chemical engineer at the plant. At first James was assigned to the filling department, the part of the plant that packaged the finished paint in cans to be distributed to stores. Later he transferred to shipping.

From the beginning, James's co-workers knew he was "a little different." In fact, one story that followed him throughout his years there was that the manager who hired him nearly decided not to because throughout the job interview James never looked the older man directly in the eyes. Bergstrom's reputation for being a little odd was only reinforced when he took to wearing a wire paint handle looped through the sweat holes of his white hard hat. "He looked like he was wired for sound," laughed Gibson.

As it had been in the days Linda's father was employed there, working at Devoe was considered a good job. Unlike so much of Houston where unskilled or minimum-skilled laborers had no union representation and were poorly paid,

Devoe & Raynolds was a union plant; the majority of its seventy employees belonged to local 4-227 of the OCAW, the Oil, Chemical & Atomic Workers. Workers were relatively well paid, and most stayed on for decades, many hoping to retire from Devoe.

The factory itself was a sprawling facility of metal warehouse-type structures painted a coffee-with-cream beige and giant stainless steel tanks of raw materials, most of which were delivered via a railroad spur that ran behind the plant. The main building was three stories high. On the top floor, the mills, a giant mixer transformed the raw materials into a basic paste. On the second, the paint was thinned and tinted in five-hundred- to three-thousand-gallon tanks. On the first, in the filling department, where James started, the paint was canned and then sent off on a maze of conveyor belts to the shipping department in the front of the building.

From the beginning, James liked working in the plant. Though the majority of the hourly workers were black or Hispanic, for the first time in his life, he felt as if he fit in. "They treated me like I was a real person," said James. "They accepted me right away."

Still, James was never really "one of the guys." In the lunchroom during half-hour dinner breaks, he almost always sat alone eating huge lunches with three or four sandwiches he'd brought from home. When he did join the others, it was to play dominoes and to listen to his coworkers gossip about their families, sports, and women. "We'd all be hoo-hawing and joking and all this stuff, and James would absorb it in, but he never had any input," remembered his friend Gibson.

There were, however, times when James would socialize with his co-workers. He joined the plant slow-pitch softball team—the Devoe Wild Bunch—and occasionally there were those afternoons when he and Linda's brother Gino would shoot hoops at a park not far from the plant. They always stopped at a liquor store and bought a twelve-pack of cold Budweiser to take along. Usually James was quiet, just wanting to play. But sometimes, after five or six beers, he would open up about himself and his family, complaining that his sisters were always causing him problems and that his family was constantly at odds.

With another of the men at work, Larry, James had a running discussion on religion. Larry was a fundamentalist Christian, a Pentecostal, and he didn't believe in many of the basic tenets of the Catholic church, such as the saints and purgatory. James seemed to enjoy acting the part of his religion's defender, bringing in books—one on the mummification of saints' bodies—for Larry to read. For his part, Larry urged James to study the Bible, suggesting he memorize Scripture, such as Romans 5:1—"Having been justified by faith, we have peace with God." James agreed but never actually committed it to memory, instead announcing one day that he had discussed Larry's views with his father and they agreed it was not wise for him to continue the debate.

"We've been Catholics all our lives," James said, ending the dialogue. "My dad's done a lot of research and he tells me Catholicism is the one true religion."

While James was comfortable around the men at work, that was not the case when it came to the few women who worked at the plant, mainly clerks in the front office. Whenever James needed to talk to them, even to do something as simple as put in a vacation request, the others noticed he was as tense as a schoolboy on his first date. "He looked real fidgety," said Gibson. "Like guys do in their early teens when girls make them nervous. Usually it's something you grow out of."

As is often the case in plants where men work with few women, every once in a while a *Playboy* magazine or its equivalent made its way into the shop. On such occasions, it passed from hand to hand through the plant. Often the others stood in a group to present it to James, who self-consciously fanned through it. He always blushed and looked uneasy. Bergstrom's co-workers laughed heartily at his embarrassment. "You ought to get yourself something like that," one would taunt. "Wouldn't that be nice, James?"

In fact, James's lack of dates and girls was a common target of the good-natured teasing in the shop. It wasn't unusual for one man or the other to say, "James, if you don't get a girlfriend, everyone will think you're queer."

"Yeah, you're right," James would answer with a sheepish smile.

More often than not, it would end with the other man slapping James on the back and walking to his assigned station laughing at Bergstrom's expense. As he had throughout high school, James went along, seeming to enjoy the joke as much as anyone. He never gave any indication that the sting of their words hit a particularly sensitive mark.

No one at work knew, but at home James heard similar admonitions, only with little show of humor. "My parents were really bothering me about dating," said James later. "Because they thought I was gay or something. My mother kept saying, 'People are going to start thinking you're funny.'"

It wasn't that James lacked an interest in women, however. Rather he felt increasingly drawn to them, like on those infrequent nights when someone smuggled a stag film into the plant. They turned off the lights in a secluded office, and many of the skeleton crew that worked the four-to-midnight shift gathered in the dark as an old movie projector lit the room. The others jeered, giving each other the elbow, as images of heavily endowed men and busty women joyfully intertwining flickered against the wall.

On such nights, James slouched in the background, watching, quiet. "He never said anything," remembers one of the viewers. "It was easy to forget James was even there. The rest of us were all hooting and hollering. Some of the movies were really pretty crude. There was one with Linda Lovelace and one where a woman had sex with a dog."

Years later, James would emulate a common theme in movies like the ones he watched with his friends: the scenario in which a masked man happens upon a lone beautiful young woman. Though she attempts to fight him off, the intruder overpowers her, binding her by the hands and feet, rendering her helpless and allowing him to do with her as he pleases. But in the fantasy of the movies, it isn't rape. Instead the actress portraying the victim quickly discards a pretense of alarm and succumbs to her own secret, sensual passions. In the thin dimension of light pulsating through film, the woman willingly and lustfully surrenders all to the actor who portrays her rapist.

Chapter Six

The week after James and Linda's first date, the phone rang constantly in the Martinez house. James telephoned from home in the mornings and early afternoon. At night, he called from work. Gibson and the others grew accustomed to finding him leaning against the concrete wall outside the break room, the pay phone's headset pressed to his ear. "Hey, Bergstrom. Aren't you going to eat?" one or the other would call out.

"I'll do it later," James would shout back. "I'm talking to Linda."

As usual, the others shrugged and laughed.

James spent much of those nights on the telephone boasting to Linda about his exploits. He recounted his tenure on the varsity basketball team, adding his teammates had dubbed him "Magic." Then he mentioned that he loved playing tennis and watching the professionals battle it out on television during tournaments, especially John McEnroe. James seemed particularly impressed with the way the explosive player threw tantrums, putting line judges on notice and shifting the momentum of the game his way.

"My little sister has a girlfriend who thinks I look a lot like McEnroe," James said. "What do you think?"

"Maybe, a little," Linda answered. "Around the eyes."

"I've been thinking about having my hair permed to make it curly like his," James admitted.

At midnight, after he finished work, James often stopped at Linda's house. He sounded the truck's horn and Linda would meet him outside, where they spent half an hour together before he headed home. One night he showed up with his hair permed in tight curls. Linda thought the curls made him look a little odd, but she answered, "It looks good," when James fished for a compliment.

"My sister says I look just like McEnroe," James said proudly.

After that night, Daniel and the rest of the Martinez family nicknamed Bergstrom "Light Bulb," joking that the tight curls made Lily's new boyfriend look as if he'd stuck his finger in a light socket.

On a Sunday afternoon, two weeks after their first date, James called for Linda at her home for a second time. Again they drove through Houston, talking. James told Linda about his last girlfriend, the ninth grader he dated in his junior year. "You're a lot prettier than she is," said James, who went on to contend that while he had given her everything, the girl had been unfaithful, dating others behind his back. Linda could hear the pain in his voice and sympathized. She, after all, understood well what it was like to be betrayed.

As always, his pickup was shining. He had, as he would before each of their dates, washed, waxed, and detailed the inside cab. It was like high school basketball. James left nothing to chance, superstitiously fearing even the smallest defect could jinx the date.

At ten-thirty that night, James drove Linda to his house, suggesting they watch television, but as they approached, he announced he could tell from lights still burning in the back that his father was awake.

"Maybe we can go someplace else to talk," James said. "Do you want to go to a motel?"

"No," said Linda. "I think it's probably time for me to go home."

James apologized, assuring her he hadn't meant to imply anything, and that he had no intention of hurting her feelings. "I don't even believe in premarital sex," he said. "I believe people should save themselves for marriage, like the church teaches."

"I'm not upset," she answered. "I just want to go home."

Throughout the ride to her house, James pleaded for forgiveness, and Linda, in vain, tried to reassure him that he had not offended her. Then she told him something she rarely spoke of, the night she was raped. As he listened, she recounted in sketchy terms how it had happened and what it had been like afterward. When they pulled up in front of her house, James turned to her and they hugged. In her ear he whispered, "I'd never let anyone hurt you like that again."

From that night on, James added a finishing touch to what was becoming their ritual. He would drive the streets of Linda's neighborhood each night after work and then call as soon as he arrived home. "The coast is clear," he said. "I checked the neighborhood and I didn't see anyone out of place."

In the span of less than a month, James Bergstrom had appointed himself Linda's protector. Though she was unsure she liked him as much as he apparently liked her, Linda felt comfortable around James. She thought she could sense a sadness about him.

Weeks and months passed, and the two continued to see each other. One day Linda called James at work and the man who answered the phone chuckled, "You're that girl James is talking about all the time. You got that guy climbing the walls." Later Caesar added his opinion. "You know, Linda, he's crazy about you," he said. "I bet you'll end up marrying James Bergstrom."

Linda just laughed. Marriage really was not in her immediate plans. She was more concerned with just going day to day, working a little and having fun with her friends. But before long, it was obvious Caesar was right about James being smitten. It was as if he couldn't do enough for her. He insisted she use his truck while he worked, and when they went out he bought her clothes, perfume, and took her to restaurants and bars. As he had in high school when he always drove and picked up the tab for the beer, James was making up for his own insecurities by showering her with whatever she wanted. When he found out she had once dated an accountant with a sports car, he traded in his truck for a 1984 metallic gold Z28 and then insisted she drive that to visit friends.

Yet there were things that made Linda feel uneasy. When James brought her home to visit his parents, James's mother often sat silently watching television. His father was noticeably absent. When James C. was home, he stayed alone in the bedroom, rarely coming out, even for meals. One night when the older man did emerge from his bedroom cocoon, he was angry and shouting, obviously drunk. His wife sat silently crying in the living room, and James took Linda home.

Even stranger was James's mother. Linda didn't know how to take it one night when she phoned James, and Irene Bergstrom answered. Before calling her son, James's mother whispered a stern warning. "James had a girlfriend once and she hurt him. If you're not serious with him, don't go out with him. Don't hurt him like she did." Then his mother added something else, that after the breakup, James was so angry, it tore the family apart. "I don't ever want to go through that again," she said.

When Linda asked what she meant, the older woman didn't answer, instead calling her son to the phone.

Soon Linda began hearing James's parents yelling in the background during his telephone calls. James told her that they complained he showered her with too many gifts, spending too much money on her. His father, he said, had told him he was living "a champagne life on a beer budget."

James's friends had also noticed a change in him. Now when they went out, he didn't always pick up the check, complaining that he had gone through much of his five-thousand-dollar savings account on the new car and gifts for Linda. Something else bothered Sam and Eddie. James seemed reluctant to introduce them to his new girlfriend. When they did run into each other, Linda appeared unfriendly and distant. They had no way of knowing James was intentionally keeping them apart. He still blamed his unpopularity in high school for the breakup of his last relationship. This time he wasn't taking any chances. "I didn't know how they'd treat me in front of her," said James. "Mock me or make me look crazy."

Yet James's generosity didn't come without strings. At night he would call, and if Linda wasn't at home, he would later demand to know where she had been. "Who were you with?" he'd persist.

Linda, who more often than not was just out riding with her girlfriends, felt he had no real hold on her. "It's none of your business. You don't need to know. I'm not married to you," she'd answer. "I can do what I want, remember?"

Then James would tell her that his family, his friends, and his co-workers were saying she was just using him. That he was being taken for a fool. That while he worked, she was driving around in his car with other guys.

"And you believe them?" Linda would ask, angered by the injustice.

James never answered.

Some of James's co-workers were, in fact, advising him that he was being taken for a fool. Especially on the nights when he would work late, until after 2 A.M., and they saw him walking the mile to Linda's house to pick up his car. Though they offered him rides, James always refused, insisting he preferred walking. One night Allen Gibson coaxed James into his truck and dropped him at Linda's house. On the way there, he turned to a sullen Bergstrom and said, "Look, James, if she's not going to pick you up, don't let her use your car."

"I'm so damned good to her," James complained, never mentioning that Linda had offered to drop the car at the plant for him and that he'd insisted that wasn't necessary. "All she does is take advantage."

To Linda's family, James seemed odd at best. Her mother felt it was strange that he never came inside their house and barely talked to her when he picked up Linda, usually waiting in his car until she was ready. When Gino introduced James to Daniel, Linda's younger brother and former protector, outside the house one day, Daniel came away wondering, *What's wrong with the guy?*

Later Daniel told Linda, "There's something strange about that guy. What's his problem?"

Linda assured him, "He doesn't have one. Gino knows him and says he's all right."

"Well, okay. If Gino knows him." Daniel shrugged. "You're a big girl now. You can take care of yourself."

Yet Linda sometimes did worry about James and what she might be getting into by dating him. Especially one night when she had forgotten they had made plans and unintentionally stood him up, instead going out with friends. About ten that night she was at home in bed when she heard the revving of an engine outside her window. She peeked through the curtains and realized that it was James and that he was driving over her mother's front lawn. *Why?* she wondered. *What is he doing?*

A visceral fear ran through her when he drove under a streetlight and she saw his face, so clouded by anger, she barely recognized him.

Minutes later the phone rang and it was James, calm, cool, like any other night. "Linda, did you forget our date?" he asked, politely explaining he was at a pay phone at a convenience store not far from her house.

"Yeah," she answered. "I did."

"It's okay. I was on my way over, but you're sleepy. I'll call you tomorrow."

Confused, Linda hung up the phone and went outside. "I ran my hand over the tire tracks, just to make sure I hadn't been dreaming," she said later. "I began to doubt it had actually happened."

Linda's younger sister, Alice, mentioned the following

day that James's mother had called the night before. "She was really upset, Linda," Alice said. "She asked me to tell you not to hurt her son. If you're just playing with him, don't see him anymore."

Despite her misgivings about that night, Linda and James continued to see each other. Linda blamed herself for forgetting the date, and to her mind most of their arguments were due not to James but the intrusion of his family or friends into their relationship. She knew he was under pressure at home. Though they'd been going out steadily for more than a year and he was now in his early twenties, James often whispered when he called her so his parents wouldn't know he was on the telephone. On other occasions, she continued to hear James C. and Irene Bergstrom shouting in the background. James admitted they were upset with him, angry about the money he spent on her. "Everybody says you're taking me for a ride," he said. "That you really don't care about me."

But Linda was beginning to care about James. For the most part, he seemed kind and considerate. He always acted like a gentleman. When it was just the two of them, he could be fun to be with. She often thought of the day they were riding in his car on the expressway. He turned to her, smiled, and said, "You're going to marry me someday." And as he had on that first night, James often told her how pretty she was. For Linda, who had never thought of herself as attractive, James's compliments were endearing.

Unlike other men she'd dated, James Bergstrom never pressed her for sex, always assuring her that they should save themselves for marriage. "That's the way God wants it," he said. "It's in the Bible."

What might have changed her feelings, had she known about it, was the way James sometimes reacted when she was not around him. Like the night he called during his lunch hour and they argued about where she had been. After she hung up, he beat the pay phone against the concrete wall and broke the handset. Another night, two of his coworkers at Devoe taunted James, claiming Linda was probably dating someone else and driving her other boyfriend around in his car. Infuriated, James kicked and pounded a pallet of five-gallon paint cans with his fists, shouting, "She's my girlfriend. She's my girlfriend." Over and over.

"Look, hey, James, settle down, man," Allen Gibson said, pulling him into the warehouse. "Don't be acting like this. You're going to get fired."

"Well, I'm tired of people always saying stuff to me about Linda," James said.

"It's not worth losing your job over," Gibson chastised. "You don't need to act like this."

As always, James nodded in agreement and looked embarrassed about his display of anger.

At home, too, James was acting increasingly irrational. "He went out with Linda and it was like she was the only one he'd dated," Adelaide said later. "They'd have a fight and it would go on for hours. He'd break phones and scream like a demon."

For Linda, everything changed one night when James came to her house after an argument with his parents. She went outside with him and they got into the car. As they rode around together, James talked about the shouting match and how he had stood up for Linda, telling his parents that she really did care for him, that she wasn't just using him. Linda listened carefully, feeling guilty, as if many of his problems were her fault. He had been spending a lot of money on her, that was true.

As she considered James's actions, Linda began seeing him in a new light. "Here was someone who was hurt, someone who wanted to be noticed and cared for," she said later. "Here was someone who cared a great deal for me."

That night, for the first time, Linda told James, "I love you."

James said he couldn't go home, the blowup had been too bad. Linda agreed and they drove to a motel and checked in.

They held each other, kissing, James touching her on the bed. "But we never even got fully undressed," said Linda. "James said someday we'd get married and he wanted to wait."

Years later James would tell Linda another story about that night. That instead of his relationship with her and the money he had spent on it, the argument with his parents had been about something vastly different. That on that particular night the young girl he'd molested told James C. and Irene Bergstrom what James had done to her while the rest of the family slept.

Without understanding why, Linda sensed that from that night on, everything was thrown into fast forward. Suddenly, James told her, his parents wanted him to follow in his younger brother's footsteps by joining the navy.

Actually, pushing their oldest son to join the service was not a total turnaround for the Bergstroms. James C., after all, talked fondly of the intrigue and excitement of his days in the air force, and James's younger brother, Chris, was climbing the promotional ladder in the navy. After Chris was on the inaugural crew of the U.S.S. *Ohio*, the country's first Trident submarine, his father talked often of the younger son's success. Chris was married, the father of two small children, and one of the youngest chiefs in the submarine fleet. The pressure mounted, and one day James walked into the house and found a marine recruitment team there at his father's request to talk to him about the opportunities in the military.

In fact, James C. had always argued that James's slot at Devoe & Raynolds was a dead end. "My father kept telling me that someday they'd have a robot do what I did and they wouldn't need me anymore," James said later. When his father voiced objections to his job soon after James began working at Devoe, James insisted he would work only long enough to save money for college. But he liked the work and stayed, much to his father's disapproval.

Since the night of the big fight and James's flight to Linda's side, the Bergstroms were pushing in earnest for their son to leave the house. Enlisting in the military must have seemed like the perfect solution. "James never came right out and said he didn't want to go," remembered his high school friend Eddie. "But you could tell it, underneath."

Before long, James agreed to enlist, but he told Linda he had one condition. There was only one way he would join the navy, he said: They had to be married before he left for basic training.

It had been clear from the night she made it that Linda's pledge of love hadn't had the effect she had anticipated. She thought it would put James at ease and allow him to stop worrying about what others said about her intentions. James, however, was not appeased but even more anxious about their relationship. As if now that she had admitted her feelings for him, he needed to have her sign it in blood.

She sensed her words also had a secondary effect; they had irrevocably tipped the scales of their relationship. If she had been the strong, independent one in the beginning, the one able to make demands, James now held that power. He needled her constantly, craving continual proof of her love. If she loved him, she needed to show it, he insisted, by marrying him.

The arguments they'd had in the past paled in contrast to James's urgent anger now. It erupted in shouting matches and enraged phone calls, ending only when Linda slammed down the phone in desperation. It was so obvious James was constantly on edge that one night at work Allen Gibson pulled him aside and suggested James and Linda take time apart from each other. "Look, James, why don't you blow it off for a while," he advised. "You know, step back and see what's going on."

As usual, James nodded agreement but then continued to pressure Linda to marry him. One night after they squabbled on the telephone, James jumped in his car and screeched to a stop in her driveway. Linda was outside when he pulled up, and James immediately continued the argument where he had left off, chasing her around the yard, thrusting his finger at her face. Daniel heard the commotion and rushed to his sister's rescue.

"You're going to have to go," said Daniel, who outweighed and towered over James.

Linda ran into the house, and James attempted to follow, but Daniel blocked him.

"If you don't tell her to come out here, I'm going to do something to you," James threatened.

"What's that?" Daniel countered.

James jumped into his Z28 and punched it, driving directly toward Daniel, who leaped out of the way. James slammed on the brakes just before crashing into an old pickup truck parked in the driveway. Daniel rushed around the side and grabbed James through the open window, smacking him in the mouth. James threw the car into reverse and sped away.

Inside the house, Linda was crying.

"There's something wrong with that guy," Daniel told his older sister. "He's not normal."

That night Santos, too, was worried about her middle daughter.

"How come he acts like that?" she asked Linda.

"I guess because he loves me, Mama," Linda answered, finding herself making excuses for James's behavior. "He was just upset. He won't act like that anymore."

"If you marry him, you better know who you're marrying," Santos concluded. "He is too possessive. He reminds me of your daddy."

Though Linda listened to her mother's words, in her view there was a world of difference between James and her father. James had never hit her and he was always sorry after they argued. One night, for instance, he had dropped to his knees on the street in front of her mother's house and shouted until the neighbors came outside to investigate the ruckus: "I'm sorry, Linda. I love you. I love you."

As the days passed, James continued to exert pressure on Linda to marry him. One afternoon he stopped at a navy recruiting station, where he was told that under the buddy plan he could request duty near his brother, who had settled in Bremerton, Washington, across Puget Sound from Seattle. "And if we end up in Washington State, Chris's wife, Tina, would be there to help you get settled," James excitedly assured Linda later that night.

Still, almost nightly he fluctuated between concluding he would enlist to ruling it out completely. Finally, he usually worked his way around to asking Linda what she wanted him to do.

"You need to do what you want to do, not what your parents want or I want," she told him. But inside she was hoping he would decide against the navy. She hated to see him go, and the prospect of moving across country was terrifying.

Finally he called one afternoon from a navy recruiting office to say he was signing his enlistment papers.

Linda cried on the phone, "I don't want you to go."

But James insisted he had to. "My parents want me to sign the papers and I'm going," he said. "But before I leave Houston, we're getting married."

Linda, unsure, agreed but kept putting the date off until one day James announced they had to get married that week. He wouldn't wait any longer. Linda was troubled, still uncertain this was the right move for her. But if they did marry, this was far from the way she had envisioned it, in a hurry with little ceremony. She wanted a church wedding like the one she had always dreamed of. But James insisted.

"Okay, James, I love you," she finally acquiesced. "I want to marry you."

On April 25, 1985, alone because they knew neither of their families approved, James and Linda drove to the courthouse in Pasadena, Texas, another of the small cities bordering Houston on the south. James was twenty-two years old; Linda was twenty-one. In the court of the justice of the peace, they married. The ceremony took less than five minutes, and afterward Linda felt disappointed. "It just wasn't the way I ever thought it would happen," she said.

After they left the courthouse, James decided they would leave things as they were, Linda living with her family and James with his, until she left to follow him wherever he was stationed. Linda didn't argue. She knew only Gino in her family liked James, and she didn't look forward to telling her mother she and James had eloped.

Still, she was confused when James drove up in front of her house to drop her off. She had thought they'd spend a romantic night together in a motel. They had yet to consummate their marriage.

"Suddenly James worried about money. He told me that this was the last day to renew his car insurance, and now that we were married, he could get a lower rate," she later said. "I couldn't believe it, but that's how he had picked our wedding date."

Despite his plan to keep their marriage a secret, Irene Bergstrom somehow guessed what her son had just done. James called Linda from a motel later that night where he sought refuge after his parents forced him to leave the house.

"They were really pissed about us getting married," he told Linda, describing the battle that had ensued after he'd admitted they'd eloped. "But I stuck up for you and I told them that now you're my wife."

Later Irene Bergstrom would say that she was surprised to learn her son and Linda had married. "They didn't tell anybody. Suddenly we just knew they were married," she said, dismissing it all with a disgusted frown and a wave of her hand.

In the Martinez home, things went on as they always had. No one realized their Lily was now married. But it wasn't long before James boasted of the news to a few friends at work. When Allen Gibson returned from a vacation, a co-worker pulled him to the side and told him James and Linda had eloped.

Gibson tracked James down and asked, "James, you got married?"

"Yeah," answered James. "It seemed like the thing to do."

"As long as you're happy." Gibson shrugged.

But in the days that followed, Allen Gibson noticed a change in James. He seemed almost giddy, happier than Gibson had ever seen him. Not contented but prideful. Gibson thought about it long and hard until he finally came to one conclusion: "All the time they were dating, James didn't have control over Linda. The marriage was a purchase that gave him title. In his mind, she was his property, and that was that. It was like he'd bought a new car. Linda was his."

Chapter Seven

In January of 1986, James submitted a request for a leave of absence to Devoe & Raynolds and packed his bags for navy boot camp in San Diego. Linda cried when he left, but he seemed optimistic and excited. Thirteen weeks later, she flew to California for a graduation ceremony in which James was one of the flag bearers. "I was really proud of him," she said. "He was making something of his life."

Since he had filed a request asking to be assigned to a Trident submarine, James was then given a battery of intelligence, aptitude, and psychiatric tests. The psychological exams were designed to determine how he would fare in the submarine corps. The navy is well aware that not everyone can take the claustrophobic confinement of months submerged at sea. In fact, many who initially request the subs wash out during their first voyages and are discharged or reassigned in other types of service.

Once his scores were tabulated and he was determined to be a candidate for sub school, James, like all nuclear submariners, became the subject of an FBI security check. Called the hundred-hours exam—because each exam theoretically consumes one hundred hours of manpower—it grants a basic security clearance. "Everybody on the sub has at least 'secret' security status," one officer later explained. "They're working with classified data and equipment. There's lots that you wouldn't want to go wrong on a nuclear submarine."

When Bergstrom's security clearance came through without a hitch, orders were issued assigning him to submarine school in New London, Connecticut.

At home, Linda maintained the charade of not being married, but soon Santos Martinez, like Irene Bergstrom, suspected that the young couple had eloped. Despite their agreement, James was evidently anxious to be sure their situation was public knowledge. From Connecticut he sent letters to the Martinez house addressed to Mrs. Linda Bergstrom. One day a saddened Santos found one such letter in the mailbox and brought it to her daughter, remarking, "I didn't know you married him."

"Yes, I did," Linda answered.

Santos said nothing more. Since her daughter had made her choice, she felt it was no longer her place to interfere. But from then on she prayed for Linda every night, prayed that she was wrong about James Bergstrom and that he would not bring her daughter pain.

The rest of the Martinez family felt much the same way. "By the time we knew she was going to marry him, it was too late," said Daniel. "We couldn't say anything. It was already done."

Inside the plain white envelopes, the letters James sent were all the same. They were written in a careful script on navy stationery with a small sailboat outlined in one corner. In each, James described his classes and training, learning to be an interior communications technician—an IC man—on a Trident submarine. Then he told of their plans once he completed his schooling, and of their impending move to Washington State. His agenda was simple: During the four years of his commitment to the navy, they would live simply and save their money, until they could move home to Houston and buy a house. Then he would return to Devoe and back to work with his friends. Before sealing the envelope, James always added one finishing touch, a black cross, like a crucifix, on the center top of each page.

As he had throughout their relationship, however, James kept some secrets to himself. Never mentioned in the letters was one particular night in Connecticut when he went alone to a bar with a big-screen television to watch a basketball game. "There were these guys playing pool—other guys from sub school. I started playing, too, and one invited me back to his place," he would later recount. "This one guy started taking his clothes off and coming on to me." James claimed he bolted and ran, just as he said he had on the other, similar incident. "But I couldn't help wondering," he admitted angrily, "why all these guys just kept assuming I was gay."

One or two weekends a month, James flew home from Connecticut. Linda spent the days before his arrival daydreaming about what they would do while he was home. He never disappointed her. From the moment James arrived in Houston, they clung together. The long absences forgotten, they frolicked like children, picnicking at the park or driving on the beach. Almost every night, they went out to dinner or to a movie. They never fought. To Linda, it was as if they were living the childhood neither had ever experienced: a childhood without the fear or violence that haunted her earliest memories.

At night they slept blissfully entwined in each other's arms in Adelaide's bedroom. Linda wouldn't learn for another three years what her husband had done in that very room—that it was there he had repeatedly sexually molested his first victim.

Although she'd had doubts before the marriage, Linda felt content and happy. Her one disappointment was in the privacy of the bedroom, where James was unimaginative. Though he had an insatiable sexual appetite—often insisting they make love as many as three or four times a day—it was always in the same way. Invariably James climbed on top of her, and in minutes it was over. Immediately after, he rolled over and fell into a deep sleep.

James had been such an ardent suitor, Linda had imagined he would be as ardent a lover. After she'd waited so long to be with him, his lack of passion and fun was disillusioning. Yet it seemed petty to complain. Instead, Linda attempted to ease James into trying new things, such as making love in the park one night under the stars or while he was sitting on a chair. Always James refused, insisting that was not "proper."

So when James asked one night if they could do something a little different, Linda was not only intrigued but hopeful.

"What did you have in mind?" she said, flirting.

"Let's play a little game," he suggested. "Can I tie you up?"

"Why?" she asked.

"It's something I've always wanted to do," he answered. "But I was afraid to ask."

Although the idea made her vaguely uneasy, Linda agreed. As she watched from the bed, James meticulously checked the room, determining the door was locked and the drapes were pulled. Then he took a perfectly rolled pair of long white athletic socks from his duffel bag and painstakingly unwound them. He pulled her nightgown slowly over her head and left her shivering in nothing but her white bikini briefs. Then he carefully knotted the first sock and bound it around her left wrist, yanking the knot tight before he looped and tied the unused length around her other wrist, ensnaring both hands helplessly behind her. She wriggled her hands to loosen the restraint as he turned his attention to her ankles. Linda was on her knees with her feet behind her as James encircled first one, then the other ankle, and pulled tightly on the ends of the second binding until they, too, were locked together.

"There was a guy in boot camp who had handcuffs," James whispered, excitedly, as he industriously tested the tightness of the restraints. "Wouldn't that be great?"

Linda just smiled. Though she was uncomfortable, she didn't want to complain. This was an adventure, an exciting new game, she told herself. "I was just glad to see him. I loved him," she said later. "He could have done anything to me."

When he was sure her bindings were secure, James started slowly. He ran his fingers lightly up and down the sides of her body. He inched closer to her breasts, then held them in his hands and kissed each of her nipples. It was a pleasant sensation, tender and warm.

Then he moved downward, toward her thighs. He glided his fingers lightly across the sensitive skin between her legs. It made her tingle and the muscles in her leg contract. In an involuntary reflex, she writhed and pulled slightly away. James looked up at her.

"That tickles," she whispered, with a nervous smile.

James stared silently at her, his eyes piercing.

Without saying a word, he untied her legs and discarded her underpants, then retied her, and bound the restraints even tighter than before. The cloth cut unyielding into her skin. Her hands and feet tingled, numbly cold.

Though she pulled against her bonds, James, absorbed in the game, appeared not to notice her discomfort. This time he ran his fingers quickly up over her breasts and down her arms. An icy chill encompassed Linda, marking her skin with thousands of tiny bumps. She shivered.

"You don't like that?" James asked.

She shook her head, no.

But rather than stop, James again lowered his hands toward the delicate skin between her legs and edged his fingers up and down inside her thighs.

Linda's flesh crawled. The sensation made her jerk uncomfortably back, and the rigid restraints on her wrists and ankles tightened, the knots pressing into her flesh.

James looked at her coolly and smiled, as if from a distance. He stared as dispassionately as a scientist inspecting a particularly interesting specimen.

A wave of anxiety swept over Linda. It wasn't only her husband's barren stare, but the hard set of his jaw. He seemed like a stranger, bewitched by his own game. Not the James she knew. *Why is he acting so odd?* she wondered. *What's wrong with him?*

Frightened, Linda drew slightly back, and James lunged forward. She turned to the right and he followed. To the left and he was beside her. She felt trapped.

"James," she whispered, finally.

But he simply gazed up at her. With that same expressionless face and distant eyes, he came at her again, running his hands up her thighs until her body shuddered. Every pore felt exposed.

"James," she said more firmly, pulling against the restraints and discovering she was powerless to break free. "Please, don't."

Suddenly James looked up at her, his eyes clear and attentive. Whatever spell held him, it was broken. He hesitated only a moment before untying her. Then he laid her down on the bed and mounted her, making love in his usual way.

Before she drifted off to sleep that night, Linda considered what had happened and why it frightened her so. James hadn't done anything particularly menacing. He had never raised his voice, never inflicted even the slightest pain. It was something else. Something less concrete. His vacant stare. The chill of his touch. But what she hated most was the knowledge that he could have done anything he wanted to her and she would have been defenseless to stop him. *James liked it,* she puzzled as sleep overtook her. *He wanted me to struggle. He wanted me to be afraid.*

PART TWO

Chapter Eight

In October 1986 James Bergstrom returned to Houston with
all his initial training completed. His orders: Report to the
Trident submarine base in Bangor, Washington, on Thanksgiving night, Thursday, November 27. James was nervous.
Linda was scared. It was one of those times when there
seemed to be too much to do to ever accomplish it all by a
given date. But then, you don't keep the navy waiting.

To get ready for the move, James needed a car. He'd sold
the Z28 before entering the navy. No longer feeling the need
to impress anyone, he opted not to commit to another car
payment, instead settling on a 1979 brown Grand Prix he
paid cash for. James worried the car would never last the
almost twenty-four hundred miles to Seattle, so Linda took
it to a local mechanic who assured her it would make the
trip. Whereas James appeared carefree, even flamboyant,
about money in the past, since the marriage he seemed increasingly concerned with family finances. The Grand Prix,
he reminded Linda, fit his overall strategy: to stay in the
navy for four years, save as much as possible of what he
made, and then return to Houston to buy a house. They
would be frugal now, and it would pay off later.

As their departure approached, they filled the car with
just the essentials, primarily clothes and a smattering of
kitchenware, including a toaster they purchased at Sears and
an iron donated by James mother. As usual, he had the
Grand Prix meticulously clean, even insisting on covering

the seat with a large towel. "I don't like to sweat on the up-holstery," he told Linda.

For their part, the Bergstroms appeared delighted that their son and his wife would soon depart for Washington. James C. constantly reminded James that his enlistment was a smart move. "You'll be worth a lot more to a company af-ter the navy trains you," he said. Linda's brother Gino voiced similar views. "This is good for James," he told Linda. "He'll get a better career. It's for your future."

Linda agreed. Naturally she felt uneasy about moving to a city where she would have no family or friends. They didn't even know where they'd be living yet. But she was excited about the future. Leaving behind Houston, with all the pain-ful memories it held for her, was not a difficult decision. What made it even sweeter was that James was moving up in the world and she was going with him. In the navy, a member of the submarine force, he would deserve a certain respect, and as his wife, she would have more of the good things in life. She had not been raised to expect success, but now that it appeared possible, Linda intended to eagerly pursue it.

Only Santos Martinez hung back, unsure. "You're going to do what you're going to do," Santos told Linda the day before the newlyweds drove off. But there was no mistaking the misgiving in her mother's tone. She knew Santos wor-ried about James and his hair-trigger temper.

At first it seemed the newlyweds would have little to transport to their new home, but on the morning they de-parted, the Grand Prix sagged under the weight of their pos-sessions. Its trunk, backseat, and the passenger's seat floor all overflowed. To fit in, Linda sat crosswise, her legs scrunched up in front of her. "I began thinking James was right and I had packed too much," she would say later, chuckling softly at the memory. "At one point I considered ditching some of the stuff on the side of the road."

The trip took four days, and James insisted on driving all of it himself. The first leg brought them to El Paso, Texas, the next to Los Angeles, and the third to Oregon. At seven on Thanksgiving evening they arrived at Chris and Tina Bergstrom's homey two-bedroom apartment on the Bangor base. Both Linda and James were exhausted, but Tina had a turkey dinner with all the fixings ready, so they stayed up to talk.

Linda had met both Chris and Tina before, in Houston, when they came home on visits. Chris was taller than James and heavier, but not as good-looking, with rougher features. He was an affable man, more outgoing than James. His parents were proud that Chris had been on the inaugural crew of the U.S.S. *Ohio*. Now James would be joining him on the *Ohio*'s blue crew and they would be setting sail together. It all fit, perfectly.

As tall as Chris was, Tina was shorter than Linda, five foot with blond hair. She was trim, probably not more than a hundred pounds, and quiet, more serious than her gregarious husband. As her two young sons played on the floor, Tina cleared the table. Perhaps assuming Linda was nervous about being away from home, she smiled reassuringly. She, too, had married in Houston, then followed her husband across country when he joined the navy. "Y'all will get used to it," she said. "Navy life is great. When the guys are away you have time for yourself, and when they come back you're always glad they're back."

To Linda it sounded like heaven. There would be an apartment of her own—her very first—and little by little she and James would work to accumulate the middle-class things she'd always wanted but never had, furniture, clothes, maybe even her own car. This was the life she had always dreamed of, with a husband, eventually children, and a place of her own.

James had worried throughout the day that he wouldn't arrive on base in time to report for duty, so immediately after dinner, Chris drove him to central command. James checked in and was ordered to report again on Monday.

With that behind them, Linda and James slept on a bed in the children's room. Though she was exhausted, days of bouncing cross-country in the car had left her head swimming and her bones aching, she drifted fitfully off to sleep. The next morning Linda awoke and walked outside. It had been dark when they arrived in Washington State, and now she beheld it with wonder. *What a glorious place to start a new life.*

What Linda discovered outside the door on her first morning in Washington State was a land rich in natural beauty. Towering fir trees and dense forests blanketed rugged hills and filled the air with the pungent freshness of wet pine. In the distance, blue-gray mountains cast a serene presence. Kitsap Peninsula, on which Bangor Base is situated, is a hilly, forested thumb of land bordered on the west by Hood Canal and the east by the blue waters of Puget Sound and Dyes Inlet. Nine months of the year, from September to May, its spectacular scenery is concealed under a blanket of clouds and nearly constant rain. Locals, who maintain their surroundings more than make up for months of dreary skies, call the drizzle "Seattle sunshine" or "liquid sunbeams." Once, these lands were the hunting grounds of the Suquamish Indians. Later they were claimed by Spain, Russia, England, and finally the United States.

The naval presence on the peninsula dates back to the late nineteenth century when the navy purchased 190 acres south of Bangor in Bremerton, Washington, for the Puget Sound Naval Shipyard (PSNS). The first vessel to dock there was the Civil War gunboat the U.S.S. *Nipsic.* By 1918 the shipyard covered 230 acres and in 1933 the U.S.S. *Constitution,* "Old Ironsides" from the War of 1812, moved in. After the attack on Pearl Harbor, smudge pots and smoke generators camouflaged the yard from enemy attack.

Then, in 1942, the navy founded Bangor Base farther up the coastline as a site for shipping ammunition to the Pacific theater during World War II. On the western curve of the peninsula, it served as such through the Korean and Vietnam wars, until January 1973 when the navy announced the more than $700 million overhaul that transformed it into the home port for the first Trident submarines.

Bringing nuclear submarines so near densely populated Seattle was not without conflict. It stirred up a nest of opposition from environmentalists who protested at base gates and blocked railroad tracks carrying missile parts, but to little avail. "We're a military-based economy," said one longtime resident. "We couldn't afford to turn the Tridents down." When the U.S.S. *Ohio* was commissioned in 1981, it pulled into Bangor Base under nuclear power. Eventually seven more Tridents followed.

When Linda and James drove through the seven-thousand-acre base later that day, she was amazed. It resembled a country club more than a military establishment. Much of the property remained wilderness. Deer, bear, raccoon, and possum roamed freely. There were oyster and clam beds and lakes stocked with trout. One of the few indications it was actually a military base was dark blue signs with white-lettered acronyms marking buildings tucked along the base's eighty-nine miles of road: TriRefFac for Trident Refitting Facilities; TTF for Trident Training Facility; SWFPAC for Strategic Weapons Facility Pacific.

A jaunty white and blue awning announced headquarters, ComSubGru (Commander Submarine Group). Nearby the commissary, barbershop, movie theater, officers' club, library, chapel, gas station, and a gym catered not only to personnel but their families. An assignment on the Bangor Base, one of eight naval stations in the area, was held in especially high regard among Seattle's naval community. Considered the "Cadillacs" of the submarine fleet, the Tridents were manned by sailors who'd placed in the top 5 percent of all recruits.

After touring the base, Linda and James drove through nearby towns in search of an apartment fulfilling his criteria, primarily that it be within five minutes of the subbase's main gates to save wear and tear on his seven-year-old car. Secondly he wanted it to be furnished and inexpensive.

Linda, who dreamed of buying furniture a little at a time and decorating her own apartment, felt disappointed. "He had this plan," she said later. "Spending money on things now just didn't matter to James."

After a weekend's search, the Bergstroms settled on the community of Silverdale, just a few minutes south of the base on Dyes Inlet. When it was settled in the 1870s, residents wanted to name the town Goldendale, but came down a notch on the precious-metal scale when they discovered another Washington State town had already claimed that honor. During Prohibition, rumrunners outran revenuers by concealing easily dismantled stills in surrounding forests. As recent as the late seventies, the town had little more than one restaurant, a tavern, and a smattering of stores bordering the waterfront. But with the influx of Trident cash, it quickly mushroomed into a burgeoning community complete with national stores and restaurants, such as Pier I and Olive Garden, an enclosed shopping mall, and mile after mile of apartments, town homes, and subdivisions.

Once they'd agreed on the town, James maintained their best choice was a small complex called Silverdale Apartments, tucked on a hill next to a strip shopping center and behind the Ryder Truck rental outlet, just a block from the waterfront. Rather than apartments, the tiny complex looked like a seedy motel. The units were inexpensive; in fact, the cheapest in the area, just $245 for a one-bedroom complete with rudimentary and battered furnishings. James's brother, Chris, had lived there when he first came to the base, and it was convenient, well within James's five-minute limit.

The complex wasn't what Linda had envisioned as their first home. "We can do better than this," she argued. "James, why don't we get something a little nicer, buy our own furniture, not this junk."

James, however, would hear nothing of it. "This is where we're living," he decreed. "It's close and it's cheap and we'll be able to save our money."

Sally and Bill Rogers had managed the Silverdale Apartments for nearly three years when the Bergstroms approached them about renting an apartment. They'd had all kinds of tenants, including a few who had been in and out of trouble. "Since the apartments were so cheap, we tended to get a lot of transients," said Sally later. "We got so leery of people, we kept a police scanner in our apartment. When anyone asked about it, we told them that we had family in the sheriff's department. It was a little thing, but we thought it might make them think twice about moving in if they were the type that caused trouble."

When Linda and James showed up on Monday, December 1, 1986, to sign a lease on unit number nine, the second-floor apartment directly next to the one the Rogers occupied, they appeared no different from other navy couples who had come and gone. "They were clean-cut—but then, most of the navy families are," said Sally. "The only thing I remember is that the husband seemed shy. Linda did all the talking. In fact, James was bashful to the point of blushing when I talked to him. So shy, he couldn't even look me in the eye."

Chapter Nine

Linda's initial disappointment over the apartment disappeared quickly. She discovered too much to do in Washington, too many places to go to spend her time fretting. James was right, she decided. Where they lived didn't matter. Rather, it mattered only that they had begun an adventure together. For the first time, she'd escaped Houston and the clouds of her past. Her new husband had given her a wondrous gift, a new life, and she wanted more than anything to seize the opportunity.

These were busy days for both of them. James worked at the base each morning, helping to ready the *Ohio* for its upcoming patrol. Linda settled in, buying pillows, knickknacks, small things to personalize their apartment with its supplied furniture—a timeworn couch, bed, and tables that appeared to have withstood the abuse of a decade of tenants. Although James had stingily insisted on their rather dilapidated housing, in every other way he continued to be generous, almost to a fault. In fact, he rarely paid attention to how Linda spent their money, allowing her to control all the household funds. James already made considerably more money than he had at Devoe & Raynolds. As his rank increased, so would his salary, plus extra pay whenever he sailed. *This is just the beginning,* Linda thought. *Pretty soon we'll have a house of our own and everything I've ever dreamed of.*

Afternoons were reserved to spend together. Usually

Linda and James played tennis a block away at courts on the hill behind the high school. Although thin, James played well, his body deceptively strong, agile, and quick; his aim accurate. Linda felt triumphant every time she successfully returned the ball. Though she was no match for him, James remained patient, giving pointers and occasionally stopping to illustrate in slow motion how to approach the ball.

At home, two or three times a day, James called her into the bedroom. "Let's do it," he'd say playfully. Always, as in Houston, he climbed on top of her and "it" rarely lasted more than a few minutes. To Linda's relief, James had not asked to tie her up since the night in Houston. Despite his unimaginative lovemaking, he was openly affectionate, insisting that they nestle together in bed, her left arm across his chest and her left leg atop his thigh. They slept entwined in each other's arms.

Linda was painfully aware time for such togetherness dwindled. The U.S.S. *Ohio*'s scheduled departure loomed, just two weeks away, on December 19. As a member of the blue crew, James would be on-board for his first patrol—seventy-two days at sea, entirely underwater.

This would be a typical patrol for a Trident submarine. Their mandate, in fact, was to stay at sea for vast periods of time, undetected. Manned by two alternating crews—the blue and the gold—the subs spent an average of 60 percent of the time on patrol, rotating seventy days at sea with twenty-five in port. "We're the fence around the U.S.," said one Trident chief. "The subs are meant to be out there at all times, a deadly deterrent."

When the subs were first included in the navy's budget in 1974, the Cold War was frigid and the Tridents were viewed as a more flexible and effective mode of self-defense than that of land-based nuclear missiles. It took seven years, two years longer than originally projected, and $1.2 billion (40 percent over budget) before the *Ohio* was commissioned. *Time* magazine dubbed the sub's construction "a seven-year ordeal of mismanagement." But when finally deployed, it became the centerpiece of the navy's submarine fleet, quieter and more deadly than its aging ancestors, the *Polaris* and *Poseidon* submarines.

Massive and black, like a giant probe, the *Ohio* went through refit on the base's Delta Pier. Only one quarter of the sub's deadly bulk cleared the water line, making it appear deceptively small. Those who had been on-board knew that from the top of its ominous steel sail it descended seven stories and weighed twice the tonnage of any other U.S. submarine. The exceptional deterrent value of the 560-foot subs came from their powerful payloads. Each carried the destructive capability of all the armaments expended during World War I, World War II, Korea, and Vietnam combined, twenty-four nuclear missiles capable of striking up to eight targets apiece, more than forty-six hundred miles away. "From Seattle Harbor we could hit Havana," boasted one Trident sailor. "And pick out our target in the city."

If more than two months undersea had once sounded romantic or exciting to James, as the blue crew's departure date approached, he became increasingly anxious. Days passed, each progressively more difficult. "He'd come home upset from the base, complaining that this wasn't going to be what he thought," Linda said later. "He was constantly angry, blaming his parents for forcing him to sign up."

"Remember the day I called you from the recruiters?" James taunted Linda. "Why didn't you tell me not to enlist?"

"We weren't married," Linda answered. "I told you to do what you wanted. I had no right to make your mind up for you."

The navy, it soon became obvious, had unknowingly resurrected James Bergstrom's old insecurities. As he had throughout his school years, he interpreted every perceived slight as an unjust personal attack. Although all new crew members toiled at menial tasks during their first two patrols—until they passed all tests and qualified on the subs—James felt singled out. One day, irate that he'd been delegated to wash dishes in the boat's galley, James came home demanding they find a lawyer to get him out of the navy. Linda picked one out of the yellow pages and called, but the attorney she consulted offered little hope. "He said the only way out was death, sickness, court-martial, or a dishonorable discharge," she relayed to James.

Furious, James picked up a glass and smashed it against the wall. "All right, I'll go out on that damned boat," he said, glaring at Linda. "But you make sure you find a way out for me. Find something, anything."

That night, in what would become a pattern of anger and apology, James begged her forgiveness. "I'm sorry. It's just the pressure, the stress; this isn't what I thought it would be," he explained.

Linda disregarded her new husband's moodiness as merely anxiety over his looming first voyage. "I figured he'd get out there, find out it wasn't so bad, and come back okay," she said later.

After all, for much of the day he was still the old James. In fact, he'd become even more protective of her than he had been before the marriage, so much so that she bridled under his ever-growing list of rules. He chastised her for the most innocent activity that he argued exposed her to jeopardy, like going to the post office to pick up mail or the grocery store to shop. "You just don't know who's out there, looking," he argued, demanding she wait until he returned home from the base so they could go together.

Every news story on the television or the radio in which a woman was victimized became fodder for his argument. She later regretted telling him about a stranger who walked up to the sliding glass door on their apartment balcony one afternoon and knocked. When Linda slid it open, a scruffy young peddler laughed, "Ho, ho, ho, I'm Santa Claus," as he pulled bottles of cleaning fluid from a bag and attempted to lure her downstairs where he said he had more to show her.

"My husband's in the shower," Linda said, although James was actually at work on the base. "He'll get really mad."

The peddler left.

When James heard the story, it, too, became evidence of how much she needed his protection. "Never let anyone inside," he ordered. "Don't even answer the door."

From that day on, James went everywhere with her, to the mall, to the Laundromat. "You can't trust anyone, Linda," he told her. "Not anyone."

As the boat's departure date drew near, Linda and James bought a Christmas tree and set it up in a corner of their small living room. On their last night together, they opened gifts. James presented Linda with a microwave oven for their tiny kitchen. She gave him a Walkman tape player to take on-board the ship. That night in bed, Linda couldn't sleep, although she felt her husband's soft, regular breathing beneath her. She wanted to be awake for their final hours together before James would have to leave.

The next morning, Linda stood at the gates to the lower base with the other wives and cried as she and James said good-bye. "I just don't want you to go," she told him. "I'll miss you."

"Just find somebody to help me get out of this," James ordered, as he walked away. "That's your job while I'm gone. I want out."

Chapter Ten

The apartment seemed empty after James left. In a strange city, her first time away from family, Linda felt afloat and isolated. For all practical purposes, she was alone. Unlike sailors working on cruisers who call home when they pull into a port, submariners remain severed from their families for the entire patrol. The only two-way communications allowed are mail drops, one two days after the ship sails and another two days before it returns. In between, wives send Family Grams, fifty-word messages that contain only happy news. "They're read by eight officers before the guys see them," said one navy wife. "You're not allowed to say anything upsetting, or the guys will never get them."

Linda had no intention of disturbing James. He had already been depressed and angry when he left. If anything, she wanted to reassure him that he had no reason to worry about her well-being while he was on patrol. "James, I love you and I'm fine," she wrote in the letter to be delivered at the first mail drop. "Please don't worry about me."

The letter she received in return included a continuation of his directives from the morning they parted. "Find some way to help me out of this," James wrote. "I've got to get out. If I'd known what it was like, I never would have signed up." As always, he topped off the page with a crucifix etched in black ink.

Despite the training and testing given submariners, or "bubbleheads" as other sailors call them, living on-board a

Trident submarine with 170 men, never surfacing for months on end, is difficult to prepare for. "A lot of the guys wash out during their first or second patrol," said one long-time Trident sailor. "They can't take the close quarters, the lack of privacy. Some just crack like an egg from the pressure."

To other members of the blue crew, James Bergstrom didn't appear to be one of those who would crack. "He was always happy, kind of carefree," said another sailor. "Nothing bothered him."

Though that may have been the impression he gave others, inside James was seething. In many respects, the incubatorlike existence on-board brought him back to high school. If to the others he was just one of a mass of bodies, James felt like an outsider, unhappy and persecuted, the butt of jokes. "We're hard on all the guys when they first start," explained one crew member. "You need to know if you can count on them. If they'll be there to back you up in a tough situation." Yet James felt singled out. When he spent the first fifty days of the patrol in the stainless steel galley washing dishes, he found no comfort in the fact that other fledgling sailors on-board had similar duty. "I was really mad, but I didn't want to show it," James said later. "I had my brother to think of. He was on the *Ohio* that patrol, too, and I didn't want to embarrass him. But I didn't go through over a year's training to wash dishes."

No matter what a sailor's duty, the months on-board can drag. The Trident, although larger than any of its U.S. ancestors and dwarfed only by the Russian submarine the *Typhoon,* is the epitome of close quarters. Men's needs bend to the requirements of the submarine and its raison d'être: the twenty-four nuclear missiles housed vertically at the very heart of the boat. The crew sleeps sandwiched among the silos, in cramped cubbyholes, each accommodating nine men. Of course, Trident accommodations are greatly improved over earlier, smaller subs where crew members "hot-sheeted,"

shared bunks by sleeping in shifts. Still, personal possessions are relegated to a four-inch space under mattresses or
in the one small drawer each sailor is assigned. During time
off, many exercise by running circles around the missile
compartment, skirting sharp turns and protruding equipment, where nineteen laps equals one mile. When two men
meet in narrow passageways, one must step aside so the
other can pass.

At the front control station the commander of the watch
oversees a panel as complicated as a jumbo jet's cockpit.
Yet unlike a 747's slick computerization, a Trident's control
panel appears crudely primitive, layered with bulky switches
and chunky red lights flashing vital information. Nearby is
the periscope, often the only link with the surface throughout the patrol. As an IC man, when not at work in the galley,
James spent day after sunless day in a high-tech cubicle
monitoring the ship's interior telephone and alarm systems.
Other sailors manned complicated systems extracting drinking water and oxygen from seawater, but the real stars of the
boat were the "nukes," the sailors who maintained the boat's
nuclear power plant, which generated enough energy to
power the city of Seattle.

From the beginning, James Bergstrom's adaption to submarine life was fraught with discontent. He viewed the
twelve-hours-on/twelve-hours-off schedule, seven days a week,
as too arduous. The ship's captain was a taskmaster, known
by navy men, even outside the sub service, as demanding.
On James's first voyage he lived up to his reputation, order-
ing drill after drill, in which the crew practiced emergency
procedures. In between, James, as a rookie, studied for his
examinations, the tests that would qualify him to move forever out of the galley and into the IC room. Three levels of
superiors would administer the oral exams during his second patrol, throwing out hypothetical situations and demanding to know how he would respond and why, during a
given situation. "The thing is, the navy is an all volunteer

force, and you have to volunteer a second time if you want to be on a sub," says one Trident crew member. "The men should know what they're getting into."

At home, Linda made adjustments of her own. Though she initially hoped she and Tina Bergstrom would become close friends, that failed to materialize. Tina, although pleasant, seemed disinterested in any real relationship with Linda. After all, Tina had lived on the base for years and already had a circle of friends, many of whom, like herself, had small children. In the beginning, Linda went to church at the chapel on base each Sunday morning and then dropped in at Tina's house on the way home, but before long she visited less often. Finally she stopped altogether.

Initially Linda had planned to find a job to fill the lonely months when James was at sea, but he had argued against it, insisting he wanted her available to spend time with him between patrols. To Linda, who was anxious to accumulate the things she'd always dreamed she would one day have—good clothes and furniture, a car—her husband's decision seemed arbitrary and unreasonable, but she reluctantly agreed. James Bergstrom had made her happy and moved her away from a life that had always disappointed her. She was determined to do the same for him. If he wanted her home, she'd find a way to fill the empty days.

At the base gym, Linda discovered just the place to whittle away lazy afternoons. She worked out with weights and jogged the track, or just sat contentedly in the sauna. "It was fun," she said. "There were people around to talk to and it made me feel good about myself."

One day on the track, Linda walked a cool-down round when a sailor slowed from running laps and approached her. "What's your name?" he asked.

"Linda Bergstrom," she answered.

"Chris's wife?"

"No, James Bergstrom's wife," she clarified. "He's on his first patrol on the *Ohio*."

"Yeah, he took my bunk on the ship," the sailor said. "I just left the *Ohio*."

They were soon walking the track together, talking. The sailor's tale sparked Linda's interest when he revealed he'd been dismissed from the ship before his scheduled tenure expired. Linda wanted to know how.

The story the sailor told that afternoon concerned a night on the *Ohio* when the boat patrolled somewhere in the Pacific. "I had this kind of out-of-body experience," he maintained. "I can't explain it, other than that I was kind of floating off above the water. While it was happening, I saw this other ship, off in the distance. When it was over and I told the others, they checked the radar and there was a ship there. It really shook the crew up."

"How can James get out?" Linda asked.

"It's really not that hard. They dump you if they think anything's wrong with you," he said. "Tell your husband to plead insanity. They'll drop him in a heartbeat."

Before she left the gym that day, Linda wrote down the sailor's phone number. When she got home, she posted it on the kitchen bulletin board. *It'll be here when James gets home,* she thought, believing she might have just fulfilled her assignment.

To meet others in her situation, Linda joined the Blue Crew Wives' Club, and became a regular at potluck dinners and get-togethers. When the wives put together a fashion show, the woman who coordinated it asked Linda to model lingerie. Thanks to her regular afternoons at the base gym, she was in terrific shape, thin and firm. Though some of the other wives had photos taken of themselves modeling for the club scrapbook, Linda declined. She knew James would disapprove. But she did mention the affair and her part in it to James in a letter she wrote to include in the mail drop the men would receive a few days before the ship pulled into port.

Yet two months after the *Ohio* sailed, she still had few close friends, until one particular potluck near the end of the patrol when Penny Jacobs approached Linda and introduced herself. "I noticed Linda standing off, kind of alone," Penny explained later. "I'd been there, the new recruit's wife at the party. So I felt sorry for her. I knew how it felt being the new person." Linda and Penny became fast friends. As quiet as Linda was, Penny was outgoing and fun-loving. She had a hearty laugh that matched her ample figure, and whenever she smiled, her blue eyes squinted merrily under a fringe of short brown hair.

Soon Linda became part of a foursome with Penny and two of her closest friends, Gayle Thomas and Diane Siler. All of the women had husbands on the *Ohio*'s blue crew and all liked having fun. If Penny was the bawdy one, Diane was the religious one, a born-again Christian who attended services at a local church. Gayle was heavyset, bubbly and fun to be with. "You need a support team when your husbands are out to sea for months on end," said Penny. "We were that for each other."

The night before the *Ohio*'s return, Linda and her new friends met at Penny's apartment for pizza. The others laughed when they saw how their friend had decorated her apartment for the next day's excitement. There were crepe paper streamers and welcome-home banners draped from the walls. Two big round red balloons with a banana poking out from between them dangled from the bedroom ceiling. Penny's guests grinned up at the whimsical symbol like schoolgirls in an arcade. "It's my welcome-home-now-let's-do-it message," Penny chuckled. Since Penny's husband had been out to sea before, she took Linda aside and assured her, "When they come home, it's like a honeymoon all over again. They can't wait to get their hands on you. You really appreciate each other."

A rivalry escalated between the friends as they tantalized each other with their plans for the next day.

"I'm going to get him home and keep him locked in this bedroom for a week," Penny laughed. "You'll see."

"Well, I'm going to get things going even before we reach the house," said Diane. "I'm going to that base with nothin' on under my coat. Wait and see."

There was a sense of competition between the wives, and soon they all joined in the fun, daring each other to wear nothing at all or something silky and sensual under their coats. Linda took it all in stride. James's months at sea had built up her appetite for his return, and one of the letters she'd included in mail drop said, "I can't wait for you to get home."

She was more than a little disappointed when the letter she received from James was less joyful, bordering on the morose. In it he complained endlessly about injustices he'd endured on-board. "I hope you've got some information for me when we pull in," he said in closing. On the top of each page, as always, he marked a black crucifix directly in the center.

Unaware of the uncertainties facing Linda, before the friends left Penny's that night, they made a pact: They'd be on the Delta Pier the following day to greet their husbands and they would all have a surprise for them—since it was February 15 and cold, they would need coats, but underneath they would wear only the skimpiest lingerie or nothing at all. Linda laughed. The idea seemed so daring. She couldn't help thinking about how surprised and pleased James would be.

The next morning, Linda woke up early and bought her own decorations for their small apartment. Like Penny, she hung crepe paper and colored a banner with markers, "Welcome Home James." Instead of a banana and balloons, Linda drew signs—"Oh, James, don't stop" and "1-Way No Fun"— to hang in the bedroom. Then she slipped on her winter coat over a burgundy silk and lace teddy. "I was so excited," she said later. "It's like, He's coming home!"

Linda met her friends at the parking lot to the lower base gates and caught one of the white buses that transported the families to the Delta Pier, where the *Ohio* docked. On the bus, everyone talked and laughed, giddy with expectation. Everyone except Linda, who sat quietly, her fingers secretly crossed in her coat pockets. She'd spent much of the morning praying James was as excited as she about his homecoming and that things weren't as bad as his letter indicated.

As the bus pulled up to the pier, Linda searched excitedly for James's face in the crush. She felt certain from his letter that he would be among the first off. As she suspected, he emerged from the bowels of the submarine well ahead of the rest of the crew. Running toward her on the pier, he grabbed her in his arms, but instead of the joyful reunion she had imagined, James clutched her elbow and whispered angrily into her ear, "This is all bullshit," clipping each word off in disgust. "Have I got things to tell you."

Surrounded by families hugging and kissing, Linda whispered, "I can't wait to get you home. You know what I'm wearing under this coat? Lingerie. Nothing but lingerie."

Instead of breaking his anger, James pulled her farther from the crowd. "What the hell did you do that for? And what the hell were you doing modeling lingerie? What's come over you?"

"I thought you'd like it," she said, trying to hold back tears. In the crowd, she saw her friends and their husbands locked in each other's arms. "I did it for you."

"Goddamn it, what the hell's gotten into you?" James answered, flushed with anger. "Go home. I've got duty tonight. I'll call you later."

In a last-ditch effort to save the reunion, Linda whispered in his ear, "I found out information for you. I met somebody who got out."

For the first time, James smiled. "Finally. That's great. Go home, I'll call you later."

Linda walked dejectedly away. When she surveyed the crowd from the steps of the bus, she saw her friends milling around her, bubbling and cooing to their husbands. Determined not to let them see her disappointment, she smiled affectionately at James as the bus pulled away.

When the phone rang later that night, it was James calling from the base. First he apologized for blowing up at her on the pier. "You just don't know what it's been like," he said. "I've got to get out of here."

Then Linda told him about the sailor she'd met, the one who had been released from the navy after claiming he had an out-of-body experience.

"Yeah, I know about him. The guys on the boat told me about that SOB," James countered, his voice thick with sarcasm. "Is that all you've got? What am I supposed to do? Plead insanity?"

"I don't know," Linda said, tears catching in her throat. "All I know is what he told me."

"Well, go to sleep," he said, disgustedly. "I'm off tomorrow. We'll talk then."

Chapter Eleven

At six the next morning, Linda drove to the base to pick up James. She didn't know what to expect, and when she pulled up to the lower base gates, he glowered at her. She slid over and he got behind the wheel. As he drove off base, Linda tried to make small talk to bring him out of his funk. James was distant. Then, once they passed the outer gates, she wiggled out of her coat, cuddled up next to him, and kissed him. As he drove, she nuzzled his neck. Finally James responded, slipping his hand under her skirt and between her legs. Linda smiled. It appeared the old James was back. When she unlocked the apartment door, he surveyed the crepe paper streamers, balloons, and the "Welcome Home" banner.

"I'm a real jerk for being so upset with you," he whispered, wrapping his arms around her. "I'm sorry."

Then he drew her toward the bedroom, pausing only long enough to laugh at the provocative signs Linda had plastered on the walls. He lay on the bed and pulled Linda to him. The anxiety melted away, and Linda relaxed for the first time in days as they made love.

Having James home made everything seem normal again. In the days that followed, each morning he drove to the base, where he helped refit the *Ohio* for the gold crew's upcoming patrol. In the early afternoon, he was back at the apartment, announcing his arrival with a *toot, toot* of the Grand Prix's horn that reminded Linda of the way Ward Clever might have signaled "I'm home" to June on the old "Leave It to Beaver" television series.

In many ways, their tiny apartment was beginning to feel more like a home. There were Linda's mementos including pictures of her family, and James had a growing collection of plaques and certificates from the navy, earned for each hurdle he passed on his way to qualifying on the sub: one for passing a fire school he attended, others for completing submarine school and basic training. Linda framed them all and hung them on a wall in the living room.

"Why are you doing that?" he asked when he first saw them.

"Because I'm proud of you," she said. "I want everyone to know how smart my husband is."

Though James said nothing more, Linda could tell he was pleased. *I'm going to do whatever I can to make sure this works out,* she thought.

As before, afternoons were their time together. They went to the movies or took long walks along the water. Just as he had before that first patrol, he insisted she wait for him each day before running errands, even going to the Laundromat or picking up their mail at the post office. "You don't know what kind of perverts are out there," he told her. Sometimes Linda thought it was odd. She was the one who had a reason to fear strangers—she'd been raped as a teenager—yet it was James who expected bad guys around every corner.

At home, James's appetite for sex was as insatiable as ever. Off and on during the day and at least once at night, he called her into the bedroom to "do it." As before, he held precisely to his routine, shunning any suggestion to try something different. The one night she came to bed wearing her burgundy lace teddy, he immediately ordered her back to the bathroom to change. "I like you better in just your bra and panties," he contended. When she reappeared in plain white cotton bikini briefs and a bra, he was happy. None of it made sense to Linda. Of course, it may have if she knew more about her husband's past, especially his early obsession with bra and panty models in the Sears catalog.

Many afternoons were spent on the tennis court, where James renewed his effort to teach Linda the game. Although the courts on base were vastly better maintained than the dilapidated one behind the high school, James insisted they play the latter. When Linda asked why, he said he preferred not bumping into the other crew members on his off hours. "I spend enough time with them," he contended. They also stopped working out at the base gym, after James insisted he'd noticed other sailors—"fucking bastards"—eyeing Linda when she ran the track or worked out with weights.

On Sundays he refused to go to the base chapel, demanding they join Holy Trinity parish in nearby East Bremerton instead. "This is a real church," he said with an all-knowing air the first time they pulled up to the sprawling complex with its mansard roof. Linda liked the church. It reminded her of the parish her family belonged to in Houston. But she couldn't help thinking James was avoiding the base as if it were the wellspring of all his problems.

Most days, James was as he had always been, thoughtful and attentive. As always, he was obsessive about spending all their time together. Still, he sometimes seemed nervous and distrustful—even of her. Once when she had just finished showering, she looked out the bathroom door and saw him searching through her dresser drawers. She had no idea what he was looking for, and as soon as he heard her pull the shower curtain back, he stopped. Then a few days later she walked out of the bedroom and discovered him tearing up the telephone number of the discharged sailor.

"Who's this guy?" James demanded.

"He's the one I told you about," Linda answered. "The one who got out of the navy. I got his number for you."

James was furious. He stormed around the apartment, his face bloodred and the veins standing out in his neck. "I know about what you do when I'm gone," he accused. "All you wives. The husbands go out to sea and you shack up with some other guy."

Linda stayed quiet, and a moment later James calmed down. "I'm sorry," he apologized. "It's just being out there like that for months. It does things to you."

The *Ohio*'s alternating team, the gold crew, sailed out of Puget Sound on March 26, and James settled into his on-shore routine of taking classes on base for six hours each day and then coming home to Linda early each afternoon. As his twenty-fourth birthday approached, Linda mentioned inviting Chris and Tina over for a party. "No. He talked me into this, and now he won't even be going out on the next patrol," James fumed. "He's been reassigned to shore duty. What a way for a brother to do a brother."

So on the morning of James's birthday, Monday, April 6, Linda baked a cake. Not wanting to celebrate alone, she approached a young navy couple who had just moved into one of the other units, inviting them to stop in after dinner for cake and coffee to surprise James. Although they'd never met the Bergstroms before, they accepted Linda's invitation. James appeared pleased when the doorbell rang and his new neighbors introduced themselves and came inside. He took it good-naturedly, blowing out his candles and cutting thick slabs of chocolate cake for everyone. Yet as soon as the other couple left, he turned to Linda and ordered, "Don't do that again. That guy's above me in rank, and I spend enough time on the ship feeling like a nobody. I don't want that when I'm home."

It was becoming a pattern with James, this not wanting to be around anyone who outranked him. They were invited often to go out with Penny, Gayle, and Diane and their husbands, but James always refused. "They're nukes," he contended, referring to their position onboard. "We don't belong socializing with them."

The only ones James sometimes agreed to see were Chris and Tina, just, he said, to keep up appearances. But each time, it was progressively more difficult for Linda.

It all began one Sunday afternoon when James and Linda stopped at his brother's after church. Chris was seated on the couch with his oldest son on his lap, and he and James were talking about their last patrol, when Linda, who was wearing a skirt that ended a few inches above the knee, walked across the room toward the bathroom. "Sexy," Chris whispered.

His four-year-old mimicked him, only louder, "Sexy." The little boy giggled, mischievously covering his mouth.

At the time, James laughed along with Chris and the child, but that night, when they were alone in the apartment, he fumed, screaming at Linda, claiming her dress was too short and that she'd knowingly elicited Chris's comment. "Keep your damn legs crossed like this," he said, sitting on a chair and demonstrating by prissily clamping his legs together at the ankles. "Keep your knees together. And no more short skirts. Who the hell are you trying to impress?"

"I didn't do anything," Linda countered. "Chris and I barely talked. You're just jumping to some kind of sick conclusion."

A few days later when James suggested she wash the car while he was at work, she called Tina to see if she could do it at their apartment, where there were better facilities. Chris answered the phone.

"Sure," Chris said. "I'll tell Tina you're coming."

When she arrived, Chris came outside and watched as she sprayed the car down and began soaping it up. "Where's Tina?" she asked.

"Oh, she just ran up to the store," he said. "She'll be right back." Chris was friendly and talked to her casually while she worked. Mostly he wanted to talk about James. "Does he like the navy?" Chris asked.

"Not really," Linda said. "But I'm sure hoping this works out for him."

"He's just got to get used to it," Chris offered. "Give it a chance."

Linda couldn't help thinking about the fight she and James had the last time she'd seen Chris. *It's all ridiculous,* she thought, when Tina, as promised, pulled up in the driveway and greeted her with a smile.

That night when Linda picked James up at the base, he whistled at the car. "Looks good," he said. "Where'd you do it?"

"At Chris and Tina's," she answered.

"Was Tina there?"

"Not when I got there, but she drove up while I was washing it."

"I suppose Chris stood around and watched you," he prodded.

"He was there," she answered, quickly losing patience. "We just talked."

By the time they reached the apartment, James was bristling, not losing control, but calmly assessing her. He jerked her inside and shoved her onto the couch. "I bet Chris had a helluva good time watching your ass," he shouted. "I bet he was thinking about what he'd like to do to you."

"We were just talking," she yelled back. "What's wrong with you? Why are you saying this?"

"I bet you enjoyed having him watch. Didn't you?" James said, strong-arming her around the room. He pushed his face within inches of hers and stared at her coldly. "You like him? I bet you're interested in him. He'll be here, you know. He's not going out on that damn sub this summer."

"I'm interested in you," Linda said, more calmly, trying to maneuver to get past him. "I married you. I love you."

To her amazement, James seized her by the shoulders and shook her.

"Stop it," she cried, her voice crackling with fear. "Stop it. I didn't do anything."

James threw her against the bed as if she were a discarded doll and walked out.

Later that night, as always, he apologized. "I just jumped to conclusions." He shrugged. "It's all the pressure I'm under."

Weeks went by with James as gentle and kind as ever, but Linda found it impossible to forget what had happened. When Tina called to invite them out for dinner, she refused. "I can't sit there with them, after what you accused Chris and me of," Linda told James. "You go. I'm not going."

"But if we don't go as a couple, they'll think something's wrong," James insisted. "We have to go."

"There is something wrong," Linda shouted back. "You think I'm having an affair with your brother. Why don't you tell them that?"

James made an excuse, but a week later, Chris was on the phone with another invitation.

"My wife doesn't want to go, she's unsociable," Linda heard James tell him.

"Tell him why," she demanded. "Tell him you think the two of us are fooling around behind your back."

James covered the mouthpiece with his hand and held it like a club. "You think it's bad now," he said through clenched teeth. "It'll be bad if you don't go."

"All right, James," she relented. "I'll go."

The night they met Chris and Tina at Azteca, a popular Mexican restaurant just across the street from their apartment, Linda felt jittery and on edge. She'd spent an hour nervously shuffling through her closet searching for something long and plain to wear, finally settling on a rather dowdy flowered dress. But as they were leaving the house, James turned to her and said, "What the hell did you wear that for? I can see your underwear right through it."

When she offered to change, he pulled her by the arm and mumbled that they didn't have time, then pushed her toward the car.

Dinner dragged on. Though the restaurant, with its festive streamers of Mexican flags and Aztec murals, was one of her favorites, it failed to lift her spirits as it usually did. Instead she stared blankly around the room. "All I could think of was, don't talk to Chris," she said. "Don't even look at him."

As the others ate and gossiped, Linda felt increasingly more uncomfortable. She pushed her food around her plate, until she feared she might explode with tension. Finally she excused herself and headed toward the rest room. Impulsively, on the way back to the table, she stopped at the bar for a drink, something to calm her anxiety. She was gone from the table for only five or ten minutes when she saw James storming toward her, followed by Tina and Chris.

"Where the hell did you go?" James shouted.

"I was on my way back. I just stopped for a drink," she said.

James seized the back of her arm and pinched so hard, pain radiated into her shoulder, until tears filled Linda's eyes.

"Hey, she's okay," the woman bartender shouted. "Leave her alone. Let her have her drink."

James spun at the other woman. "Listen, you bitch, this is my wife. Stay out of it."

On the way home in the car, James berated her. "You pulled a good stunt, Linda," he hollered. "You embarrassed me in front of my family."

"I just wanted a drink," she said, trying to calm the tremor in her voice.

"I owe you one, bitch," he concluded. "I owe you one."

"How did you expect me to sit there after what you've accused me of with Chris?" she asked bitterly, as they entered the apartment.

Deadly calm, James forced her into the bedroom and onto the bed, then stood above her, glaring.

"This is not my fault," she protested. "This is all in your mind."

Soon she was afraid to say any more. "I never saw James like that before. He was so angry, the veins in his neck and arms were throbbing, and his eyes, his eyes were popping out at me," she said later. "He looked like an angry dog. Like a Doberman pinscher."

As always, later that night he apologized.

Weeks and months passed, and on June 9, 1987, the gold crew returned from their patrol on the *Ohio*. Once the boat pulled into Bangor Base, James appeared under increasing pressure. He'd go days at a time as the old James: gentle and caring. Then he'd be on edge, agitated by even the smallest things. To calm him, Linda tried to do everything he suggested. Instead of working out on the base, she joined a women-only gym, Living Well Ladies, in a storefront not far from their apartment. At aerobics class one day, a woman whose husband was on the *Ohio*'s gold crew casually mentioned, "Bet you were sorry to see the ship come into port. That means your husband will be sailing soon."

Linda didn't answer. Unlike her sadness the first time James pulled out of port, this time she wasn't entirely sure how she felt. If pressed, she would have had to admit she was anxious to see James go, so she could try to decipher the reasons everything was going so wrong. She couldn't help thinking that he seemed increasingly irrational.

Like the afternoon the phone rang while he was on base. When Linda answered, James roared at her, "Come down here. I can't make it. I can't do this. Chris won't be there this time. I'll be all alone."

When she arrived on base, he jumped in the car and ordered, "I know this is crazy, but let's just pack up and take off for Canada. They'll never find us."

Linda let him drone on about how they could escape, leaving no trace, as she drove home. He had thought it all through, how they could start a new identity across the border. She said nothing until she pulled up in the apartment parking lot. "No, James. We aren't running away," she told him firmly. "I'm not going to spend my life on the run."

James said he understood, but the subject of fleeing came up continually after that afternoon. Always James would be angry. "If you loved me, you'd do it," he'd demand, much as he had two years earlier to convince her to marry him.

One night during a particularly heated argument, James slammed her against the apartment wall. Linda, reeling under the blow, fell onto the bed. James left her there, crying. Afraid at what he might do next, she waited, sobbing, for some sign from him, some indication the violence was over. Before long, she heard a strange moaning in the living room, a mournful wail almost like that of an injured animal. When she peeked around the corner, Linda saw her husband, his hands covering his face in despair, crying. It sent a shudder through her.

Minutes later, James ambled back into the bedroom, acting as if nothing particularly surprising had happened. As always, he apologized, blaming his actions on the stress he was under. "It's not that bad," he said, wiping away Linda's tears. "Why are you crying? Stop it."

As she quieted her sobs he assured her, "It's just the navy. Everything will be all right when I can get out of the navy."

On Tuesday, July 7, Linda drove James to the *Ohio*. They held hands in the car and she hugged him and kissed him good-bye at the gate. "You'll be all right," she assured him. "Just hang in there."

James looked fine, smiling, as if nothing in the world bothered him.

On the drive home from the base, Linda went over the last few weeks again and again in her mind. "I figured he was right. James had never acted like that before. It had to be just the navy and all the pressure he was under. I was angry at his brother and his parents for forcing him to sign up," she said. "And I decided he was right. Once sea duty was over, he'd be fine."

Later that morning Linda's landlord knocked on the door.

"Are you all right?" Sally Rogers asked, her voice filled with concern. "I heard you two fighting the last few days and I could barely sleep wondering if you were still alive."

"Yeah, I'm fine," Linda assured her. "We've just been under a lot of pressure with James leaving. He's gone now. It'll give us a little time to cool off."

"Well, if you're sure," Rogers replied, uncertain.

"I'm sure," Linda said. "But thanks for asking."

Still, later that afternoon in her own apartment, Rogers couldn't help reflecting on the sounds she had heard emanating through the thin apartment walls. After years of living beside all kinds of people, she was used to loud arguments, but this was something else. The moaning and the screaming. When she saw James Bergstrom coming and going around the apartment complex, he looked like such a shy, pleasant, even timid man. It was hard to imagine he was the one wailing into the night. "I could only come up with one way to describe what I was hearing," Sally said later. "It sounded not human."

Chapter Twelve

Linda's prediction that the patrol would give her and James time to put things in order never materialized. Days after the boat set sail, the phone rang in her apartment. It was the wife of the *Ohio*'s COB (the chief of the boat), Sandy Sirles. Her husband was the highest-ranking enlisted man on board the *Ohio,* and Linda knew immediately something must be wrong. "Linda, I'd like you to come over for a visit," she said. "We need to talk."

When she arrived at the COB's home, the other woman invited her in. "The thing is," said Sandy, a petite, polite woman with long, dark hair, motioning for Linda to sit beside her on the couch, "I've just received a letter from my husband, and it seems James is having a hard time. As a matter of fact, he's acting rather childishly. We need your help to get him through the patrol."

She then explained to Linda that almost immediately after the boat pulled out, James began insisting he be returned to shore, claiming that because of their volatile last weeks, he feared Linda would leave him while he was at sea. "We'd like you to send James a Family Gram," Sirles went on to say. "Something cheerful to let him know you'll be all right."

"Sure," Linda agreed. "I'll do it today." Still she left the COB's home feeling exhausted and confused. *Why is James doing this?* she wondered. *What's wrong?*

Linda never imagined things could go far enough for the COB's wife to be involved. She was worried about James. She was also concerned about herself. She had grown to love navy life, the friends she'd made, her new home. James was jeopardizing all of it. If this didn't work out, they'd end up back in Houston with little hope of ever getting ahead and making something of their lives. She drove back to the apartment to get one of the eight Family Grams she'd been issued for this patrol. It had room for just the briefest message. She sat down at the kitchen table and wrote:

James,

> *I love you. Everything is fine. I hope you're okay. Please don't worry about me. I'm looking forward to seeing you when you get back from patrol.*

> > *Love, Linda*

She drove back to the base, where she slipped her note through the slit in the silver mailbox marked with the *Ohio*'s designation.

Then she went home. Just moments after she walked in the door, the phone rang. This time it was Penny calling to invite her to her apartment "just to talk." Eager not to be alone, Linda got back in the car and drove over.

Linda sat at the kitchen table in Penny's bright apartment drinking a Coke and trying to make sense of it all. "Why is James doing this?" Linda asked her friend.

Penny shrugged, then went on to explain that she already knew something of James Bergstrom's problems. In the mail drop she'd received that morning, her husband had written asking her to check up on Linda. "Your husband mentioned that we're friends, and the COB suggested James might be more at ease if I promised to keep tabs on you," Penny said, laughing. "I figured we'd be together anyway, so what the heck."

Linda shook her head. *What's going on?* she wondered. "James was upset about sailing, that's all," she assured her friend. "The fight was just because he was so stressed out about going out to sea. I don't understand what he's doing."

Penny looked sympathetic. "None of the guys like to go out to sea. Would you?" she asked. "Seventy-two days underwater? I'm sure James was just overreacting to the pressure."

"I really want this to work out for James and me. I don't want to end up back in Houston," Linda concluded.

Determined to make the best of the situation, Penny said, "Let's forget about all this. Your husband tells my husband that you like to play tennis. I can't say I know a damn thing about it, but I've got a racket and I'll give it a try."

From that point on, Penny and Linda were together almost daily. They played tennis on the courts in Penny's complex or went to wives' club functions. Often they became a foursome, with Gayle and Diane. At one get-together, a garden party, everyone wore formals. Just for fun, Gayle came in her wedding dress. Late at night the four friends ordered pizza and talked, sometimes about how wonderful it would be when they all had children. When Linda said her period was late, they all smiled expectantly. But inside, Linda was sure a pregnancy now would be far from wise. When she began menstruating a month after James left for sea, she sighed with relief.

"I just wasn't sure yet," she later said. "Things were too unsettled. I figured everything with James was going to be all right, that we were just going through a rough spot. But I didn't want to add any more pressure."

One afternoon, Diane started a conversation about all the sailors who had "cracked" while at sea. "One even shot his wife and himself when he was on shore duty," she added. Penny noticed Linda flinch and sensed how uncomfortable the conversation must be making her. Though they never discussed it, Penny understood Linda worried constantly about James and how the patrol was unfolding.

In fact, Linda spoke about her husband as reluctantly as one might a particularly troublesome child. All three of the friends had noticed that whenever the conversation turned to spouses, she almost always remained silent. Though she revealed little, their perception was that something was terribly wrong. Wrong enough that once when Linda was not with the group, Gayle asked the others if they thought James battered Linda. "It's the way she never talks about him," she said. "It's like there's something there."

Penny said only that she would not be surprised to find out that was true.

The week before the *Ohio* was scheduled to return, the four women took a trip together, one last fling before the *Ohio* pulled into port. That morning they drove around the sound and then headed toward Mount Rainier National Park. It was one of those clear blue days so rare in the Pacific Northwest, and the mountain, majestically streaked with snow and ice, was visible miles before they arrived in the park. While they traversed the winding mountain roads, Linda gulped it all in, the clear sky, the imposing fir trees, the massive rock formations, and the spectacular rivers and waterfalls. Before they left the park, they pulled off the road for a panoramic view of the mountain surrounded by wildflowers. In the cool breeze, Linda breathed in the crisp air and the smell of a fleeting summer day.

Still, shadows of her malaise lingered. A few nights later, the four friends were gathered as usual at Penny's house, wolfing down a large pizza with extra cheese and sausage. Penny told stories about her childhood and they laughed uproariously, their mood heightened by the fact that in only two more days, the *Ohio* would pull into home port with their husbands on-board. At one point, Penny looked over and realized that though the others tittered with excitement, Linda sat quietly beside her, a wide but empty smile plastered on her face. "You worried?" she whispered.

"Maybe just a little." Linda grimaced. "I just don't know what to expect. But somehow, I'm going to make it all work out."

Linda never could have anticipated what happened the following morning, Wednesday, September 16, 1987, a full day before the *Ohio* was scheduled to dock. The apartment, to her chagrin, was a mess. She'd spent so much time at Penny's, her own place looked as disheveled as a parade route after the final float and the crowd had passed. Clothes lay where she'd undressed, and absolutely, everything needed a good scrubbing. Dark, thick hair piled atop her head, in an old pair of shorts and an oversized T-shirt, she was on her hands and knees scouring the bathroom floor when suddenly she instinctively knew she wasn't alone. She turned slowly toward the patio door and saw the figure of a man silhouetted in the bright afternoon sun. He stared at her, watching. Linda squinted and looked again. The man looked vaguely familiar but frightening. *Who is it?* she wondered.

"James," she suddenly whispered. Standing outside the door as if in a trance was her own husband. She hadn't even recognized him. "My God, it's James."

Once Linda coaxed James inside, she led him to the couch and sat beside him. "What are you doing here?" she asked softly. "I was planning to meet the ship tomorrow."

James didn't answer, just stared straight ahead. Linda looked at him closely and realized that what made him look so different was his eyes; they were distant, as if he peered through a haze.

"What's going on?" she demanded.

"I can't take it anymore," James answered, flatly. "I can't go back. It's too hard."

That was all James would say. For fifteen minutes, Linda sat beside him talking, trying to eke out even minimal information about what had happened. Her husband's lips remained still until he finally turned to her and whispered in a hoarse, quiet voice, "I'm supposed to go to the doctor. I can't drive. You'll have to take me."

In the car, James stared silently out the window at Silverdale—the place they'd lived for nearly a year—as if he recollected little of it.

"Talk to me," Linda pleaded. "This isn't like you, James. What happened?"

There was only silence.

Linda drove James to the naval hospital a few miles south of the base where he'd been ordered to undergo a psychiatric evaluation. She still had no idea what could have happened to throw him into such a zombielike state when they pulled up in front of the hospital, an imposing cement and glass structure virtually hidden amongst the forest. Inside, they were directed to the seventh-floor psychiatric unit, where Linda waited in a hallway while James went into an examining room. An hour later, he emerged and walked toward her. "We can leave now," he said. There was no explanation; no doctor approached her.

At home that night, James sat transfixed on the couch. He stared blankly at the television, as if its images hollowly reflected off his eyes. As he peered at the screen, Linda watched James, studying him with such concentration, the ringing of the phone jarred her back to reality.

"Aren't you coming over? Diane and Gayle are already here," Penny asked.

Linda could hear her friends laughing and celebrating in the background. She cupped her hand over the phone and whispered, "I can't. James is home."

"Is he all right?"

"It's really bad," she said. "But he won't tell me what's wrong."

Linda hung up the phone feeling disappointed and alone. Her friends were so excited about their husbands' return. She knew it was selfish to think of herself when James was so troubled, but she longed to feel as they did, without the continual pain that haunted her. As that night lingered on, James never made a move toward her, said little if anything. She couldn't help thinking it was like he was barely there. *He's like a ghost.*

The silence continued like a presence between them, until the following afternoon when James, sitting timidly in a chair, finally blurted out, "I really thought I would kill myself." Kneading his hands and staring downward at the apartment's worn beige tile floor, his eyes rimmed in tears, he talked in disconnected and fitful terms about his second voyage.

Linda finally pieced together a terrifying chain of events. In James's words, it sounded as if he had suffered a breakdown or a deep depression. The sub had been a pressure cooker for him, his mind continually drifting back to Linda and arguments they'd had, blowing them up until they loomed insurmountable. "I was sure you'd be gone, that you'd leave me," he said. "It was all I could think of." Shaking and crying, he sought out Jim Sirles, the ship's COB, and asked to be taken back to port. Sirles, an intensely businesslike man, listened to James ramble on about his fears, then assured the young sailor his wife, Sandy, would look in on Linda. "She'll be all right, James," he said. "She'll be waiting for you on the pier when the boat pulls in."

In the following weeks, Sirles occasionally sought out Bergstrom for a "climate check," a few minutes to ask how things were going. James always smiled pleasantly at him and assured Sirles he was fine. Sirles would later say he worried about his young recruit, but not overly so. It wasn't unusual for sailors facing months at sea to have doubts about their ability to handle the confinement. When there were problems at home, the situation became only more complicated.

But halfway through the patrol, Sirles heard through the sub's grapevine that Bergstrom had taken a turn for the worse, that he had a knife hidden under his mattress and that others had heard him threatening to use it on himself. Sirles went to Bergstrom's bunk and confiscated a small paring knife James had apparently lifted during galley duty, then took his charge to sick bay. They talked for an hour, James crying that the submarine corps just wasn't for him. He couldn't take the confinement, being so far from home, and so far from Linda, for long periods of time. As before, Sirles managed to calm James down and convince him to hang in through the last month of the patrol. "But I was worried," said Sirles later. "I didn't know what Bergstrom might do."

Besides Sirles, the only one Bergstrom confided in on the *Ohio* was the chief petty officer in charge of the IC unit, Steve Swartz, a lanky, somewhat balding man who had the manner of a concerned neighbor. It was Swartz's job to take care of his men, to make sure their personal problems never interfered with their duties. Swartz, too, worried that Bergstrom might wash out of the corps.

Whatever was going on inside James Bergstrom's head, to those not in immediate contact with him, he maintained a cool and jovial exterior, just as he had throughout his painful school years. "Everybody on the boat seems to settle into a particular role," Sirles would later explain. "James was this boyish, quiet guy. The guys liked to kid him because he'd blush and get embarrassed. Some of them used to call him 'Wild Man,' not meaning any harm, but just out of fun."

In fact, Bergstrom camouflaged his feelings so well that outside his division, few knew he was undergoing any kind of crisis. One longtime submariner, Telford Weister, helped James study for his qualifying exams during that patrol, and he remembers little of the chaos the others describe. "James seemed fine. He was studying hard and always appeared to be okay," Weister said later. "In fact, one thing I remember about Bergstrom is the way he was always smiling. He had this sappy grin." James did hold it together well enough to take his oral exams and pass, qualifying as an IC, interior communications, man during the patrol.

Still, Sirles was worried, and he ordered Swartz to keep a special eye on the young IC man from Houston. He wasn't sure when or if James Bergstrom's buckling veneer would crack again. For his part, James was acutely aware that his superiors now had doubts about him. "For the rest of the time on the boat, they had someone looking out for me at all times," James told Linda. When the *Ohio* neared port, a concerned Sirles ordered Bergstrom to leave early with the mail drop and issued orders for him to report to the psychiatric unit of the naval hospital "for a checkup."

Jim Sirles was reassigned to other duty, and that was his last patrol on the *Ohio*. If he had stayed, he wasn't certain how he would have felt about taking Bergstrom out to sea again. "I had some doubts about letting him continue onboard," Sirles said later. "I felt he had some real problems. Though he seemed to settle down after that night with the knife and he did do his work, I wasn't sure he should continue to serve on a nuclear submarine."

The day after James's unexpectedly early arrival, Linda drove him back to the naval hospital for a second appointment. She was worried, about both James and his future in the navy. Again she waited in the hallway for nearly an hour, but this time the doctor called her into his office, where James was seated quietly on a chair.

"Your husband is all right," the boyishly young navy doctor in the white coat assured her with a smile. "It's just anxiety from being out on patrol."

The doctor went on to discuss their marriage and the importance of sticking together to work things out. "I couldn't get over the feeling that James had blamed all this on me," Linda would later say. "But I didn't care, just as long as he was all right and things were going to be okay."

As far as leaving the navy, the doctor didn't recommend it, but the decision was up to James. "It could mean you won't get an honorable discharge," he cautioned. "That can make it tough to get a job later."

James looked at Linda and asked, "What should I do?"

"It's up to you," she said quietly, holding her breath as he decided. "It's your call."

After a moment's hesitation, James said, "I'll stick it out. I've just got two years left."

Although she tried to look noncommittal, Linda was relieved. She had no desire to return to Texas, at least not yet. Since arriving in Washington, she'd felt progressively stronger and freer. Even the occasional turmoil of her marriage wasn't enough to cloud her new enthusiasm. It was as if the crisp mountain breezes had blown away the old Houston cobwebs that had imprisoned her. "For the first time in my life, I wasn't afraid," she would later say. "The nightmares were gone."

After that second doctor's appointment, James settled into his regular routine onshore. It took almost a month for the *Ohio* to go through refit before the gold crew set sail on October 14. Then there was school each morning, and in the early afternoons he'd leave the base and head home to be with Linda.

For her part, Linda treated James as if he were in a fragile, hand-blown glass bubble. "I would have done almost anything to make him happy," she would later say. "I wanted so much for our marriage and his career in the navy to work out."

In some ways as the months passed, James seemed changed. There were small things, little indications that something preyed on his mind. Often he disappeared in the afternoon or at night, saying he wanted to take a walk. "I just need to be alone," he explained. Later he became obsessed with emptying the wastebasket in the kitchen. Even on nights when it held nothing more than a single sheet of paper, James would be gone for fifteen or twenty minutes until he walked up the steps to their apartment dangling the empty basket in his hand. Though the complex's heavy brown metal Dumpster was less than two hundred yards away on the side of the complex, Linda wasn't too worried. "I figured he was just outside thinking," she later explained.

But what she did find disturbing was days when she found James staring vacantly out the front window at an apartment opposite theirs. Startled by her presence, he hurriedly planted himself in front of the television. Curious, Linda went to the window and glanced down as her husband had moments before. There in an apartment catty-corner to theirs, she saw a young woman, a navy wife, sitting alone in her own living room.

Days later, James disappeared with the kitchen wastebasket, and when he didn't immediately return, Linda followed him down. She couldn't help being curious. *What could he be doing?* she wondered. Linda rounded the end of the complex near the Dumpster, and James wasn't there. As she turned the corner to the back of the apartments, she thought she saw him, on his tiptoes, peering through one of the bedroom windows that lined the building, five feet from the ground. Perhaps sensing her presence, James immediately bobbed down and picked up a window screen that lay nearby on the ground. Standing up, he smiled at Linda as if he'd just noticed her. "Look what I found," he shouted, holding up the screen. "I bet it'll fit the bathroom. We can have cross ventilation."

Linda wasn't sure what she had just walked in on, but she had the unmistakable feeling that until she arrived, her husband had been watching someone through a bedroom window. When she confronted him, he only laughed. "Why would I want to look at anyone else when I have a wife as gorgeous as you?" He smiled. "Come on. Let's go upstairs and have some fun."

By the end of October, Linda had set aside most of her fears as James acted more like himself. They played tennis again, took long walks on the shoreline. If it weren't for his continual disappearances in the evening—always saying he just needed to be alone—and his obsession with emptying the wastebasket, he was nearly the old James, with a sex drive as strong as ever. It was as if he couldn't keep his hands off her.

Then something happened that she had half expected ever since that night in Houston. One afternoon when he called her in to make love, James held two long, white athletic socks. Tentatively he asked, "Can I tie you up?"

Linda considered for a minute before answering. She felt a sense of dread welling up inside her, yet James had been so volatile in the past few months, she hated to refuse him. "Okay," she said, solemnly. "I guess it would be all right."

Linda kneeled on the bed in her bra and panties and, as he had that first night, James cinched her wrists, then her ankles, together, but this time he didn't stop there. Before she realized what he was doing, he reached down and grabbed a balled-up third sock and jammed it into her mouth, binding it in place with a fourth.

A sense of apprehension settled over Linda. *My God, what is he doing?* she wondered, as James began mechanically fondling her, running his hands over the white lace of her bra. He seemed stiff, robotlike, almost disengaged from his actions, but it wasn't until he leaned over to unhook the back of her bra and let it droop softly from her shoulders that she saw his face. Inches away, his breath hot against her flesh, James gazed down at her and smiled. The man she saw above her was the other James, the James with the blank eyes of that night in Houston, the dazed and transfixed James who leered at her from the balcony the day he'd returned from sea. Unable to cry out, she swallowed, hard.

As before, James ran his hands over the sensitive skin of her inner thigh, downward to the arch of her foot until her leg muscles contracted. Linda recoiled, shrinking away from him, and shook her head, *No.* James smiled noncommittally at her, intensely caught up in the game. He laid her down and leaned over her like a cat eyeing its prey. Smiling, he pulled a pillow from the bed, and placed it over her eyes. She attempted to draw away from him and shook her head, harder. "No, no," she shouted, her cries muffled by the gag.

"It seemed like it lasted forever," she'd later say. "I could see him from underneath the pillow. His eyes were dead, cold. He kept running his hands over me. It gave me the chills, and I began shivering, so I couldn't stop. I was sobbing under the pillow."

James appeared as if nothing were wrong, fondling and stroking her though she pulled away, showing not a glimmer of understanding. Finally, when she'd given up hope, he noticed tears running down her cheeks. He wiped them away with the back of his hand, untied the gag, and gave her an embarrassed smile.

"Not the gag, okay?" she pleaded. "I can't stand the gag or the pillow."

"Okay, not the gag," he answered sheepishly, untying her hands and her feet. Still frightened and confused, Linda lay beneath him trying not to cry as James satisfied himself and then rolled over and fell instantly to sleep.

Splotches of red and gold dotted the forests, and on Halloween day, Linda's twenty-fourth birthday, they carved two pumpkins. James fashioned one with long, pointed triangles for teeth. Linda's had a big smile and one winking eye. That night they drove through subdivisions of one-story houses not far from their apartment. Goblins and witches and gypsies and pirates were afoot, the neighborhood children trick-or-treating. As they circled the quiet neighborhoods with porch lights lit and saw neighbor after neighbor answer a doorbell with a bowl of candy, James talked about going back to Houston. "I can't wait to go back to the plant to work," he said. "Just to be able to spend a night with Sam and Eddie again. I can't help thinking about all the great times we used to have."

"I wish we could stay here," Linda said sadly. "I love it so much."

"Well, we can't," said James, angrily. "We're going to fin-ish the four years and get out. You'll see, I'll get out of the navy and we'll go back to Houston. Everything will be all right again."

By mid-November, the leaves had all dropped, exposing skeletal trunks and branches against the green of the tower-ing pines, when James came home from the base one after-noon and, as usual, called her into the bedroom to make love. He had the drapes pulled and two pairs of Linda's leg warmers in his hands. "Strip and lay down on the bed," he said excitedly.

"You want to play this game, we'll do it, James," she said, firmly. "But no gag."

"Okay, no gag," he agreed.

She undressed, then kneeled on the bed, expecting him to tie her as he had in the past—arms and legs together—only instead he pushed her onto her stomach and straddled above her. He laid the leg warmers beside them on the bed and then held the first one by the ends, its weight sagging be-tween his grasp, until he snapped it between his hands, the weave tightening like a child's finger snake. He knotted one end tightly around her left wrist, as he had before, and cinched her right wrist to it. Then he rolled her over.

"What are you doing?" she asked.

"You'll see," he answered. "Relax. You'll like it."

As Linda wriggled her hands behind her, James turned his attention to her legs. One at a time, he bound her ankles with one of the leg warmers, then tied them individually to the bed frame, awkwardly anchoring her to the bed, helpless to move more than inches in any direction.

"What's this?" she asked, fighting the panic she felt well-ing inside her.

"It's just a little different game," he said. "You're too up-tight, Linda. Just settle down and you'll like it."

Once he had her tied, he lay beside her and fondled her breasts, then looked down at her quizzically, cupping his hand over her mouth. Glaring at her as if he didn't have his creation right yet, he recovered a rolled-up sock from between the mattress and bed frame and forced it solidly into her mouth. As Linda felt alarm rising within her and struggled to spit it out, James retrieved a second sock from its hiding place and banded it around her jaw, tying it above the nape of her neck, fixing the gag in place.

Linda protested, shaking her head, no, and pulling away from him, but she couldn't move, bound as she was to the bed. James laughed quietly at her predicament, then became sternly serious, running the back of his hand along the soft curve of her breasts and lightly down her belly. She shivered and he smiled complacently at her.

"You really don't like that, do you?" he asked, grinning down at her.

She tried to answer, but the gag strangled her words. Instead she shook her head again, more sternly, insisting, No.

James gazed vacantly at her. She could have been a stranger, someone for whom he had no feelings and to whom he had no ties. As amusing as a mouse winding its way through a fickle maze. To her surprise, he then coolly stood up and pulled on his jeans.

"I'll be right back," he said, nonchalantly walking out the apartment door and, without further explanation, closing it behind him.

Linda lay there, she wasn't sure how long, staring up at the ceiling, cold and alone. As minutes ticked away and James failed to return, she could no longer keep the fear from rising up inside her. *What if someone sees me like this?* she thought. *What if he never comes back? Why is he doing this? What is he going to do to me?*

In a panic, she pulled at her bindings until the cloth dug into her flesh, but her efforts only wedged the knots tighter around her wrists. Calming herself, she tried to relax, working her hands one fold of flesh at a time through the knotted leg warmer that immobilized both. They were bound tight.

If she pulled, the cloth cut into her skin, denying the circulation in her hands, but if she moved slowly, the knit had some play in it. Finally her right hand broke free. She pulled off the gag and began gulping in the air, her body heaving. She was untying her legs, her hands trembling, when James walked through the door.

"Where were you?" she asked, her voice breaking with pain.

As before, he appeared detached and preoccupied. "I just had to go outside for a minute," he said with a shrug.

Indifferently James leaned against the doorframe and watched as she untied her ankles.

"Where the hell were you?" she demanded again, this time shouting between sobs. "Why are you doing this to me?"

James looked like he had on the balcony the day he'd returned from sea, distant, as if through a fog. His expression was blank. Finally, in a toneless voice devoid of emotion, he explained, "I just wanted to see if you could get out."

Chapter Thirteen

Thanksgiving came and passed. Linda roasted a turkey with stuffing, the first she'd ever attempted, and James ate heartily, commenting that it was superior to Tina's efforts on holidays past. They rarely saw Chris or Tina anymore, only when James determined they had to visit to keep up appearances. Though Linda urged him to call home to Houston, James rarely did. "Why should I call them after what they did to me?" he'd ask, portraying the injured victim. "They forced me into the navy. It's their fault and Chris's that I'm stuck for another two years."

In fact, almost everyone was off-limits. James argued he didn't want to share her and insisted on every available minute alone together before he left for sea, so Linda gave up suggesting she spend any time with Penny, Gayle, or Diane. Of course, couples' activities were out of the question because of their husbands' higher ranks. The only friends James was willing to see socially were Earl, whom he'd known since boot camp in San Diego, and his girlfriend. Earl tended to drink too much and was sometimes crude but had an offbeat sense of humor. The only word to describe his girlfriend was "young." Often, in the evenings, they would go to Earl's apartment to watch movies, usually comedies, on his VCR.

The gold crew was scheduled to maneuver the *Ohio* back into Puget Sound and around Hood Canal to the Delta Pier just two days before Christmas, and time was passing before James would again be at sea. Linda was sure that explained his jumpiness and irritability. She tried to be sympathetic; the last thing she wanted was a repeat of her husband's last patrol. "I thought if I kept things on an even keel before he left, he'd be okay," Linda later said.

But as December neared, Linda noticed James acted increasingly agitated. Just the mention of the ship's impending arrival was enough to send him into his old diatribe against the navy: that he'd been lied to and that the submarine service was nothing like he imagined it.

One night in early December, Earl and his girlfriend invited James and Linda over to drink and play cards. When they arrived, Mack, a tall, blond shipmate of Earl's whom Linda had never met before, was also there. Earl brought out a board game and they all sat in a circle at the table, ready to play. It was a drinking game, the kind wherein every time a player loses a hand, he has to chug a beer or throw down a shot of whiskey. The object was to collect the most cards.

It wasn't long before all five of them were giddy from liquor. Linda's face felt flushed and she laughed uncontrollably at the silliest things, like once when James got up to go to the bathroom and almost toppled over the board. Before long, Mack, too drunk to play, casually pitched his cards toward Linda and said, "Here, they're yours."

By the time Linda got up and walked to the bathroom a few minutes later, he was almost asleep on the couch. Without thinking, she paused and bent over him. "Thanks for the cards," she laughed, flirtatiously. "Maybe now I'll win."

James barreled up from behind and pinched her arm until she winced with pain. "Wait until I get you home," he whispered in her ear. "You goddamn bitch. I owe you one."

Because the others were embarrassed or simply lost interest, the gathering broke up after that, and Earl left to take

Mack back to the base. A few minutes later, Linda was putting the game back in its box when she noticed Earl's girlfriend on the balcony pitching dirt from a flowerpot onto cars parked below. James stood behind the girl, rubbing her shoulders. Confused and angry, Linda grabbed her coat and went outside for a walk to clear her head. She wasn't outside for more than a few seconds when James bolted down the apartment stairs after her, grabbed her shoulder, and flung her around to face him.

"Just let me get some fresh air, okay?" she shouted, resentfully.

"You're coming back inside," he demanded.

"Let me take my walk," Linda said, straining to pull her coat free from his grasp.

"You're coming upstairs with me, now," he persisted, yanking so hard, the coat's shoulder seam ripped open.

James wrenched her toward him, and Linda toppled to the ground. Suddenly she was flat on her back in the parking lot, James on top of her. He slapped her over and over, as she kept shouting, "No, stop it." Then he seized her hair in his fists and beat the back of her head against the asphalt. Neighbors in the complex rushed out and pulled them apart.

Dazed and crying, Linda followed James back into Earl's apartment to collect her things, when a squad car pulled up outside, lights flashing. James answered the door and a uniformed officer peered in at both of them. Linda could feel him sizing up the situation, the stench of alcohol and her torn coat and tear-streaked face.

"Someone called about a disturbance," the cop said, warily. "Let's all step outside, down to the squad car."

"It's okay," Linda said, quickly, not wanting James in any trouble that could backfire and hurt his career with the navy. "He's my husband. We just had too much to drink."

But she was bruised and her pink and gray wool coat had a wide rip across the shoulder.

"It looks like more than a little argument to me," he said. "Come on."

Outside, Linda talked to one officer, while the other interrogated James.

"I'm okay," she said. "I'll be all right."

"From the look of things," her officer said, "I think we'd better take him in."

With that they frisked and cuffed James, directing him toward the squad car. "We had a couple of drinks," Linda heard James say. "I just wanted her to come back inside."

Linda felt groggy from the alcohol and the beating, but she couldn't believe what was happening. "It's just the booze. He's a little drunk," she said again to both officers. "I'm okay, really. Please don't arrest him."

"He's going in," the first officer concluded. "We're going to book him."

Linda's eyes followed as the squad car pulled out of the parking lot with James in the backseat. *James was just drunk,* she thought. *That's all.* But she could see him staring back at her, glaring. "If I didn't know better, I'd swear he hadn't had a thing to drink," she'd later say. "He looked sober. Stone cold sober."

The next day at the apartment, Linda saw James drive up in a van. He got out, and another man, tall and lanky with glasses, climbed out of the driver's seat and followed James up the stairs. Linda pulled on a sweater to conceal the red and blue bruises that covered her arms, and opened the door. The other man offered her his hand. "I'm Steve Swartz, your husband's chief," he said. "I picked him up last night at the jail and he spent the night on the base."

Linda invited Swartz, whom she'd heard James talk about but never met before, inside, and James followed.

"The thing is, we've had a talk, Linda," Swartz said, nervously. "James promises me he won't do anything to hurt you. That it's all right now. Is that okay with you?"

Linda nodded yes.

"Well, then, I'll go," said Swartz, turning to talk to James. Pointing a stern finger at him, he ordered, "Be good and don't lay a hand on her."

Swartz left.

Linda was relieved to see James. More than anything, she wanted to sit down together and talk, to figure out what went wrong the night before. The way she saw it, they were both at fault. Her main concern was what the navy might do. Penny and the others had told her stories about sailors who got in trouble and were summarily shuffled out of the submarine corps. She'd been frantic all morning, imagining that James would be dishonorably discharged and they'd be headed back to Houston, the promise of his career in the navy lost.

James, however, didn't seem in the least concerned about his situation, just angry. "Steve says a lot of women get drunk and act dumb," James said to her derisively as he walked toward the bathroom door, ready to take a shower. "You know what I was thinking about when I was hitting you, Linda? How you bent down and thanked that guy for his lousy cards."

"What was wrong with thanking him? What did I do—" Linda started.

"It's up to you, Linda," James cut in. "Do you want me to get kicked out of the navy?"

"No," Linda answered. "I don't."

"If we're going to get them to drop the charges, you better come up with a story. Tell the prosecutor it was your fault," he warned. "Tell them that you were drunk and that I pulled you back because I didn't want you to get hit by a car. That you just don't remember what happened, except that I was trying to help you."

James turned and left; minutes later he was in the shower. Without saying another word, he then pulled the shades and climbed into bed, where he stayed, sleeping the rest of the day. For a long time that afternoon, Linda sat alone in their apartment, trying to make sense of her husband's actions. Her body ached under the patchwork of bruises that covered it. But more than anything she felt stunned by James's indifference. *He didn't even apologize,* she thought. *He wasn't sorry.*

Christmas came and James and Linda decorated a small tree and brought gifts to Chris and Tina's for their two sons. Everything was so tentative between them, neither bought the other a present. "He was acting like I had beat him up," Linda said later.

It was weeks before the icy silence melted. At first, James kept his distance from Linda. Then, as his court date approached, he cajoled her, flirted, and suggested, "Let's just say it was the booze."

Steadfastly silent, she fumed that so much had happened and he remained unrepentant.

Finally, in early January with his next voyage imminent, Linda gave in and agreed to consult an attorney to make arrangements to have the charges against him dropped. As James instructed and with him at her side, she recounted how her husband had only been trying to protect her, to keep her from walking in front of a passing car, and that the officers had misread the situation. "I couldn't even look at the lawyer while I was telling her the story," Linda remembered later. "It was all such a lie."

"So in other words, you were intoxicated, Linda," asked the attorney.

"Yeah," Linda said. "I was."

James's lawyer later met with the prosecutor, and all charges against him were dropped.

It seemed an unsatisfying finish to Linda. Yet as the days before James would go off to sea drew to a close, she became increasingly concerned that they had not yet really made up. More than anything she wanted to avoid a repeat of last summer's patrol. Finally one afternoon she approached him. "James, I'm sorry about the fight and everything that's happened," she said. "I did have too much to drink."

To her surprise, James answered, "I don't know if I can

ever get over it. I'll always remember you bending over to thank that son of a bitch."

"James, all I can say is, I'm sorry," she said, weary of the entire episode.

After that day, Linda and James eased back into their old routines. Linda was anxious to put it all behind them and she tried to forget that he had never really apologized for hurting her.

As always, the day before the *Ohio* was scheduled to sail, January 20, 1988, was family night, the one opportunity spouses and children had to tour the submarine. Although James had never agreed to bring Linda on-board before— claiming he couldn't stand the lascivious way other men looked at her—this time when Linda asked if she could come on-board like the other wives, he agreed. That evening, Linda walked through the *Ohio*'s tight passageways among the throng of wives. Fascinated, she inspected the galley, the front control station, and the small IC station where James worked. Then he escorted her to the nine-man cubicle where he slept. Except for one rolled-up magazine carelessly thrown on the bunk, everything in his cubbyhole was neat and orderly, just as things were at home.

"That's another guy's," said James nervously as he picked up the magazine and discarded it on a lower berth. "He's always leaving things around."

Flirting, Linda playfully jumped on his bunk and motioned for him to follow. James did and she pulled the curtain behind them. Over the years, she'd heard many navy wives fantasize about making love to their husbands onboard the sub. At the wives' club functions, she'd met a few women who bragged that they had done just that. Linda had often wondered what it would be like, stealing forbidden moments together.

To her astonishment, in the privacy of James's curtained berth, he shushed her to stop giggling and then kissed her. One thing led to another, and before long they were making love. Linda was exhilarated by the spontaneity of such un-planned, dangerous passion and the joy of telling her friends about it later. The night wore on and the other sailors and their families left. James and Linda made love twice more after the boat fell quiet, then, without intending to, they slept.

Morning came and the boat filled with the hubbub of men shouting orders. James panicked when he awoke and saw her beside him and realized what had happened. "God, I'm going to be in deep shit for this," he said. "We've got to get you off."

They dressed hurriedly and then he pulled the curtain back, checking to be sure the area was clear. It was. As he frantically pulled her from his bunk, Linda's gaze fell on the discarded magazine from the night before. It was a detective magazine, the kind with grisly tales of murder. On the cover was a woman, young and beautiful, bound and gagged. It sent a shiver through her.

But James yanked her by the arm and she followed him from his quarters. Though he tried to smuggle her out, the boat was filled with his crewmates and it was impossible to hide. The other sailors laughed and called at Linda as James pulled her toward the back of the sub, where she climbed up a two-story ladder to the deck. To Linda, it seemed a great adventure as they sprinted toward the gangplank and off the boat, surrounded by catcalls.

In the navy jeep as James drove her to the gates, Linda's thoughts flashed back to the magazine.

"Was that yours?" she asked. "The detective magazine?"

"No," he assured her. "I told you. It belongs to one of the other guys."

Relieved, Linda shrugged off her apprehension. It was too glorious a day to ruin it. She felt naughty and free, so much so that she grinned with pleasure. "It was so not James. So full of fun," she said later. "I couldn't wait to tell Penny and the others. They talked about it all the time. How great it would be to make love to their husbands on the boat. I couldn't believe that James and I had actually done it."

Chapter Fourteen

When the *Ohio* pulled out of Puget Sound on January 22, 1988, Linda felt good about the future. She and James had made up, and he should have little reason to worry about her while he was gone. She was going to make this work. As insurance, she packed an eleven-by-fourteen-inch envelope with twenty cards for the mail drop. Each bore orders on the front, instructing James to wait until a certain Monday or Friday before opening it. Once a week, she stopped on base to send a Family Gram that always concluded with "I love you and I can't wait until you get home."

Certain that she had done all she could, she settled into her regular schedule, working out at the gym. She was finding navy life much as her sister-in-law had first described it: "When the guys are away you have time for yourself, and when they come back you're always glad they're back." When James was gone, she was free to do as she wished, unhindered for the first time in her life by anyone or anything. She ate when she wanted to, read when she wanted to, slept in if she felt like it, didn't clean if she had other things to do. It was heaven.

Not to mention the camaraderie of the other wives. She'd grown so close to her friends, she felt as if she could tell them almost anything. There were many of those afternoons or evenings, usually at Penny's house, when the women just sat and talked for hours. Sometimes Diane or Gayle would pop in, but often it was just Linda and Penny, drinking

Cokes and talking about life. Like on one afternoon when the talk turned to sex, and Linda, in a hushed, embarrassed tone, told Penny something she had never revealed to anyone else.

"James has this thing he likes to do," Linda confided.

"What?" Penny asked.

"He likes to tie me up, during sex," she said, hesitantly, too self-conscious to go into more detail.

"Some of the guys like to do different things," Penny said, dismissing her friend's concerns with a wave of the hand. "They're away so much, they get strange ideas. Don't let it worry you."

Unsure, Linda didn't respond.

"There's probably nothing to it," Penny pressed on. "It's like ice cream. Who wants to always eat vanilla?"

This time Linda nodded in agreement. *Penny's probably right,* she thought. *I'm probably being a prude and there's absolutely nothing wrong with it.*

At the first wives' club function, Linda signed on a list of volunteers willing to help out in an emergency, and early in February she was called. Mitzi Swartz, the wife of James's chief petty officer, Steve Swartz, suffered with asthma and needed help caring for her two young daughters, eight and eleven.

The two women hit it off almost immediately. Mitzi, a short brunette who had remained spunky despite her illness, had followed her husband from base to base during his career in the navy. She'd met many navy wives, but she particularly liked Linda. "Linda could be really outgoing and fun, if sometimes a little quiet," explained Swartz later. "I understood she was trying really hard to keep things together."

Linda spent days caring for the girls while Mitzi rested. Often she'd stay to cook supper. When Swartz was hospitalized for a week, Linda moved into the house to help, even taking the two girls to mass at Holy Trinity on Sunday morning.

Before long, Linda began thinking about having children of her own. "I wanted a family, and seeing Mitzi with her girls made me think more and more about having children," she later said. "I suddenly had this overpowering urge to have a child of my own."

Sometimes, after Mitzi returned home, the two women sat in the backyard in the early evening, drinking strawberry daiquiris. Steve had told Mitzi about James Bergstrom's troubles, both his dismal second patrol and the beating he'd administered to Linda in the parking lot. One day when Linda revealed how much she enjoyed Washington and navy life, Mitzi cautioned her, "Steve has some doubts about James. He's not sure James will be able to make it in the navy."

Linda looked downcast.

"I understand you're trying to help James," Mitzi continued. "But you have to think about yourself, too."

What neither woman knew was how James was faring on his third patrol. Later Steve Swartz would tell Mitzi that on-board James was withdrawn, rarely talking with anyone. Bill Haberstock, the COB who had taken over the *Ohio* from Jim Sirles, would later describe Bergstrom in even harsher terms, as almost pathologically quiet. "James always did an average job in his work. He never let it get in the way," Haberstock, an avuncular man with a soothing manner, said later. "But he was so balled up inside himself, you never had any idea what he was thinking."

On a team where every man counts on every other man to do his job, James didn't seem like a team player. In fact, in many ways it was like going back to his high school years when he viewed himself as estranged from the other students. It was also similar in that James was the one who judged his situation most harshly. To the others, he was just a nondescript, shy member of the crew. In his own judgment, he was an outcast. "I knew I had failed them and that they were all talking behind my back. They all knew I wasn't the kind that would stick in the navy," he said later.

He would also later admit that something else changed during that third patrol. Though he had always had the urges, with little to occupy his mind, he increasingly escaped to the fantasy world of his adolescence. Whenever he was alone, even standing watch in the IC unit's small cubicle, he would daydream about catching women unawares, watching them from a distance, and something new, entering their homes, tying them up, and forcing them to do anything he wanted.

When the *Ohio* pulled into port on March 30, Linda and Mitzi arrived at the pier late. They'd lost track of time while celebrating their husbands' arrival with margaritas at Azteca, and James and Steve were standing side by side on the dock, obviously annoyed, when their wives drove up. All of the other wives and sailors were gone, and Linda immediately feared the reception she would get, but James was only upset for a moment before wrapping his arms around her. "Thanks for all the cards and everything," he said. "It really helped."

It was an auspicious homecoming when compared to the ones before it.

As always, with James home, the days returned to their routine in which he spent mornings at the base and arrived home in the early afternoons. Linda usually slept late, and once out of bed, she'd tackle the housework. In the afternoons James nearly always wanted to make love; often that included tying Linda up. Sometimes he bound her ankles together and her arms behind her, as he had that first time in Houston. Other times he ordered her to lie on her back, then he bound her carefully to the bed frame, her legs and arms spread.

Linda hated it. Each time she felt as if she were being violated and raped. She bristled at the way he glared at her while he played out his fantasies. It was humiliating and frightening. James appeared cruelly oblivious to her feelings, and she forced herself to play along, hoping that if James was happy in bed, other aspects of their lives—including his performance in the navy—would improve. For months now, she had felt as if she were married to two men: the quiet, thoughtful, shy James she had fallen in love with, and the uncaring man with the distant eyes who haunted their bedroom and had exploded in anger that night in the parking lot.

Yet she had lived with a truly domineering man, her father, and it was hard to imagine anything James did was beyond what she had grown up knowing. Oddly, Linda felt more hopeful. James no longer mentioned getting out of the navy early. Secretly she hoped he might even decide to reenlist, giving her another two to four years of the life she'd grown to love.

Despite all the blowups, the thoughtful James, the one who wanted desperately to please her, was the one with whom she spent most of her days and nights. She never doubted how important she was to him. Though he initially balked when she broached the subject of children, James relented when he realized how desperately she wanted a baby. Excitedly she stopped taking precautions to prevent a pregnancy. But months passed. Each time her period arrived she became despondent. "James would pat me on the back and say, 'Don't worry. It'll work. You'll see,'" she'd later recall. "But I wanted a baby so much, I couldn't think of practically anything else."

She tried to ignore the other James, the one who held her workout tights in his hands one afternoon when he called her into the bedroom.

"All right, but no gags," she warned him, as she always did.

She undressed and lay down on her back, and he tied her—arms and legs spread—to the bed frame. Then he retested each restraint to make sure it was tight. It was becoming almost routine for Linda now. She tried to concentrate on other things, having a baby or playing tennis, so she wouldn't feel as vulnerable and humiliated, as he fondled her breasts and ran his fingers over her body. And she tried not to look closely at James. She didn't want to see that distant gaze that always shot a tremor of fear through her.

But then, to her amazement, like that one other time months earlier, James suddenly stopped. He stood above her, fully clothed, and stared down at her. "I'll be right back," was all he said before he turned and left.

Minutes passed. Linda tried not to panic. "I knew he'd come back like the time before; I figured it would just be a little while," she would say later. But James didn't return. As she watched the second hand on the clock sweep its way around and around, Linda began wondering what would happen if a fire broke out in the complex. What would happen to her. *Where can he be?* she wondered.

Later James would describe what he had done when he left Linda helplessly tied to the bed that afternoon. As she counted off the minutes, he furtively circled to the back of the apartment, peering in one window after another. Doing just that, he found Theresa George, a statuesque half-Sioux woman, in unit number four. Just emerging from the shower, she had finished her day job working as a utility clerk at a store in the nearby Silverdale Mall. In another hour, she had to report to a fast-food Chinese restaurant where she worked evenings. The apartment was quiet. As she reached down to untie her robe, she suddenly sensed something awry. She had the unmistakable impression that she wasn't alone. George glanced up at the window and saw—frozen forever in time—the frenzied face of a man, watching her. She screamed and ran toward him to close the curtain, but by the time she'd reached the window, he'd vanished. "He had the strangest look in his eyes," George later remembered. "They were ice-cold."

Looking back, Linda would judge James had been gone for ten minutes when he returned to the apartment. Again she had managed to free her hands and feet from the restraints, but her wrists were sore from the strain.

"Where the hell have you been?" she asked, sobbing.

"I just had to run out," James answered. "I see you got loose."

"James, don't tie me up anymore, okay?" she said. "I don't want it. I won't have it."

"People do this all the time, Linda," James scoffed, plainly irritated. "It's no big deal. You just don't like it because of the rape. If I could find that guy that raped you, I'd wring his neck. Because of him, we can't have a normal sex life."

Linda said nothing more, but held her ground a few days later when James again wanted to tie her. The truth was, she had become increasingly frightened during James's sex games. The way he looked at her, that distant, vacant gaze. The way he insisted on putting his hand across her mouth to gag her. *If I screamed, no one would hear me*, she often thought. And then there was the way he would tickle and prod at her. Though she pushed him back, struggling against the bindings, he came at her until she thought she could take it no more and gave in to the tears. She could never have explained to anyone why it seemed so menacing: the inability to move, to get away, to make him stop. Having no control over anything once he slipped that final knot around her wrist.

At such times, Linda remembered a deer that had emerged from the darkness of the forest along the highway one night when she rode home from a gathering with her friends. She'd had to swerve to avoid hitting it, as it stood blinded by the headlights of her oncoming car.

If anyone had asked, she would have told them that was how it felt to be tied to the bed, helpless to escape, and at the mercy of the James who emerged at such times, the James with the vacant eyes and the cruel smile.

Theresa George saw that same man a few weeks later when she was again dressing in her bedroom. Unlike the first episode, this time it was early morning and she was in a hurry to report to work at the department store. In her bed-room, she dropped her robe, slipped into her briefs, and fastened her bra. Then she stepped in her jeans and pulled a blue striped T-shirt over her head. Just as she finished dress-ing, she heard a low whistle from the direction of the win-dow. George looked up and saw the dark-haired man with the frenzied expression and the haunted hazel eyes. Again she screamed and he disappeared. George slammed the window shut, locked it, and shut the curtains. "I couldn't get over it," she'd say later. "He wanted me to see him."

This time, George reported her run-in with the Peeping Tom to Sally Rogers, the landlord. "He looked familiar, but I'm not sure where I've seen him before," a shaken George told her.

"Is it someone who lives here?" asked Rogers.

"It's possible."

Sally listened calmly and tried not to reveal any undue concern. They'd had drifters make trouble off and on over the years, or it could even have just been a tramp who'd ducked behind the building to relieve himself. Rogers hated to admit it but knew that happened occasionally. But George wasn't the first upset tenant. Others had complained of a man who hung around outside the complex, and a few had reported that their bedroom screens were bent as if someone had tried to pry them loose to get inside.

The following day something else happened, and though she couldn't prove it, from then on Sally Rogers felt certain the man at Theresa George's window was James Berg-strom.

It was the following morning when another tenant knocked on Rogers's door. This time it was Shane, a young sailor who had moved into unit seventeen two months ear-lier. Heather, his seventeen-year-old wife, Shane told Rog-ers, was being harassed. "The guy in unit nine—James Bergstrom. He's coming around knocking on our windows and our doors. I'm afraid to leave her home alone," he said.

"She talked to him at first, to be neighborly, but now he's coming around all the time, knocking on the window and asking to come in. He says his wife doesn't have enough time for him, that she ignores him, and that he's lonely."

That afternoon, James came home from the base raving angry. One of their neighbors, he said, had filed a complaint with central command about his behavior. Before long, word got back to the officers on the *Ohio*, and Bill Haberstock called James in to get his side of the story. James denied everything.

"That bastard got me called on the carpet," James grumbled to Linda. "I haven't done a damn thing to that woman. She's just using me to make her husband jealous."

Not sure what to believe, Linda questioned James repeatedly about what the man and his wife were claiming. Through it all, James kept insisting the woman was crazy. "I wouldn't even look at another woman," he maintained. "I love you so much, I even hate to leave you to go on patrol. We're trying to have a baby. We're a family. I wouldn't risk that."

Linda then telephoned next door to ask Rogers where Shane lived, but before she could say much of anything, the landlord informed her that Shane had made similar accusations—charging James was harassing his wife—to her. "How can that be?" Linda asked, incredulously. "James has always been obsessive about me. He almost got thrown out of the navy because he didn't want to go to sea and leave me alone."

Rogers said nothing, but she was predisposed to believe Shane and his young wife. The Bergstroms' loud arguments and James's mournful cries had often disturbed both her afternoons and her nights, and her husband, Bill, mentioned when she'd relayed Shane's complaint to him that he'd sometimes noticed James Bergstrom's Grand Prix parked behind the complex. "It's like he doesn't want his wife to know he's home," Bill had said. "Maybe he has reasons."

As Sally Rogers listened, Linda kept going over Shane's

charges one by one. "Why would James do that?" she asked. Rogers understood Linda was groping for answers but felt unable to help her. She pitied Linda. Lately she'd noticed that whenever she saw James and Linda walking together, Linda always stared down at the ground. "It was like she was afraid to look at anybody," said Rogers. "Afraid he'd get mad if she did."

With James peering nervously from the balcony, Linda walked down to unit number seventeen. Shane answered the door and she introduced herself. "I'm having a hard time believing this," Linda said. "Is it possible your wife is lying?"

"I guess it's possible," Shane mused. "But I think she's telling the truth."

When Heather arrived home later that afternoon, she called Linda. "I am telling the truth," she maintained. "There's something wrong with that husband of yours. I want him to leave me alone."

Linda was in a quandary, not knowing what to think.

That night, James was despondent. She had to believe him, he insisted. Wasn't she *his* wife? Shouldn't she take *his* side? Why would he bother with Heather when Linda knew how much he loved her? "I'm not getting in trouble because of that lying bitch," James shouted. "I'm tired of her lies."

By the next day on base the situation had escalated. Shane refused to back down from his complaints, and Haberstock issued an order; James and Linda had to move from the apartment by the end of the week. Not sure why she was the one being uprooted, Linda called Steve Swartz and asked if he thought James was guilty of Shane and Heather's charges. "Steve told her no, and later, when she asked me, I told her I didn't believe James had done it either," said Haberstock. "The guy was just too quiet. It was hard to imagine."

Feeling somewhat reassured by Swartz's and Haberstock's certainty that the charges against James were trumped up, Linda began to see a bright side to the situation. She'd wanted to move from the Silverdale Apartments since the day they'd moved in. They were cramped and run-down. Only James's refusal to spend money kept them there. Now she had a week to find a new place. With no time to spare, Linda settled on the Central Park Apartments, a sprawling complex on a bucolic setting in a suburban area of Central Kitsap County, on the corner of Fairgrounds and Central Valley Roads. Like surrounding subdivisions of ranch-style houses and a small shopping area across the street, the apartment complex was carved out of the forest, each unit over-looking a parklike setting with a gazebo.

That Saturday, Steve and Mitzi Swartz pulled up into the parking lot of the Silverdale Apartments in their van, and Bill Haberstock arrived in his truck, all intent on moving the Bergstroms to their new apartment without further incident. Linda had everything packed and ready, and since they had little furniture, it took only two trips to move their possessions. Then, in Haberstock's truck, Linda and James drove from the parking lot of the Silverdale Apartments one last time. Heather and Shane were outside their apartment, watching.

"As we passed them, James slipped his arm over my shoulders," remembered Linda later. "He gave them this defiant look. It was like he was telling them he had won."

The next Sunday, as always, James and Linda drove the short distance to Holy Trinity Church. Reverend Joseph P. Erny was saying mass that morning. Father Erny, with soft white hair and glasses, was known throughout the congregation for his sermons utilizing Charlie Brown comic strips. Snoopy, the good father maintained, was an acute observer of life.

After mass, James pulled Linda toward the priest, who shook hands with parishioners in the vestibule.

"I want to set my wife's mind at ease," James said nervously to the priest, with Linda listening. "We've been going through a lot. A girl who lives in our apartment complex made allegations that I was pursuing her. I want you and

Linda to know that I don't care about that person. I don't know her. She's lying. I love my wife."

The priest looked sympathetically at Linda. "Does this clear your mind and take care of it for you?" he asked her.

Linda considered James and the way he idealized the church, quoting prayers to her and talking about his faith in God. She couldn't believe he would lie to a priest. "Yes, Father," she said. "It does."

Father Erny made the sign of the cross over their heads— in the name of the Father, and the Son, and the Holy Spirit.

"Then bless you both," he said. "And may God be with you."

Chapter Fifteen

A month after their hasty move, James was on patrol again and Linda tried to put all the summer's pieces into a pattern that made sense. That James had sworn in front of a priest that Heather had lied made her confident he was telling the truth, but not confident enough to forget what the seventeen-year-old had alleged. "If there was a scale of one to ten to measure how much you loved someone, before that incident, I loved James a ten," Linda would say later. "After that summer, it was never more than a six. I just couldn't forget."

Still, even if it was true, it wasn't something she wanted to break up the marriage over. She, after all, had not been raised to expect an untroubled life, and she had known all along that as time passed, she might have to make some adjustments. The important things were still there; James loved her and they were building a family together, the kind of life she had always wanted.

To keep busy and take her mind off the past, she applied for a part-time job at the day-care center in the Puget Sound Naval Shipyard. If it had been up to her, she would have worked years earlier, but James always wanted her home and accessible. In fact, when she told him she planned to look for work, he was not pleased. Linda persisted, pointing out their new apartment needed furniture and came with a higher rent, until he reluctantly gave in. But his approval came with strings. James ticked off a list of three acceptable occupations—jobs with little contact with men: Linda could work in a fabric store, a women's gym, or a day-care center. Because she yearned to have a child of her own, Linda decided on day care.

It was everything she'd hoped.

On the outskirts of the shipyard, the PSNS day-care center was housed in a converted brick barracks, one story with a newly added annex. It was always noisy and hectic, with as many as two hundred children divided by age into sixteen rooms. Each morning when parents dropped their young charges off, the halls filled with the squeal of laughter and the pounding of sturdy young feet. As a floater, Linda rotated between rooms. Sometimes she helped in the kitchen or the office, or with diaper changes in the baby room. There she met Carmen Mirano, whom Linda nicknamed "Grandma." At forty-nine, Grandma, a diminutive woman who'd emigrated from the Philippines and still spoke with a heavy accent despite decades in the States, was the wife of a retired navy man and the mother of two teenage children.

The other friend she made at the day-care center was Patricia Ingersoll, heavyset with long, straight, dark brown hair and glasses. Pat had a self-deprecating sense of humor and was always overly solicitous, speaking with a steady, thoughtful tone.

But more than anything, Linda enjoyed the children. Especially the toddlers. She'd roll the ball across the floor to one, with another tucked securely under her arm, as a third hugged her from behind. How she wished to have one of her own.

More and more, however, Linda feared that might never materialize. Now that she was ready to raise a child, it just wasn't happening. In the past six months, she'd been in and out of the base hospital consulting one doctor after another. They had her taking her temperature and charting her menstrual cycle, but to no avail. James was sympathetic but uninvolved. "There's nothing wrong with me. I'm fully stocked," he'd say brusquely, whenever she mentioned the subject of their infertility.

"He knew how desperately I wanted a baby," she'd later say. "I don't think he ever cared himself. He agreed to make me happy. To give me whatever I wanted."

Unexpectedly, for the first time since James had started making patrols, the *Ohio* surfaced that October in Hawaii, docking in Pearl Harbor for its biennial torpedo reidentification, a series of exercises and exams in which the crew practiced firing the boat's MK 48 torpedoes at dummy targets.

A ringing phone woke Linda's friend Gayle from a deep sleep at two A.M. the first night the ship pulled into port. It was James looking for Linda. "He sounded frantic, like he had to talk to her immediately," Gayle said later. "James was always that way. He obsessed about her." Gayle said she'd left Linda at Penny's earlier that evening. When she asked how he'd gotten her number, he said, "I copied the numbers of all Linda's friends out of her telephone book before we sailed," as if it were a natural thing for him to have done.

When James finally reached Linda at home later that night, he demanded to know where she had been and with whom. She told him about her night with her friends and that Gayle had left earlier than the rest. "I didn't do anything special, James," she said. "We just sat around and talked."

"I worry about you, Linda," he said. "Everybody on the boat is talking about some guy running around wearing a ski mask, peeping in windows. Maybe he's even a rapist. You've got to be careful, lock your doors and windows. Be on the lookout for him."

James then kept her on the phone—long-distance from Hawaii—for what seemed like hours, talking about nothing in particular. When she was too tired to talk and wanted to hang up, he refused, saying, "I just want to hear you breathe."

There had, in fact, been complaints pouring into the Kitsap County Sheriff's Department since June about just such a dark-haired man in a red ski mask plaguing subdivisions surrounding the Bergstroms' new apartment. It would be many months until the police discovered the sightings began just after James Bergstrom moved into the neighborhood and until Linda realized that the night James called from Hawaii, he had warned her about himself.

As James's fourth patrol drew to a close, Linda found her emotions about his return mixed. "I was happy, sad, excited, and scared all at the same time," she'd later remember. "I didn't know what to expect when he got home. All I was certain of was that our marriage was in trouble."

To do what she could, Linda read books and watched "Oprah," "Donahue," and "Sally Jessy Raphael" every time the talk shows centered on how to breathe life into a foundering marriage. She took some of the money she was making at the day-care center and bought herself lingerie, and then had Patricia take provocative Polaroids of her, including one in filmy white baby-dolls with a telephone to her ear. At the last minute, Linda bought a *Playboy* magazine and included it with the Polaroids in James's mail drop. "I wanted to spice things up," she explained later, almost defiantly. "I didn't know if James would like it, but it was something all the other wives were doing. I did it for fun."

But when Linda met the *Ohio* with the other wives on September 28, 1988, her husband's reaction wasn't what she had hoped. She knew from the minute she saw him walking toward her—from his jutting chin and the glare in his eyes—that James was angry. As soon as he reached her, he grabbed her by the arm. "What the hell was the magazine and those pictures for?" he demanded. "You looked like a goddamn whore. I don't know what you've been up to, Linda, but I'll pay you back. I owe you one."

Linda swallowed her tears as they drove back to the apartment. She'd suspected James would react just as he did, but she'd wished for it to be different. More than anything she wanted the type of relationships she saw her friends having with their husbands, playfully sexual and carefree. She didn't understand that the pictures weren't sensual for James.

It would be years before she finally realized he didn't want her willing participation. What stimulated James Bergstrom's sexual appetite wasn't love but humiliation and fear.

As she suspected he would, James demanded almost immediately after he returned home that she quit her job at the day-care center. "I want you here when I'm here. You're ignoring me," he insisted. "I'm making money. We ought to be able to live off what I make."

Though in the past she had always given in to James, agreeing to everything he wanted, she now refused. "It's wonderful. I love working," she told him. "There is nothing you can do to make me quit. We need the money and I'm staying."

In truth, the money had little if anything to do with Linda's determination to work outside the home. Seeing other people every day, playing with the children, made her focus on something other than her growing doubts about their marriage. "The truth is, working gave me some control over my life," she'd later say.

James was angry when she refused to adhere to his mandates, but then, he was often angry those days. In the back of her mind, Linda wondered how much of his anger stemmed from her refusal to play his "game," since that last afternoon when he left her tied to the bed. Whenever she refused to submit, he became furious, often accusing her of being unfaithful.

Everyone, including James's superiors on the ship, had heard him complain that Linda took him for granted, spent too much money, and ran around with other men when he was on patrol. Those who knew Linda discounted it as James raving. "James always thought Linda was fooling around," said Mitzi Swartz, his chief's wife. "And she never was. He never really had anything to worry about. I've known navy wives who play around while their husbands are off at sea, but Linda wasn't that type."

One day James came home early from the base on Linda's day off. She was cleaning, as she often did in the afternoons.

It was one of the ways she tried to keep the peace in the house, although it was often fruitless. James was even more compulsive than in the past, requiring that everything in the apartment be arranged just so. If a knick-knack was turned differently from usual, he'd immediately reposition it. His fetish with neatness was a nearly superstitious preoccupation. This day, however, he stormed into the apartment and flung open closet doors. He searched the bathroom and under the bed.

"Where is he?" he screamed.

"Who?" Linda asked.

"Chris," James persisted. "Where are you hiding Chris?"

Linda was shocked. She hadn't even heard from Chris or Tina.

"I don't know what you're talking about," she insisted, disgustedly. "All of this with Chris isn't real. It's just in your mind."

With the turn of his head, James was furious. He grabbed her arm, forcing her from the living room into the bedroom, where he shoved her against the wall. When she swung at him, he knocked her in the chest so hard, she fell to the ground. The last thing she would remember hearing as she collapsed was the sickening thud of her head hitting the corner of their new dresser.

When Linda came to, she wasn't sure how long she'd been unconscious. She ached all over, and she had a tender knot the size of a half dollar on the back of her head. She looked around in a daze. There was James, in a frenzy, muttering to himself and stalking around the room. His suitcase was open on the bed and he had armfuls of clothes piled about him. In a haze, Linda felt confused but suddenly understood. *He thinks he's killed me. That I'm dead*, she thought. *He's packing to run away.*

When James noticed her watching, he seemed relieved. But instead of comforting her or apologizing, he simply unpacked, as calmly as if he'd just returned from a weekend away. Then he strolled into the living room and turned on the television, as if nothing of importance had occurred. An old "Happy Days" rerun was playing and Richie and the Fonz were kibitzing in the auto shop when Linda entered the room. She ran cold water onto a washcloth in the kitchen and pressed it against the throbbing bump on the back of her head. She was standing in the kitchen doorway when James turned to her, his voice dead calm. "You know, Linda," he said, "I could kill you. I could throw your body out into the woods, and no one would ever find it. No one would ever know. I'll never let you leave me, Linda. I'll see you dead first."

Linda leaned against the wall for support, afraid her legs would buckle beneath her.

Complaints about a Peeping Tom from women in Central Kitsap had died down for nearly three months, but in late October, after the *Ohio* pulled into port, the switchboard at the sheriff's office lit up with reports that the man in a ski mask had again been spotted peering into homes.

Undersheriff Chuck Wheeler was stunned. When the first wave of sightings stopped last summer, he'd hoped whomever was behind it was a drifter who had moved on. Now he was back. Red ski mask and all. *Damn,* thought Wheeler, *this isn't good.*

When Wheeler, who'd worked his way up through the ranks, considered the almost three-month lull, his instincts after twenty-two years in law enforcement clicked in. "I knew most of the boats went out on patrol for seventy days," he explained later. "I figured there was a pretty good chance we were dealing with a guy on a sub." Wheeler lived near the Parkwood East, where the voyeur was seen. The subdivision, with its rambling streets of modest one-story wood and brick homes, had been settled twenty years earlier by retirees, but now many of the homes were owned by young navy couples, families in which husbands went on patrol for months at a time, leaving their wives and children home alone. With a wife and two daughters of his own, Wheeler took the case seriously. "It was personal," he said later.

Working his hunch, Wheeler called an acquaintance, a master chief who worked in Bangor Base's central command.

"Have you got any guys there, someone who just recently came back from being at sea—someone you've had problems with?" asked Wheeler. "I've got a feeling this Peeping Tom we're after is a navy guy."

"Not that I know of," the master chief answered. "But it's possible. I'll ask around."

As days passed and no one on the base called with any leads, Wheeler grew impatient. He'd already assigned extra deputies to patrol the area each morning between six-thirty and seven-thirty, the hour the incidents all took place. He even routinely drove the streets of Parkwood East himself each morning in his unmarked squad car before coming to work. It was the most Wheeler could do. Kitsap County, like many sheriffs' departments, was understaffed and overworked. The county's population had nearly doubled in the past two decades, and when a carrier docked at the shipyard, it could mean an influx of thousands of sailors.

What nagged at Wheeler most was that the interloper was becoming increasingly bold. He knew that it wasn't unusual for a rapist to begin as a voyeur. In fact, one FBI study estimated 68 percent of all serial rapists began as Peeping Toms. "It felt to me like the thing was going to escalate," said Wheeler later. "That this guy wouldn't be satisfied just looking in windows for very long."

Since they only had one car, most mornings James dropped Linda at work at the day-care center at six and picked her up after she helped feed the children lunch and put them down for their naps. As far as she knew, James spent the hours they were separated working on base. That he seemed so changed worried her, but she still made excuses for him. "I figured it all had something to do with the navy and the pressure they were putting him under," she said later. "I couldn't believe James meant to treat me like he was. I was just there, handy for him to blow up at."

Winter came and it snowed, a rather infrequent occurrence in Seattle. Linda built a snowman with the three-year-olds at the center. Sometimes, when things were the worst between her and James, the only ones who could cheer her up were the children. They'd call her Miss Linda and pull her hand until she bent down, then they'd plant firm if sloppy kisses on her cheeks. She began to feel as if these children, the offspring of strangers, depended on her. It made her proud that she was responsible for their care.

When December came around, James was home more than usual. There was little to do on the base with the *Ohio* still out and his classes over for the holidays. Often she'd come home to find he had rearranged everything in the apartment, including her closet and her clothes. Linda noticed some of her things were missing, especially her belts, which James meticulously coiled in a blue plastic laundry basket. First it was the one from her white terry cloth robe. A few days later, the cloth sash to one of her favorite dresses was gone. When she asked James about it, he shrugged. "I don't know where it is," he'd say. "If you took care of your stuff, they wouldn't be missing."

It bothered Linda that James went through her things while she was gone, but she dared not complain. James was too volatile now, becoming angry at the slightest affront. Many times her mother's words came back to her. "James reminds me of your father," Santos Martinez had said. The thought made Linda shudder. She could never have imagined anything worse.

One day while she was at work and not there to see, James watched a movie on television, *Jagged Edge,* the 1985 thriller staring Glenn Close and Jeff Bridges. In it, Bridges played a homicidal husband who enters his own home in a mask one night with a knife and in a bloody rampage ties down, gags, then eviscerates his wife. "It was after that movie that I started thinking about going in houses," Bergstrom would later say. "About how easy it was to get in through an unlocked door or window."

The first article in the *Bremerton Sun,* Kitsap County's daily newspaper, about an attempted rape in the Parkwood East area appeared on December 21, 1988. Under the headline "Man enters house, tries to rape Bremerton woman," the story detailed how a thirty-six-year-old woman fought off a ski-masked assailant in her home. The would-be rapist entered through an unlocked garage door and an unlocked connecting door. She was alone.

"The woman struggled with her assailant, and when she partially removed his ski mask, he fled," according to the newspaper. "The victim was not injured."

The victim gave police a description. Her attacker, she said, was a white man, nineteen to twenty years old, approximately five feet nine inches and weighing 150 to 160 pounds. He had brown eyes and wore blue jeans.

The next morning another article ran under the headline "Sheriff fears serial rapist after second attack." A man wearing a red ski mask had broken into the second home in two days, this time in a mobile home development on Old Military Road, within a half mile of the first attack and a mile of the Bergstroms' new apartment. Again the victim was a woman home alone in the morning. Suggesting the women had been watched, the paper quoted a "very concerned" Kitsap County Undersheriff Chuck Wheeler as surmising, "It's unlikely the targets were chosen at random."

As in the previous attack, the would-be rapist entered through an unlocked door or window, attacking the woman from behind in her bedroom. She struggled and he eventually gave up and ran, but not before injuring the woman's face in the fight. "Wheeler urged all residents to keep doors and windows locked and to call 911 if they saw anyone suspicious," the article concluded.

Privately Wheeler was even more worried. His gut instinct told him this guy was one and the same with "the lowlife" who'd been peeping in windows. Wheeler felt certain his prediction had come true. He knew the guy wouldn't be satisfied just looking and not touching for long. Even more troubling was that with the second attack, the would-be rapist had come later in the morning than usual and changed the location, choosing an area near but not in Parkwood East. "It was like he was branching out. He knew we were watching for him," Wheeler explained later. "The guy was smart. He'd changed his MO."

Linda never saw the newspaper articles, but the "Parkwood Rapist" was all the women at work wanted to talk about. Carmen, Patricia, and Linda all lived within blocks of the subdivision, and at lunch the other women gave them pointers on avoiding attack, especially about locking their doors and keeping their windows secure. Carmen pulled Linda to the side that afternoon. "You'd better be careful," she said. "It's young, pretty girls like you he's after."

But despite her history, Linda wasn't too frightened. On James's orders, she always kept their doors and windows locked. "I'll be all right," she assured the older woman. "I'll be careful."

That night, James asked Linda if she'd read the articles about the attempted rapes in the paper. "No," she answered. "But I've heard about it."

"You'd better be careful," he cautioned. "Sounds like this guy is crazy."

A few nights later, when James was in an uncharacteristically good mood and agreed to stop for drinks with Monique, one of the women from the day-care center, and her husband, the subject came up again. It started with James and Monique arguing about abortion.

"Are you for it or against it?" Monique challenged.

"Against it," James countered.

"What would you say if this son of a bitch who's raping women raped Linda and got her pregnant? Wouldn't you want her to abort it?" Monique challenged, not knowing Linda had lived through a rape years earlier.

"First of all, no one will rape Linda. I won't let that happen," he said, firmly, covering Linda's hand protectively with his own. "Secondly, if that did happen, my sole purpose in life would be to kill the SOB. He'd better be looking in all directions, because I would be after him."

The next morning at the day-care center, Monique whispered in Linda's ear, "James is a nice guy. You're lucky. He really wants to take care of you."

Though she said nothing, Linda was having many doubts. She didn't tell Monique about her husband's violent temper or how much she feared him. The only thing that made their marriage tolerable anymore was that James would be leaving for sea in just a few days. "I'd grown to believe it was possible," Linda would say later. "James could kill me. He could throw my body into the woods, and no one would ever find it. I would just have disappeared. And I understood that if I ever tried to run—no matter where I went—he would find me."

Linda felt trapped. It didn't help that in the past weeks, James had repeatedly gone to Holy Trinity to talk to Father Erny about marrying Linda in the Catholic church. Whenever he brought up the subject of a church wedding, Linda tried to deflect the conversation. There was too much happening in their marriage and she was too uncertain to take what seemed such a permanent step. James had always been the churchy one, the religious one, but Linda felt her faith deeply. A Catholic wedding was a commitment she wasn't sure she wanted to make.

"We have to do it the right way. If we're going to have children and a family, we need to get married in the church," he insisted. "I want to be married to you, forever and in the eyes of God."

Chapter Sixteen

January 30, 1989: The *Ohio* pulled out of Puget Sound. It was James Bergstrom's fifth patrol. Though he'd been irritable in the weeks before he sailed, James seemed to dread this particular voyage less than the others. In fact, he said he was anxious to go and get it over with. He was counting down. There would only be one more patrol the following summer and his commitment to the navy would be over. He would be discharged and free to return to Houston in the following winter.

Linda, too, had been counting down the days until James left. "I was having a tough time even being around him," she said later, recalling how James would indiscriminately push and shove her against the apartment walls. "I didn't know what would set him off."

When Penny and Gayle dropped in unexpectedly to see Linda at her new apartment on Fairgrounds one afternoon not long after the *Ohio* sailed, they caught her cleaning. "James is a neat freak." Linda shrugged. "I've got to keep things up." The apartment was spotless and airy. Linda had already furnished much of it out of her earnings from the day-care center: a dinette set, country French furniture in the bedroom, and tables in the living room. The two women sat on her beige overstuffed couch talking, but instead of admiring their friend's new furniture, they stared at her legs. Linda had on shorts and her flesh was mottled with fading bruises. Linda never acknowledged their stares and her friends left without asking, but from that afternoon on, they were both certain their suspicions had been right. James Bergstrom was battering Linda.

Though she had always tried to hide her marital problems from her family, she called her mother that February and complained bitterly that marriage to James had not turned out as she'd imagined. "She said James would get mad all the time and hit her," Santos remembered later. "I told her, 'Why don't you come home?' But she said maybe it would get better once he was out of the service. She told me, 'Mama, I'm all right. Don't worry. I'll see what I'm going to do.'"

Then she called her oldest brother, Gino. "James and I fight all the time. He's jealous," she complained. "Every time he goes out to sea, he figures I'm home seeing someone else."

"Come home, Lily," Gino urged.

"I'm not sure what to do," Linda admitted. "I'm going to try to work it out."

Gino hung up the phone and had the unmistakable impression that his sister was frightened.

The only one Linda was truly open and honest with was her friend from the day-care center, Grandma. One night as the two women met over pizza at a little restaurant on Silverdale's main drag, Linda showed the older woman her bruises and told her about her husband's violent temper.

"It's bad when a man beats a woman," Grandma advised. "Why do you let him do this to you?"

"I don't know how to stop it," Linda said, her eyes wet with tears.

"Why don't you just leave him?" she asked.

"He'd find me," Linda said, resolutely. "I couldn't run far enough to get away."

For the most part, Linda was trying to live day to day, waiting for James's time in the service to end. "The last hope I had was that once he was out of the service, things would change," she'd say later. "Part of me still believed that what was happening to us was because of the pressure James was under."

The one decision she had made, however, was that this was not the time to get pregnant. The base doctors had wanted to do more tests, including assessing James's sperm count and inserting a tube through Linda's abdomen to examine her fallopian tubes. James, as always, refused to be involved. "It's your body that's screwed up, not mine," he'd insisted. Without discussing it with him, Linda silently dropped the entire pursuit.

Months passed. Easter approached and Linda surprised the children at the center by dressing as the Easter Bunny. The little ones took turns sitting on her lap, tweaking her nose and pulling her whiskers. She felt happy and content. With James gone, these were the quiet days. Until the *Ohio* pulled into port in mid-April, Linda had time alone to think and recharge.

The Kitsap County Sheriff's Department was also rethinking during an unexpected quiet time. The complaints in Parkwood East had died down shortly after last December's attempted rapes. Some detectives wondered if the "Parkwood Rapist," as he was being called in the papers, had moved on to other hunting grounds. Wheeler didn't think so. "I figured he was out at sea again," he'd later say. "I figured this was just a pause and then he'd be back, probably more dangerous than before. After all, he would have had three months to think over why he had failed to rape those women, and how to get what he wanted next time around."

The *Ohio* pulled into Puget Sound on April 11, and Linda tried to make the best of it. Since James was out to sea on his birthday, she baked him a cake. For fun, she used trick candles that relit when he blew them out. Even James laughed when the candles kept relighting until the frosting caught on fire. In desperation, he finally threw the cake in the sink and turned on the faucet. For his present, she gave him something he'd often talked about, a graphite tennis racket, along with a small color television and some clothes.

Forms Father Erny had given James to send to their families' parishes in Houston were waiting for him when he returned from sea. Santos Martinez and her pastor had signed one verifying Linda was a practicing Catholic. The second form, from St. Helen's Parish in Pearland, bore the signature of that church's pastor and those of James C. and Irene Bergstrom. James talked incessantly about setting up a wedding ceremony at Holy Trinity. The one time Linda said she'd really prefer just renewing their vows at the chapel on base, James was furious. "That's not a real church," he scolded. "We're going to do this the right way, so it sticks."

Most mornings, as before, James would drop Linda at the day-care center and then drive off, ostensibly to work on the base. But rather than be there to pick her up, he often ran up to an hour late in the afternoons. Linda concluded the only sensible thing to do, now that she had an income of her own, was to buy another car. James was against it but soon agreed. On April 20, 1989, she signed loan papers and drove home in her new light blue Mitsubishi Precis. It was the first time she'd had a car of her own and she loved it.

At home, James was as demanding as ever. When he watched television, he insisted she sit beside him on the couch holding hands. If she refused, preferring to read a magazine, he'd become incensed and scream obscenities until she gave in. The only time she had any real peace was when he disappeared on and off during the day for his regular jogs. In a sweat suit, he left the apartment for nearly an hour each night. "I was so grateful he was gone for a little while," she said later. "It never occurred to me to wonder what he might be doing."

One evening he came up to her while she stirred a pot of spaghetti sauce, put his arms around her, and affectionately nuzzled the back of her neck. Linda sensed immediately that James wanted something.

"I've been thinking," he said, cautiously. "You know that tennis racket you gave me for my birthday?"

Linda nodded, yes.

"Well, I really don't need it," he said. "I've thought it over and there's something I'd rather have."

Linda turned and scrutinized his face. "What?"

"A gun," James answered.

"A gun?" she repeated.

"Yeah, a gun," James said, smiling.

"Why?"

"For protection," he answered.

The gun became the topic of conversation in their apartment from that day forward. James had a friend who owned a nine-millimeter Beretta he wanted to sell for three hundred dollars. "It's a steal," James said. "A real bargain."

Linda was against it. They didn't have the money right now, she argued. They'd just bought the new car and his birthday gifts.

"I understand a gun can be protection," Linda argued. "But one of us will end up getting mad and using it against the other. Having a gun in the house, James, I'm not sure it's a good idea."

But James would tolerate no arguments. The gun was for sport, to practice at the range, and for protection. "What about that rapist?" he asked Linda. "Wouldn't you feel better having something here with you the next time I go out to sea?"

"I don't like it, James," she said.

"Why not?" he shouted, walking to the television set and picking up a crystal bowl he knew Linda loved. It was one of his latest tricks, circling the apartment during an argument looking for something she cherished to destroy.

"Not the crystal, James," Linda pleaded. "Don't break it. It was a gift from Gayle."

"I've never asked for anything," he said, fingering the deep grooves in the bowl's pattern. "Now that I want something, really want something, you won't get it?" he shouted.

As Linda knew he would, he smashed the bowl against the wall, where it splintered into hundreds of pieces.

Days later, Linda finally acquiesced. Not because her gut instincts had changed, but because she could no longer tolerate the continual arguments. They agreed that on May 15, when he was next paid, he would take three hundred dollars to his friend and purchase the nine-millimeter semiautomatic pistol.

James was thrilled.

The switchboard at the Kitsap County Sheriff's Department began lighting up with calls from women in and around Parkwood East again the last two weeks of April. "Our guy's home," Wheeler told his deputies and detectives. In a *Bremerton Sun* article that ran on Monday the seventeenth, Wheeler cautioned residents: "We're certain this is the same guy. Keep your doors locked and be alert."

The last week in April, Linda and James were out driving after church when he insisted they stop at Chris and Tina's house. While the two men talked in the bedroom, Linda went in the kitchen to visit Tina. "What made James buy a gun?" Tina asked.

"James hasn't bought it yet," Linda corrected her.

"Sure he has. He told Chris about it," her sister-in-law insisted.

The two women walked toward the bedroom, and Linda found James and Chris inspecting something. When she got a clear look, she realized James was holding a nine-millimeter in his hands, turning it from side to side so his brother could admire it.

"Nice gun," Chris said, taking it from him and holding it up to look through the sights. "Feels good."

Linda was stunned, but Tina patted her on the back.

"You're lucky to have a gun in the house with that rapist on the loose," she said. "Chris and I were talking about buying a house, but now I'm glad we're still living on base. That guy scares me."

James, Linda realized, was smiling and nodding in agreement.

Chapter Seventeen

Thursday, May 4, 1989, *Bremerton Sun:*

MASKED INTRUDER RAPES CK WOMAN

A ski-mask-clad intruder held a Central Kitsap woman at gunpoint early today and raped her, the Kitsap County Sheriff's Office reported.

The rapist is believed to be the same man who tried to rape two other women in the same neighborhood last December and was seen peeking into several homes earlier this week.

This is the first attack in which the intruder was successful in raping his victim and the first time he was armed with a gun.

A woman in her mid-20s who lives near the Kitsap County Fairgrounds told sheriff's deputies a man wearing a red ski mask broke into her home about 8 A.M. He was armed with a small-caliber handgun.

The woman told police the man tied her up, placed a pillow case over her head and raped her.

"I predicted last fall that things might escalate," Undersheriff Chuck Wheeler said, noting this was the first attack in which the man had been armed with a weapon. "Now that a gun is involved, this thing is really taking on a different tone today. And always before, his attacks were unsuccessful. Now we've an armed rapist who was successful."

Wheeler was plainly worried. He had reason to be. Like any officer who had been around for a while, he knew about rapists, understood their learning curve. This rapist was following a familiar pattern of trial and error. He'd started with the peeping, then moved into entering houses. He knew how to watch to know when a woman was alone. He knew how to get inside. The first two attempts hadn't worked because the women had fought him off. This time he was armed—with a gun—and he'd succeeded. "If you cooperate, I won't hurt you," he'd told the victim, a young wife who cried throughout her interview with detectives. The Parkwood Rapist was now a very dangerous man.

Chapter Eighteen

The next day, all of Central Kitsap County buzzed about the rape. It was the topic of conversation in homes, offices, and restaurants, in grocery store checkout lines, and over the whine of dryers and the swoosh of washers in local Laundromats.

Even more residents learned of the rapist that night when the *Bremerton Sun* carried a feature on the women of Parkwood East under the headline "I'm going to kill this guy." In the doorway of her meticulously kept home surrounded by flowers, one mother of two told reporter Jack Swanson how, on four occasions since last Christmas, a man who fit the description of the rapist had tried to break into her house. "My stupid ex-husband has my .357 or I'd have shot him [the intruder] the last time he tried to break in," she said. "As soon as I have money, I'm going to buy another gun and, Lord forgive me, I'm going to kill this guy."

Two navy wives in shorts jogging up a hill told Swanson they, too, were armed and ready. One woman's husband conducted nightly emergency drills in which he attempted to break into their home while she reached for her revolver and dialed 911. "I've got a snub-nosed .38 and an NRA certificate that shows I know how to use it," she warned. "Anybody trying to break into my house is going to get stiffed [sic] in the face."

Underneath all the bravado, the women of Parkwood East were clearly shaken. "I didn't know what would happen next," one later said. "I was living in fear that he would come after me. I had all the doors and windows locked, the drapes closed. I wouldn't even let my children go out and play. I hate guns, but for the first time in my life, I thought seriously about buying one."

At the sheriff's office, phones rang continually with nervous women reporting unexplained noises, strange cars on the streets, or just wanting reassurance that if they needed help, the deputies would be there. "We had everything we could spare in Parkwood East," one detective who worked on the patrol later said. "If we'd had a helicopter, it would have been hovering over that subdivision."

But in truth, there was little concrete for police to build a case on. They had Wheeler's gut telling him the rapist was a navy submariner, and they had residents who thought they'd noticed a man who fit the general description of the rapist—white, early twenties, five feet nine inches, 150 to 160 pounds—jogging in a sweat suit with a towel over his neck in the area near the time of the rape. But though they arrived at the scene within minutes of the victim's call and brought police dogs to assist in the search, they uncovered no real physical evidence. The Parkwood East victim had reportedly showered before police arrived, but even if she hadn't, it might not have mattered. In Kitsap County in 1989 police didn't yet have the capability of matching suspects' DNA. "That was still a year away," explained Wheeler later. "God, I wish we'd had it then."

The sobering fact was that Wheeler and his staff needed a break. Without it, there was a good chance the Parkwood Rapist might just get away.

If a furor over the rape preoccupied Silverdale and Bremerton, Linda was oblivious to much of it. She had other, more personal troubles to deal with. James, though his remaining months in the navy dwindled, was becoming increasingly violent. It was commonplace for him to respond to any perceived slight from her with a barrage of obscenities and threats, throwing her against the apartment walls, or destroying something she loved. In the blink of an eye, he could change from the gentle man she married to a raving and bitter madman.

The many friends she had made in Washington stood back, not knowing how to help. Most were beginning to suspect just how tight a rope Linda walked. When Grandma invited her to stop at her house one afternoon after work, Linda refused. "I can't risk it," she told the older woman. "If James gets home before I do, he'll be angry. And I don't want to give him any reason to hit me."

Others around the Central Park Apartments noticed the young husband in apartment number eleven seemed exceptionally on edge. An engineer who lived alone in the unit directly above the Bergstroms saw James outside washing the Grand Prix one afternoon. He'd heard loud arguments and shouting from the Bergstroms' unit since they'd moved in the previous summer, but had never actually met either James or Linda. "I figured it would be a good time to introduce myself," he'd later recall. "So as I walked past, I said, 'Hi.' The guy must have jumped two feet. He looked startled, jittery."

Much of the quarreling filtering up through heating ducts concerned the nine-millimeter Beretta. If they owned a gun, Linda wanted it registered. James agreed, but never did it. Day after day, he invoked the same excuse: His work kept him too busy on base, and he just didn't have time to get it done. Once he insisted the gun didn't need to be registered to be legal. Calling his bluff, Linda dialed a nearby police station.

"Do we have to register a gun in the state of Washington?" she asked.

"All right, so it has to be registered," James admitted after she hung up the phone. "But I don't feel good about it. What if somebody used this gun to commit a crime? I could get in trouble for just trying to register it."

"James, you know the guy you bought the gun from and you've got the receipt showing when you bought it," Linda assured him. "Get the gun registered."

As always, James nodded in agreement, but when he came home the following night, the gun was still unregistered and the argument was replayed.

The night of May 17, 1989, was an exceptionally quiet night for the Bergstroms. Weary of the continual haggling, Linda never mentioned the gun. For dinner, she ordered a pizza. For once, James skipped his nightly jog and they both went to bed early.

That calm, however, didn't last through the next morning. As always, the alarm went off at five and Linda reached over and clicked it off. James was already awake.

"You were on the other side of the bed last night," he said, reproaching Linda for not sleeping draped across him as he demanded.

"I'm sorry," she said, sensing from the flat tone of his voice that he'd awakened angry. "I must have rolled over."

"Sure," he said, sullenly as a spoiled child. "You haven't hugged me. Kissed me. You never pay a minute's attention to me."

Linda leaned over and gave him a quick hug and a peck on the cheek. "I'm really sorry, James," she said, gently. "I guess I just got preoccupied with getting to work."

In the bathroom, she turned the radio on softly and then showered and dressed. She was putting on makeup when James thrust his arm through the bathroom door and switched off the radio.

"What the hell are you doing to your face?" he demanded. "Why are you wearing all that stuff? You looking for somebody?"

Linda, who routinely dressed in the dark to avoid waking her husband, knew she was in trouble. Without saying a word, she picked up her purse and walked outside to the car.

"You sorry bitch," James bellowed as he shadowed her outside. "I can smell the goddamn perfume. Who the hell are you wearing perfume for, anyway?"

Linda said nothing. She knew there was no way to reason with him. She'd seen James like this too often. His jaw set, his dark eyes flashing with anger. The veins on either side of his neck stood out and his fists were clenched. Saying nothing, Linda opened the car door and sat down behind the wheel.

"You sorry bitch," he said again, then pulled back his foot and kicked the back fender of her new car.

Fearing he would destroy the new car as he had everything else she held dear, Linda returned to the apartment. She wasn't crying. She knew better. If she cried, it would only get worse. "What do you want James?" she asked, once they were inside. "Do you want me to quit my job? Is that it?"

James silently turned toward the bathroom and stalked inside, stripped and turned the water on in the shower. He glared at her before stepping inside. To Linda he looked as detached as he had that first day he returned from the second patrol, the time she'd had to take him to the psychiatric unit at the naval hospital. She sat down on the couch and tried to concentrate enough to rethink the morning, all the time fighting back the fear congealed inside her chest.

"James, the kids count on me," Linda shouted nervously over the hot running water, steam billowing from the bathroom door. "I love what I'm doing. Please don't take it away from me."

The pounding of the water stopped and James walked out, blotting himself with a towel. "Okay, Linda. Go to work," he said, evenly. "I'll go to work. Everything is okay."

He appeared cool and remote, as if his attention had drifted off to other matters. Linda sensed he barely noticed her.

"Are you sure?" she asked, fighting a disquieting apprehension.

"Yeah," he ordered. "Go. Everything is just fine."

The morning at the day-care center went quickly. Since she'd arrived late, Linda had to work hard to catch up on her rounds. At ten she was called to the phone; it was James.

"Listen, I'm sorry about the blowup," he said. "Are you okay?"

"Yeah, I'm fine," she answered. "You didn't even dent the car."

"Good," he said before hanging up. "I'll see you when I get home from work."

Linda left the PSNS day-care center at one-thirty that afternoon. She was happy if tired, an effect the children often had on her, and she was again wondering if she should reconsider her decision to postpone having children. "I wanted a baby so much," she said later. "But I just knew I had to get things straightened out with James first."

When she pulled into the apartment parking lot she noticed James's Grand Prix near the walk-through to their apartment. Since she planned to pick up license plates for her new car that afternoon, she went inside to ask James if he wanted to drive across town to the dealership with her. But though she called out his name, he didn't answer. He wasn't inside. In the kitchen she noticed the bag from inside the wastebasket was missing. *This must be another of his daily disappearances*, Linda thought. She checked outside at the apartment mailboxes to see if he was picking up mail. He wasn't. She decided to go on without him.

Linda drove off, but a few miles down on Fairgrounds Road, she passed Steve and Mitzi Swartz driving in the opposite direction. Though both appeared to see her, neither smiled or waved. Later Linda would describe her instincts after she saw the Swartzes as a premonition, the distinct impression that something was terribly wrong. She thought again about the argument they'd had that morning, and dread settled over her when she recalled her husband's strange aloofness when she'd left for work. Though she was within a mile of the dealership, she swung an abrupt U-turn and rushed back to the apartment. *I'm sure everything is fine,* she told herself. *I'll just go back and get James.*

But when she pulled into the apartment parking lot for the second time that afternoon, Linda saw two men, strangers in suits, standing outside her door. At first she thought maybe they were friends of James's, although she'd never met them before, and they didn't have the look of someone paying a social call. She waited in the car for a few minutes, assuming they would leave, but instead they disappeared inside.

Moments passed. Linda eventually opened the car door and walked into the apartment, calling out, "James. James. Are you here?"

No one answered, but inside she discovered one of the men sifting through her closet as the other talked on the phone. Still certain James must be close by, Linda walked into the bedroom. He wasn't there, or in the bathroom. When she again passed the kitchen a second time, the man talking on the phone flashed a badge at her.

"Are you Mrs. Bergstrom?" he asked, hanging up the receiver.

"Yeah," Linda said. "Who—"

"We're detectives," he explained. "Have you caught your husband peeping in windows before?"

"I . . . Once I thought I did."

"Your husband was arrested this afternoon," the detective said, sympathetically. "He was watching a fifty-three-year-old woman undress."

Linda said nothing. She was thinking back to the way James stared out the windows, the time she thought she'd seen him at the old apartment complex, looking through a bedroom window.

"Mrs. Bergstrom," the detective said, coming forward and dropping his voice to just above a whisper. "We think there's more to this. Can we step outside?"

Stunned, Linda followed him outdoors to an unmarked squad car parked next to the Grand Prix. Then the detective cocked his head back at the man searching inside her apartment. "Your husband signed a consent-to-search form," he said.

Smiling weakly, Linda nodded that she understood.

"The thing is, Mrs. Bergstrom, we don't think your husband is just a Peeping Tom," he said. "We believe your husband is the Parkwood Rapist."

"How can you say that?" Linda asked.

"Mrs. Bergstrom—"

"No, no. A Peeping Tom, maybe. But a rapist?" she scoffed. "It's not true."

"Mrs. Bergstrom, your husband tells us he has a problem," the detective continued. "That he likes to watch women undress. He likes watching women in lingerie."

"That's not possible," she shouted. "He doesn't even like watching me in lingerie."

"I can't explain that," the detective said. "But, Mrs. Bergstrom, I've got one more question."

Numb, Linda looked up at him.

"Mrs. Bergstrom," the detective asked, "does your husband own a gun?"

The heat radiated up from the cement. Linda's head had already begun to ache and her heart hammered in her chest, as if she'd stopped running midsprint.

"Yes," Linda said, without hesitation. "He does."

"Mrs. Bergstrom," the detective said, an edge of impatience cutting his voice. "Your husband told us he didn't own a gun. Why would he say that?"

Chapter Nineteen

In his then seventeen years in law enforcement, Undersheriff Wheeler had worked more cases than he cared to remember, but none that had drawn out so long or terrorized the community as much as that of the Parkwood Rapist. Later, Wheeler would credit hubris and a twist of good luck for James Bergstrom's arrest that clear May 1989 day. He would also describe it as one of the most frustrating cases of his years on the force.

"We had every officer we could afford to have in that area," says Wheeler. "I was patrolling it on my way to and from work. The switchboard in the office lit up constantly with residents calling to report anyone suspicious. Anyone moved in or near that subdivision, we heard about. The whole area was on guard." Still, the police came up dry.

The hubris that trapped Bergstrom was his own. A description of the Peeping Tom was plastered over local papers and detailed on radio news reports. It matched that of the rapist. It also described Bergstrom. If he had lain low, at least until the media moved on to other stories and vigilance waned, he may never have been caught. But it was obvious to Wheeler and everyone else, as sightings of the peeper continued to pour in from Parkwood East, that whomever this man was—and Wheeler was convinced the voyeur and the rapist were the same guy—he wasn't hiding out. This fellow believed he was good, good enough to skirt around unseen in the midst of one of the biggest manhunts in Kitsap County's history.

The lucky breaks began a few nights before the arrest, when James, dressed in sweats, told Linda he was going for a "jog." That night, a deputy circled Parkwood East in an unmarked squad car. She saw Bergstrom in his brown 1979 Grand Prix and made a note on her log. Remembering the car resembled the description of one spotted near some of the incidents, she took it one step further and called it in. "There's a guy," she radioed into headquarters. "I don't know if he's connected or not connected. But I don't like the way he's driving around looking at houses." Before signing off, she relayed the license number, make, and approximate year of the car. At headquarters, it was only one of a flood of possible leads, and a notation was made to check out the car and its owner as soon as time permitted.

On May 18, while Linda looked for James in the apartment and found only the wastebasket missing its bag, a switchboard line lit up at the sheriff's office. A Parkwood East woman wanted to report another sighting of the Peeping Tom. "I saw him," she told police. "He just left here." In seconds, marked and unmarked squads from the entire area descended on Parkwood East, combing the streets. Deputies drove the winding blocks, peered in backyards, knocked on doors to talk to neighbors. Women who had been home caring for their children flocked out in the unusually warm May day and clustered together, their fears only exacerbated by yet another sighting. Everyone was on edge.

Still, no trace of the intruder was found.

Though deputies arrived within minutes of the report and had Parkwood East covered, it appeared the man had slipped through their grasp again. As on all the other sightings, it was as if he'd simply vanished.

Unaware, Linda left for the car dealership to claim her license plates as police called off the search. Minutes later, a sergeant driving down Fairgrounds Road noticed a dark-haired man matching the description of the Peeping Tom walking out of the convenience store at the Cedar Valley Plaza shopping center. The sergeant called for backup and then followed in his squad car as the man loped casually across the street to the Central Park Apartments. In the parking lot, outside unit number eleven, the officer noticed the 1979 brown Grand Prix that had been called in a few nights earlier. He screeched to a stop and got out. The man in the sweat suit looked at him calmly.

"Can I help you?" James Bergstrom asked.

"Yeah, is that your car?" the officer said, flashing his badge.

"Yeah," he answered. "Is there a problem?"

"We're looking for a guy who's been peeping in houses," the sergeant said. "I'd like to see some identification."

"Sure," Bergstrom said, politely handing over his wallet.

Other squad cars and unmarked cars converged on the apartment parking lot, surrounding Bergstrom.

One of the detectives got out and introduced himself.

"We'd just like to take a little look around in the apartment and your car," he said, holding out a clipboard with two forms. "How about signing a search warrant for us?"

"No problem," James said, signing them with his careful scrawl. "Anything to clear this up."

As one group of deputies searched the apartment, another combed through the car. All the time, James stood to the side, casually answering questions.

"What do you do?" asked the detective.

"I'm in the navy, on the *Ohio*," said James. "I'm an interior communications man."

"Must be interesting work," said the detective, noting a navy man fit the on-again-off-again rapist's MO.

Just then another squad drove in. When the door popped open, the woman who had called police to report seeing the Peeping Tom jumped out.

"That's him," she shouted, pointing at Bergstrom. "That's the guy."

James Bergstrom's eyes opened wide and his face blanched as he looked from officer to officer.

"You've got the right to remain silent," the sergeant began

as he removed handcuffs from his belt. "If you choose to speak, anything . . ."

By the time Linda met with detectives that afternoon, James had been transported to the Kitsap County Sheriff's Department in Port Orchard, at the base of the peninsula, for further questioning. Faced with a positive identification, he confessed to the peeping incident but maintained that was all he was guilty of.

"I didn't rape anyone," Bergstrom, seated in an interrogation room at the station, told Wheeler. "I'll admit I've got a problem, but I'm not a rapist."

Wheeler wasn't buying Bergstrom's protestations. The department had already run a check on the days Bergstrom had been out at sea and knew his onshore dates corresponded with both the peeping incidents and the rape and attempted rapes. That only bolstered Wheeler's conviction that the Peeping Tom and the Parkwood Rapist were the same man.

"What about the gun?" Wheeler asked. "What did you do with the gun?"

As he had whenever the subject of the gun came up, Bergstrom went as silent as the rock in the nearby cliffs.

"James, we know you have a gun," Wheeler said. "Your wife even gave us the receipt for it. Now you need to tell us where it is."

Still, James was mute.

As they did whenever a navy man was arrested, Wheeler had notified authorities on base of Bergstrom's arrest. His two chiefs from the *Ohio*, Swartz and Haberstock, had rushed over and stood nearby, watching. Swartz, who had been the only man on the *Ohio* occasionally able to crack Bergstrom's shell, stepped forward. "Let me give it a try," he said to Wheeler. "Maybe James will tell me."

Nodding, Wheeler moved back and let Swartz take over. The undersheriff was willing to do whatever he needed to do to get the gun and the ski mask worn during the rape. Without them, Wheeler was painfully aware that he had no physical evidence linking Bergstrom to the rape or attempted rapes.

Swartz moved forward and sat down next to his shy crewman. Wheeler watched with Bill Haberstock from a distance as Bergstrom and Swartz whispered. Wheeler didn't ask Haberstock what he thought about the young crewman. If he had, Haberstock would have told him that he believed they'd probably pulled in the right man. "I had a hard time with it," said Haberstock later. "But I thought, deep inside, that yeah, he was capable of doing it. I remembered the way he had beaten his wife and the complaint at the apartment complex. I figured he was capable of it."

When Swartz and Bergstrom stopped whispering, Swartz walked toward Wheeler. "James says he threw the gun in the water," said Swartz. "He says it's in the sound."

"That right, James?" Wheeler asked.

"Yeah," said James. "I threw it out."

"Why did you do that?" he asked.

"Just seemed like a good idea," said Bergstrom.

Wheeler looked at the young man seated before him and shook his head. "I didn't believe it for a second," said Wheeler later. "He had no idea we were on to him and he was still operating. He had no reason to dispose of that weapon. I figured he had it hid somewhere; the question was where."

Chapter Twenty

As soon as she'd handed the detective the receipt for James's nine-millimeter handgun, Linda got on the telephone. First she phoned Chris, who told her to stay put while he went down to the sheriff's office. Then she called her mother in Houston. "Linda was hysterical," Santos would say later. "I couldn't understand what she was saying, something about James being a Peeping Tom and maybe a rapist. I said to her, 'No, Linda, that can't be right.'"

It was hard for anyone who knew the shy, quiet James Bergstrom to believe. Even Linda, who had experienced his angry, violent side, couldn't reconcile the man she knew with the allegations police were making. "I was out of hand," said Linda later. "I knew James could be mean, but I couldn't believe what they were saying about the man I married."

The detectives treated her patiently, realizing the young navy wife was stunned by the accusations. One assured her they would try not to disturb her apartment any more than necessary. "It's a nice place," he said, kindly. "You've really fixed it up." Then he bent toward her. "Listen, you're too emotionally upset to be alone. Why don't you call someone to come be with you?"

Numb, Linda dialed the phone again. This time she called Patricia, one of her friends from work. When Pat answered, she tried to explain what had happened, but it was like stumbling through a maze. How could she explain what she didn't understand? Finally she said, "Just come over here. I need you to be here."

Since she lived only blocks away, Patricia arrived just minutes later. At the door to Linda's apartment, a deputy stopped her, spilled her purse out on the cement, and checked its contents before motioning her inside. When she entered, she saw more deputies and detectives pawing through Linda's possessions, and Linda seated on the living room couch, crying.

Between sobs, Linda explained to Patricia in skeletal terms what had happened, that police claimed James was the Parkwood Rapist. "I told her that couldn't be right," Pat said later. "James was just this thin, shy guy. It wasn't possible that he was the one."

To Linda, it seemed the rest of Silverdale learned about her husband's arrest only moments after she did. When the *Bremerton Sun* arrived on area doorsteps at five that afternoon, it contained a hastily written bulletin, banded in a thick black box: "Parkwood rapes suspect arrested." Though the *Sun* identified Bergstrom only as "a navy man stationed at Bangor," reports blaring out over local radio stations were more specific. They reported that James Bergstrom, a sailor on the U.S.S. *Ohio,* had been arrested that afternoon. "Police sources say he is a suspect in a series of incidents including a rape in Parkwood East," the newscaster announced.

As soon as the news broke, the phone began ringing continually, with Linda's friends offering help. She talked briefly to each, glad to hear friendly voices, but hung up as soon as possible. It was too painful talking to anyone. Finally she handed the phone to Patricia, who took over fielding calls. Linda simply didn't feel up to talking to even the most sympathetic caller just then.

"I didn't know what was happening or who to trust," she would say later. "I was so confused, I'm not sure that if anyone had asked me, I would have been able to tell them my own name."

That night Linda couldn't sleep. She woke up continually in a heavy fog, drugged by stress and fatigue. "I kept going over it in my mind," said Linda later. "I kept thinking about why this was happening. That the woman who'd been raped was tied up and gagged. Maybe it was James. But why? Had I done something? Then I'd think, *No, no, this can't be.* It just wasn't possible. Maybe James was a Peeping Tom. But a rapist? Never."

Patricia, who stayed to do what she could, watched her tossing and turning. She offered to get her aspirin or a glass of water. Linda just stared off into the darkness. Although thankful for the small kindnesses, she was exhausted, barely able to nod yes or no to her friend. "I could hardly walk," Linda recalled later. "It was like someone had turned the world upside down and I was holding on by my finger-nails."

The following morning, Chris picked Linda up and the two of them drove to the sheriff's office together to see James. In the car, her brother-in-law turned to her and put his finger to his lips. "Chris told me, 'Keep your mouth shut,'" said Linda later. "He said, 'Just don't say anything.'"

When they arrived at the headquarters building, James was seated in a room, alone. After asking permission, Linda went in to talk to him for the first time since her world had shattered with the previous day's accusations.

"Did you do this?" she asked him. "Did you do what they're saying?"

His eyes rimmed in red, James looked up at her. "No, I didn't," he said. "The peeping, yeah. But not the rape. I didn't do the rape. I've got a problem, yeah. I like to watch women undress. But I'm not a rapist."

Not knowing what to believe, Linda obeyed when Undersheriff Wheeler motioned for her to join him in another room. She felt Chris slip in silently behind her as they went through the door.

"Now, this gun, Mrs. Bergstrom," said Wheeler. "Do you have any idea where we can find this gun?"

"No." She shrugged. "No idea."

"Tell me why your husband bought the gun," Wheeler pressed on. "What did he need one for?"

"He said he needed it for protection, that's all," said Linda.

"For protection?"

"Yeah."

"I don't think your husband bought that gun for protection," Wheeler pressed. "I think he knew exactly what he was going to do with that gun when he bought it."

"How can you know that?" she asked.

Wheeler then went over the evidence: James's schedule matched the occurrences of the peeping, the two assaults, and the rape; his description and that of the car matched accounts given by witnesses; he was identified by the final victim. "The reason we had such a hard time catching him is that you lived so close to Parkwood East," Wheeler went on. "He was ducking into your apartment and hiding out after each attack."

Though up until now he'd been silent, Chris Bergstrom suddenly cut in. "You've got the wrong guy," he insisted, angrily. "My brother's not your rapist."

Despite her brother-in-law's objections, Linda reluctantly tabulated the similarities. "I don't know who to believe," she told Wheeler. "Let me talk to James again. Maybe I can find out about the gun."

Alone again with her husband, Linda asked, "Tell me about the gun."

"What about it?" James replied, softly.

"Where is it?"

"I threw it away," he maintained. "In the water."

"Why?"

"Because we kept arguing and I was afraid if I kept it, I might use it to hurt you," James said. "I didn't want to take the chance."

Linda had to admit James made sense. She'd repeatedly warned him of the dangers involved in having the gun in the house. *God, if there was only some way for me to know the truth,* she thought.

"Well?" Wheeler asked, when she rejoined him.

"He says he threw it in the water," Linda answered.

"Well, we searched the coastline, and guess what—no gun. I don't believe him, and don't you believe him either," said Wheeler. "Your husband knew exactly what he was going to do with that gun, and he did it. He used it to rape."

Years later Wheeler would look back on that afternoon and remember how disoriented and confused Linda seemed. "You could tell she just didn't know what to believe," he said. "We'd have her halfway convinced he was guilty and then she'd talk to her husband and he'd convince her that he was innocent."

Just a day after James's initial arrest, it was determined that there wasn't enough evidence to charge him with the attempted rapes or the rape. Wheeler reluctantly agreed with the county prosecutor that they could prosecute him only with second-degree trespassing on the peeping charge and allow him to make bail.

"If we would have found the mask and the gun, we would have had a good case against him," said Wheeler later. "Without it, we had no choice except to turn him over to the navy."

May 19, 1989, *Bremerton Sun:*

EVIDENCE TO CHARGE MAN WITH RAPE LACKING

Sheriff's investigators don't have the evidence to prove that a suspect arrested yesterday in a Peeping Tom incident is the same man who raped one woman and attempted to rape two others in a Central Kitsap neighborhood . . . The man will be released to the custody of the navy following a district court appearance early in the afternoon.

That afternoon, James went before a judge and was charged with a misdemeanor, second-degree criminal trespass. With his release imminent, Linda conferred with his brother, Chris, and his chief, Steve Swartz, about what to do next. "I don't want him coming home," Linda told them, more frightened of James now than she had ever been in the past. "I think the navy needs to do something."

"Well, I could suggest he check into the naval hospital for psychiatric evaluation," offered Swartz. "We can't order him, but we can suggest it."

Linda agreed and that afternoon put down five hundred dollars, plus the registration slips on her car and on Chris's truck, for James's bail. Once he was freed, Swartz drove him to the hospital, while Linda and Chris followed behind in Chris's truck.

Chris Bergstrom would later decline when asked to discuss any of the events surrounding his brother's arrest. He refused comment on what was discussed that afternoon as he and Linda rode down the highway toward the naval hospital or what he may or may not have later done to ensure his brother's freedom. But as Linda describes their conversation, it introduced fears that would haunt her for weeks to come.

Linda recounts the conversation this way:

Angry and confused, now that she knew her husband to be at the very least a voyeur, she reexamined the last few months, remembering how James frequently disappeared. And she considered again the denial he'd made the day she saw him looking through a bedroom window. Then she thought back to their abrupt move from the Silverdale Apartments and the allegations that caused it.

"I guess the girl at the apartment was telling the truth," she said, wiping tears from her eyes. "James must have been harassing her."

"I don't know, Linda," Chris replied.

"Don't bullshit me now," she told him. "Isn't it obvious?"

"Yeah, he probably did it," Chris said, turning toward her, his face solemn. "But I'm going to do whatever I need to do to keep my brother out of jail."

Chapter Twenty-One

That Wheeler and his staff hadn't been able to charge James with rape gave Linda no comfort. The details of the attack haunted her. The rapist had tied up his victim and placed a pillowcase over her head. "It was just like what he had done to me," said Linda. "It just sounded like James." Still, every time she tried to understand what had happened, what could have driven him to do such a thing, she was left without answers. And then there was James, tearful James, reassuring her that while he had "problems," being a rapist was not one of them. "I didn't do it," he continually repeated. "I didn't rape anyone."

Linda wanted to believe he was telling the truth, that he wasn't capable of such an attack. It was possible, after all, that this was a case of mistaken identity. "I kept looking for something to grab on to," she said later. "Something that would prove one way or the other who was telling the truth."

The questions occupied her mind, filling every cell, until they controlled the very fabric of her thoughts. Linda slept rarely, never well. Looking for answers, she turned to the person she believed knew James best, Steve Swartz.

"Do you think James did it?" she asked one afternoon when they were pacing the hall at the naval hospital together.

"No," said Swartz confidently. "I'm sure he didn't."

In retrospect, Haberstock would wonder if Swartz might have been blinded by friendship and a sense of responsibility for Bergstrom. "When you've worked with a guy, tried to help him, sometimes there's a tendency not to want to believe the bad stuff," he said. "You want them to do well, partly because it's your job to see that they do."

Whatever the reasons, Swartz's assurances didn't reflect the sentiments of Haberstock or others on the blue crew who gossiped about Bergstrom often that June as they readied the *Ohio* for its next patrol. "I'd have to say, the consensus was that he was guilty," said Haberstock. "Most everybody was convinced that Bergstrom could have done it."

Not sure what to do or where to go, Linda notified her landlords that she would move out of their apartment at the end of May. They agreed to overlook the few months remaining on her lease. Like everyone in the tightly knit community of Silverdale/Central Kitsap County, the couple who ran the Central Park Apartments knew what their tenant had been accused of. All the notoriety the case received made Linda feel tainted and ashamed. "I hid as much as I could. . . . I stayed away from everyone," she said. "I was embarrassed and hurt. I'd drive to another town to shop if I needed anything. I just couldn't face running into anyone who knew me."

When Linda tried to work, the day-care center no longer offered the refuge it once had. She could barely function and was so preoccupied, she often struggled to remember the names of even her favorite young charges. Most of her co-workers were sympathetic. Many approached Linda to assure her that James's arrest was undoubtedly a mistake. "I've seen your husband," said one woman. "He's not capable of doing anything like that. He's not big and powerful enough."

"But he had a gun," said Linda.

"No," insisted the woman. "It can't be him."

Her friend Monique, the one James had once assured he would hunt down and kill any man who raped Linda, offered a similar assessment. "Linda, it's just not him," she said. "Remember what he said about rapists? He hates rapists. He couldn't be the one. They've got the wrong guy."

Still, Linda couldn't enter a classroom without wondering what others were whispering. In the lunchroom, she felt all eyes turn and everyone stop talking when she walked through the door. One co-worker scoffed to her face, "So your husband's a rapist, huh, Linda? What's the matter? You weren't giving him enough at home?"

Too confused and exhausted to even defend herself, Linda simply walked away.

Through it all, her good friends stuck by her. Patricia often slept over. When Linda woke up screaming in the night, her friend comforted her. "It's all right, Linda," Patricia would console. "He didn't do it."

Linda held on to her friend, sobbing, and wondering if she would ever know the truth.

One day at the day-care center, Grandma told Linda she worried about her. "You look so pale and nervous all the time," said the older woman. "Linda, you don't even eat like a bird, your stomach is always upset. Why don't you go to the doctor? Maybe there's more going on here. Maybe you're pregnant."

"I'm not pregnant," Linda assured her. "I tried to get pregnant and I couldn't."

"Do me a favor," Grandma said, placing her hand on top of Linda's. "Take a test."

Linda did go to the naval hospital for an exam and a pregnancy test; it was negative. While she was there, she told the doctor she suffered from anxiety attacks throughout the day and night. He listened sympathetically and pressed a prescription into Linda's palm. A prescription for Valium.

The tranquilizer helped, but couldn't erase her fears. For that, she needed answers. Her good friend Penny was visiting family in California, but with Diane and Gayle, Linda spent hours sifting through her memory, reconstructing her activities on the days when the two attempted rapes and the rape took place. "She kept trying to remember what she had been doing and where James was," said Diane. "She was looking for clues." Sometimes Linda thought she remembered those days and that James had been with her. Other times, she'd admit she had little recollection of the exact times they had been together and whether or not the attacks occurred during one of her husband's frequent jogs. "I just couldn't remember," she said later. "I tried and I tried, but I couldn't."

Almost every afternoon or evening, Linda drove to the naval hospital to see James. Usually she found him seated in the psychiatric unit's dayroom. Wearing clothes she'd brought him from home, jeans or a jogging suit, James shuffled along much like the other patients who dotted the room. He often appeared dazed. Linda, always crying, would sit next to him.

"Did you do it?" she'd ask, prodding. "I've got to know."

"Sure, I was watching that woman," James pleaded with her. "But I didn't rape anyone. I just went around looking in windows, that's all."

Then he droned on about his "problem," how he couldn't stop himself, that he was compelled to watch through windows as women dressed. "I've had this problem a long time," he admitted. "I can't control it. But maybe with therapy, if you'll help me, I bet I can be cured. I'll go in for counseling. You'll see. I'll get better and we'll have the family you want."

One afternoon, James shook nervously and stared around the room, pointing at other patients and the staff. "They keep trying to get me to say what I've done," he told her. "But I won't. See that nurse over there?" he whispered, indicating a uniformed woman talking to a patient on the other end of the room. "She told the doctors I was watching her, that I made her nervous. Damn bitch. Who the hell would want to watch her?"

Always the conversation turned around to the gun. Often James's brother, Chris, would be with them, and he, too, asked question after question about the mysterious disappearance of the nine-millimeter Beretta. Linda sensed Chris was as determined as she was to find the weapon and anything else that could be used as evidence of his brother's guilt. While she wanted the gun to settle her own doubts and to turn over to police, she felt uncertain of her brother-in-law's motives. "I knew he wanted it and that he was pressing James to get it," she'd say later. "I was afraid Chris would get it and not even tell me. That I would never know for sure what to believe about James."

Only three people know what happened next. Years later, Chris Bergstrom would refuse requests for an interview. James would continue to insist he'd disposed of the 9mm in the water. But Linda would give a very different account.

According to Linda, a few nights later, she and Chris finally persuaded James to open up about what had happened to the gun. The two brothers talked, heads together, in the antiseptic atmosphere of a hospital corridor, as she listened. James described a field minutes from the apartment. He told of a patch of bushes, a cluster of three trees, and a pole. That night, she and Chris drove in Chris's truck to a field that matched the description. Though they searched, no gun was found.

Two nights later, Linda would later describe walking into the hospital and meeting Chris in the hallway. He gave her a thumbs-up. "I've got it," he said as she followed behind him and took the elevator down to the lobby.

"You don't have to come," Chris told her.

"I'm coming," she insisted.

It was a drizzly, cool night thick with the smell of forest, and the moon skirted the treetops as Chris drove back to the field, the site of their previous futile search. He pulled over, just as they had the other night. Linda watched from the truck as Chris walked perhaps a hundred yards toward a cluster of trees. Her heart pounded and her throat tightened. She at once hoped and feared he would find the gun. Since that first day, she'd decided that the gun was the key to everything.

Arms folded against the brisk night air, Linda stood near the truck, watching for Chris. It was dark, and though she sometimes thought she saw him, his figure was obscured by shadow. Suddenly she realized he was walking toward her, clutching something, she couldn't yet make out what, against his chest. She walked out to meet him as he neared the truck. A chill ran through her when she saw he cradled something heavy in his hands. Chris hurried toward the truck, and she climbed back into the passenger seat. As Chris got inside, she looked down at what he'd retrieved. It was dark and bulky, covered with bits of leaves and dirt. She reached down and picked it up, realizing it was something rectangular tucked inside a green mask, the type used for welding onboard the sub.

"Don't touch that," Chris ordered.

Linda ignored him. She peeled back the mask, and found another identical one inside. When she peeled back the second mask, something jangled. She stuck her hand in and pulled out a handful of bullets. *God*, she thought. *Oh my God.*

Then she turned her attention to the box. She opened it. Inside was the nine-millimeter Beretta, the one James had so proudly shown off to his brother just a few weeks earlier. Linda picked it up and held it nervously in her hands. It felt heavier and colder than she expected. It was terrifying.

Linda dropped it back inside the box, slammed the top shut, and replaced it between them. She was shaking.

"I never really believed James was guilty until I saw the gun," Linda said later. "That he had lied about the gun meant the sheriff was right. Everything he said was true. James was the rapist."

Linda was about to ask Chris what he was going to do with the gun and suggest they take it to the police when he turned to her, his eyes as piercing as bullets. She realized how much he resembled James, especially in the intensity of his gaze as he focused on her. She could feel every ounce of his will bearing down on her when he spoke calmly and slowly, emphasizing every word. "He told me, 'I'll do whatever I have to do, no matter what,'" she later recalled. "Then he glared at me and said, 'My brother is not going to jail. I don't care what he did, or to who.'"

Linda maintained she never saw the handgun again. "Chris dropped me off at my car at the hospital and drove away," she said. "I have no idea what he did with it." For a while she considered going to the police to tell them that her brother-in-law had the weapon they so desperately sought. But without the gun, it was her word against his, and she was afraid now, not only of James, but also of his brother. She'd later say that as the days passed, she thought often of Chris's words as he held the gun in his hands: "I'll do whatever I have to do, no matter what. My brother is not going to jail. I don't care what he did, or to who."

Chapter Twenty-Two

After that night, all Linda's doubts disappeared. In a visceral, concrete sense she accepted James was guilty of everything the undersheriff suspected—not only the peeping and the attempted rapes but the rape itself. Instead of facing uncertainty, she had to deal with a new reality: her conviction that her husband was indeed the Parkwood Rapist.

"You did it," Linda said to James when she went to the hospital early the next day. "You raped that woman."

"I'd be careful who you tell," James said, smirking at her. "I'd be careful for my own good, if I was you."

Linda looked at him sitting there in his hospital-issue bathrobe and pajamas and thought about the time he had knocked her out and she awoke to find him packing. *He could do it,* she thought again. *He could kill me.* Raw fear settled within her. After that day, it never left.

In need of help, Linda corralled the psychologist treating James and asked for a diagnosis. Afraid to tell him everything that had happened over the past twenty-four hours, she said simply, "I think James needs help. I'm not sure he didn't rape that woman."

To her surprise, the doctor answered, "Well, we know he raped that woman, we're sure of it. But we've got no way to prove it. As far as I can tell, he'll be discharged from the hospital soon, and after that, from the navy."

"Isn't there anything you can do to treat him?" she begged. "Maybe he needs to be hospitalized for a while."

"We're not equipped to handle this," the doctor said, dismissing her concerns. "Your husband has a problem, a serious problem, but it's not one we can fix."

Undersheriff Wheeler, too, followed up with navy doctors treating James Bergstrom. "They told me that they couldn't keep him, that he was going to be released. And when I told them I was sure that without some form of treatment, he'd rape again, they said that whatever Bergstrom did, once he was out of the navy, he was no longer their concern."

Convinced she had no decisive proof to turn over to investigators, Linda concentrated on more personal issues. James would soon be released from the hospital, and she knew he would come looking for her. She couldn't bear the thought of seeing him again. The thought of his touch repulsed her. Somehow, she had to get away.

In need of a place to hide, Linda accepted an invitation from her boss at the day-care center, Jane Richards, and moved into an attic bedroom in the Richardses' rambling ranch house across the street from the high school, where in happier days she and James had idled away long afternoons on the tennis court. She told no one where she was staying, not even her best friends. "I wanted to be out of the apartment. I didn't want to be alone," she said. "I was confused. All I knew for sure was that I didn't want James to be able to find me."

Anxious to find a way out, she called Steve Swartz and asked if the navy would move her back to Houston if she and James divorced. Swartz recited the regulation answer: that the navy was only responsible for moving James to his next destination. If she wanted help moving, she would have to stay with him at least long enough to get home.

Despondent, she called her mother.

"Mama, James did it. He raped that woman," she said.

"Oh my God," said Santos. "How can you be sure?"

"I'm sure," she answered.

Though she considered asking her mother for the money

Ashley Bergstrom was a beautiful, perfect baby girl and Linda fell instantly in love with her. She wanted nothing more than to protect her daughter from the pain she herself had endured as a child. *Courtesy of Linda Bergstrom*

Appearing the dedicated father, James holds Ashley at a family baptism with Linda standing far left. *Courtesy of Linda Bergstrom*

Much of James's and Linda's families gathered to help Ashley celebrate her first birthday. It should have been a joyous occasion, but by then an undercurrent of fear and violence haunted Linda's life. *Courtesy of Linda Bergstrom*

James sitting with a crucifix over his head. At one point James counseled with a priest, but nothing the holy man said lessened James's fixation on violence. *Courtesy of Linda Bergstrom*

Ashley dressed as a cat for her first Halloween. James insisted on taking her door to door. It was important to him to appear a devoted husband and father, as it allowed him to hide the monster he'd become. *Courtesy of Linda Bergstrom*

James holding Ashley on his lap in their apartment, staring at the camera. *Courtesy of Linda Bergstrom*

Linda snapped this photo of James as he got ready to leave the apartment for what he told her was a jog. Later she discovered his intentions were far more sinister.

Courtesy of Linda Bergstrom

As Ashley grew, Linda worried for her daughter's safety, especially when she left the toddler alone with James.

Courtesy of Linda Bergstrom

Frank Fidelibus, a detective for the Friendswood Police Department at the time, remembers: "I looked at the knots and thought, *This guy's been in the navy.*"

For nearly two years, a dangerous sexual predator hunted women in Houston's southern suburbs. An apartment complex security guard described the man to a forensic artist who drew this sketch. *Harris County Sheriff's Office photo*

Chuck Rosenthal, the prosecutor who took on the case, was later elected Harris County's district attorney. *Photograph by Kathryn Casey*

The naval hospital where doctors described James as "dangerous" and recommended he be discharged from the service. *Photograph by Kathryn Casey*

Charles Dunn worked for the Houston P.D. as a detective at the time Linda Bergstrom's accusations were relayed to him. Later, Dunn earned a law degree and a lieutenant's badge. *Photograph by Kathryn Casey*

Sergeant Rusty Gallier later retired from the sex crimes division of the Houston Police Department, but he never forgot the Bergstrom case.

Photograph by Lain Clements

Sergeant Robert Tonry, pictured here, along with then-Detective Charles Dunn, moved in on their suspect.

James Bergstrom in 2006.

Linda, here in 2007, remembers too clearly the horror of her years married to a dangerous psychopath. *Photograph by Manuel Fernandez*

she needed to move home, she knew the older woman wouldn't have it. Santos had been sick off and on lately, keeping her from work. Linda knew her mother was having a difficult time paying her own expenses.

These days, Linda lived with a permanent knot in her chest that tightened whenever she thought of James or the previous month's events. On the few quiet moments when she briefly buried her troubles watching television or reading, the pain would return without notice, wrenching inside her until she sometimes felt it would strangle her. "It was like I was living in a nightmare and I couldn't wake up," she said. "Sometimes during the day, it would pop into my mind, and just for a second I'd think, *This can't be true. It must all be a dream. It can't be happening.*"

As she slept alone at night in the small attic bedroom, the real nightmares came. Always she envisioned James in the distance staring through a window at the figure of a woman asleep alone in her bed. In the dream, Linda cried out to warn the stranger, but the woman slept on, oblivious to her cries. Instead James turned toward her and grinned, then opened the window and disappeared inside. Linda awoke to a shrill scream, only to realize it was her own voice that reverberated off attic walls.

"I knew what the woman James raped felt like," she said later. "I was raped. I found myself wondering about things like whether or not that woman had screamed like I had, and what she was thinking when she saw James coming at her with the gun."

On May 30, 1989, eleven days after he arrived at the hospital, James was discharged from the naval hospital. The attending physician noted in his chart that Bergstrom had been uncooperative throughout, barely participating in group therapy. His demeanor had been much as it was onboard the *Ohio*: He was withdrawn and uncommunicative. The doctor also noted that the then twenty-six-year-old sailor struck him as possessing "a violent temper and episodes of uncontrolled aggressiveness," and expressing "fear and hostility toward women" and the need to have a woman "helpless in a sexual relationship."

A neatly typed "Narrative Summary" was attached to the front of Bergstrom's file. It concluded:

> This individual is, in this examiner's opinion, totally unsuitable for continued naval service. He presents with uncontroverted evidence of a major personality disorder which is self-destructive and he represents a continuing danger to himself and others and probably others in the community, particularly his wife.

The diagnosis: "Paranoid personality disorder and voyeurism." And the recommendation: "Serious consideration should be given for administrative separation from the service, as expeditiously as possible consistent with the wishes of his command."

James was dangerous, the doctor was saying. How dangerous, he didn't speculate. Although James Bergstrom had another half year of his enlistment to serve, the captain's only recommendation was not treatment but to quickly discharge him, making him someone else's problem.

In early June, Linda learned James had been released from the hospital. She was still living in the Richardses' attic and working, whenever she felt strong enough, at the day-care center. Once she knew he was free, she began taking even more precautions, like checking her rearview mirror as she drove to the Richardses' each day after work. As she knew she would, one day she glanced back and discovered James following her in the brown Grand Prix. Her heart racing, she wove amongst the busy Silverdale traffic until she finally looked back and he was gone. Trembling, she drove on.

Despite her efforts, one afternoon she pulled into the

driveway after work and looked toward the street, drawn by the plaintive honking of a horn, only to see James driving past the house. He was staring at her, waving. Somehow he had found her hiding place. After that, she glimpsed him often, cruising leisurely up and down the busy street that ran in front of the Richardses' house. Always she would draw the drapes and hide.

Jane Richards and her husband were good people, considerate and kind. Though they had opened their home to her, Linda tried to keep them separated from the terror that enveloped her life. She never told Jane how much she feared James, just that she wanted it to be over with him. When the phone rang at their home a few nights after James had made his reappearance, Jane answered it and looked at her expectantly.

"It's Chris," she said. "Do you want to talk to him?"

"Okay," Linda answered, wondering how James's brother had tracked her down. "I guess I'd better."

But instead of Chris, she heard James's voice on the other end of the line.

"You think I can't find you, can't get to you?" he challenged. "I can find you anywhere. I can come in that house and kill you and everyone in it."

"What do you want?" Linda implored.

"Meet me behind the high school track. Five minutes," he said, calmly. "If you know what's good for you, you'll be there."

Linda drove across the street to the high school and took the road that led to the track. When she arrived, James was waiting. He walked around and got inside the passenger seat beside her.

"Drive to the park," he snarled. "Now." Beating the car roof with his fist, he bayed at her as she drove: "You know too much, Linda. You know too fucking much."

"Then let's just forget it," she said. "You go your way and I'll go mine."

"Just drive, you bitch," he hissed. "Drive."

The park James referred to was a small, wooded area on Hood Canal, miles up the road from their first apartment. It had always been one of Linda's favorites, a haven she sometimes ran to when she and James fought. There she had once walked and considered the dismal turnaround in her marriage. On this afternoon, the park was deserted when they arrived.

James motioned for her to follow and he led her to a picnic table near the water. Linda was terrified, her heart galloping with fear as she sat down next to him.

"What do you want?" she asked, finally. "Can't you leave me alone? Haven't you hurt me enough?"

"Linda, shut up," he shouted.

"You go your way, James, and I'll go mine," she insisted. "This isn't a marriage anymore. The marriage is over and finished, and I never want to see you again."

"Shut the fuck up," he screamed.

"I saw the gun. Chris has the gun," she shouted. "How could you have done this? How could you have raped that woman?"

"You do what I say," James said, pushing his face at hers, "or I'll kill you, that man and woman you're living with, and anyone else I have to. I'll move to Greece and stay with my mother's family. They'll never find me."

James was angry, as angry as she had ever seen him. Linda knew she was only an impulse away from violence. She surveyed the seclusion of the park, the water and the forests. When she closed her eyes, she could picture the gun in her mind. *You did it,* she kept thinking. *You raped that woman.*

"I've told you before and I meant it," he said, opening and closing his fists until the veins in his muscles bulged and twisted like blue highways on a map. "I could kill all of you and no one could stop me."

"I won't tell anyone about the gun. Just leave me alone," she pleaded, gulping back the tears.

Then, according to Linda, James looked at her coldly and deliberately. "He said, 'Chris says I should just get rid of you. You know too much. I could kill you right now, Linda. Right here. And no one would ever know.'"

Trying not to cry, Linda stared down at the water lapping lazily against the shore. *This can't be happening,* she thought. *God, if I could only wake up.* Where she'd felt panic earlier, resignation now overtook her. *I'm never getting away from him.*

Docilely Linda followed when James ordered her to her new car and directed her toward the driver's seat. She got in as he rounded the car. Linda surveyed the forest, its towering, pencil-straight pines standing as if at attention all around her. She felt no hope. No escape. She reached into her purse and pulled out the Valium the navy doctor had prescribed and devoured a handful of pills, flushing them down with the bitter, warm remnants of a leftover Coke. "I figured he was going to kill me," she said later. "I didn't want to feel it, to feel anything, ever again."

James didn't appear to notice. He ordered her to drive and she did, waiting for the pills to have their deadly consequence. The rest of that afternoon she would remember through a drugged haze. She later recalled pulling to the side of the road and James loping off into the forest. Before long, he returned, put something in the trunk, and took over the driving, stopping at another spot in the woods. Later he would tell her he had been collecting evidence, ski masks and ropes he destroyed. But Linda paid no further attention. She drifted into a drugged sleep, expecting never to reawaken.

Afternoon sunlight glinted in the window when Linda awoke the following day. She had a pounding headache and her throat was raw with pain, the bitter taste of vomit coating her mouth. Squinting, she opened her eyes. It took a few seconds before her mind cleared enough to register that she was in a motel room, alone, before she once again surrendered to unconsciousness. The second time she awoke, James was coming through the door.

The next thing she would remember was walking on rubbery legs, and James helping her to the car, as he whispered in her ear.

"Did you think I would let you get away from me?" he said, eerily calm. "You're not ever getting away from me, Linda. Not ever."

Chapter Twenty-Three

In mid-June 1989, James Bergstrom pleaded no contest to a misdemeanor charge of second-degree criminal trespass and went before a judge, promising to seek counseling when he arrived home in Houston. He was sentenced to one year's probation. Things were moving quickly now. The *Ohio*'s executive officer, following the recommendation of naval doctors, offered Bergstrom a deal: stay in and the navy would investigate and possibly seek a court-martial, or take an early out and get an honorable discharge. Bergstrom took the early out.

As his discharge date approached, Linda agreed to meet with him to discuss plans for the trip back to Houston. He always talked hopefully about their future together, and she said little to contradict him. Since that day in the park, she no longer believed she would be able to walk out of James Bergstrom's life. Instead, she reasoned, her best hope was to move with him back to Houston so the navy would pay their expenses. She would then stay with him just long enough to contact an attorney and get her affairs in order before filing for divorce. At home, with her family beside her, Linda knew she would feel more secure, less vulnerable to her husband's violent threats.

In the meantime, she stayed on in the Richardses' attic alone and continued to work sporadically at the day-care center. Jane and the rest of the staff were supportive, never questioning when she felt too ill to come in. They all noticed the change in Linda, the dark circles under her eyes, the way her hands shook whenever she talked about James. Her confidante, Grandma, understood more. She knew that Linda was losing weight and that she had difficulty keeping anything on her stomach.

Continually she whispered to Linda when they were changing diapers in the nursery, "Have you had a pregnancy test?"

"I can't be pregnant," she always protested, although she hadn't had a period in months. "That's impossible. James and I haven't been together since before his arrest—and I had a pregnancy test after he was arrested. It was negative."

"Linda, have another test," the older woman advised. "Call it intuition, but I think you should have it checked."

Finally, on June 16, the date James was being discharged, Linda drove to the navy hospital. Since she'd soon be losing her medical benefits, she reasoned it was only prudent to get a complete checkup. When the doctor came in she pleaded with him to do a pregnancy test. "I need to know, today," she told him. "I know you guys can do it. Please, help me."

For an hour she sat in the hallway outside the hospital lab awaiting the test results. Sometimes, when the waiting was too much, she paced, trying to remain calm. She was supposed to meet James behind the commissary at three to make final plans for their trip home, but still the findings weren't in. She looked down at her watch and then prayed. "God, not now," she whispered.

Half an hour later, the door to the lab was still shut. This is ridiculous, Linda thought. *I know I'm not pregnant.* She was approaching the receptionist, planning to tell her she was leaving, when the lab door swung open and a nurse motioned for her to step inside.

"Mrs. Bergstrom, you're pregnant," the woman said eagerly.

An anxiety that now always stayed close to the surface overcame Linda and she sat down in a nearby chair, feeling like a puppet whose strings had been cut.

"You're pregnant," the nurse said again. "Isn't that wonderful news? You've been trying for so long."

Linda looked up at the nurse, wondering if she could possibly be one of the only people in Central Kitsap County who didn't know about James and that this would not be welcome news. "Thanks," she said, smiling weakly. "That's great. Just great."

On the drive to the commissary, Linda considered the haphazard twists fate had dealt her. If she'd been enacting this tragedy onstage, this is the point when the gods would have looked down from Mount Olympus and laughed heartily at her plight. The unfairness of it all astonished her. To have wanted a child and been denied for so long, only to discover she was pregnant now, was a cruel joke. *I find out my husband is a rapist,* she thought. *Then I discover I'm carrying his child. And the only way I can get home is if I stay with him long enough for the navy to move us.*

When she arrived at the commissary, James was there, and as usual, he was angry.

"What the hell took so long?" he demanded.

"I told you I had a doctor's appointment," she said. "I had another pregnancy test."

"And I told you to be here at three, and I meant three," he shouted. "Did it have to take so long?"

"Well, it did," she said. "I'm pregnant."

At first James looked shocked, but he quickly recovered. To her surprise, smiling and clearly exhilarated, James Bergstrom swept her up in his arms. It was the first time he'd touched her since the arrest, and her body stiffened with revulsion, but he appeared oblivious to it.

"We finally did it," he shouted, giddily. "We finally have what we've always wanted. We're going to be a real family."

In mid-July, James and Linda packed their cars for the drive back to Houston. The moving van was scheduled to pick up the rest of their things from the Richardses' house and Chris's apartment later that week. Before they left, many of Linda's friends tried to talk her into aborting the baby, but she decided she just couldn't do that. "I wanted a baby," she'd say later. "I desperately wanted a baby. I was not going to abort the baby."

What puzzled Linda was the way James acted, as if he expected them to stay together. He babbled on constantly about the new life they'd have in Houston and about how good it would be to see his old friends. James was happy, crowing about the early out and their arrival home. All she could think about was how long it would take to file for divorce.

Linda couldn't help but see the paradox. For many years she loved James, so much she once cried when he went out to sea. But he never understood how she felt, instead continually accusing her of being unfaithful and not caring for him. Now that she found his very touch odious, he appeared unable to recognize her loathing. James Bergstrom, she realized, couldn't understand either love or hate.

The week of James and Linda's departure, Bill Haberstock heard through the navy grapevine that the Bergstroms were headed back to Houston. Momentarily he wondered what would happen next. "I kind of figured James would go back to Texas and start a new life," the COB would say later. "I was hoping he'd turn it around."

When Undersheriff Chuck Wheeler heard Bergstrom was leaving Washington State, he had no such illusions about what lay ahead. One day in the office he made a prediction to the county prosecutor. "You and I both know what's going to happen. He's going to go back to wherever he goes and he's going to do it again," said Wheeler, shaking his head in frustration. "There's no doubt in my mind. He will do it again."

PART THREE

Chapter Twenty-Four

Linda and James Bergstrom's twenty-four-hundred-mile drive back to Houston from Seattle in July 1989 was like a funeral procession. James drove the lead, headlights on, in the Grand Prix, and she followed behind in her blue Precis. For Linda it was as if there had been a death in the family. Her marriage was, for all practical purposes, over, her dreams shattered. "Nothing was there for James," she said later. "Everything I had felt for him was dead."

She knew James had different plans: to return to Houston and to move in with his parents until they found a place of their own. Pragmatic as ever, Linda wasn't arguing with him. She had a baby coming and she needed to be practical. Besides, she was now more afraid than ever that if she left, he might carry out his threat—hunt her and the baby down and kill them both. Who could protect her? There'd been enough stories in the newspapers and on television about women who went to the police for protection from an abusive spouse and ended up dead. Afterward all the editorials asked, How could it happen? Linda knew. It happened.

The best thing, she reasoned, would be to go along until she had everything in place, and then make the split. To move into the Bergstroms' just long enough to find a way out.

That almost didn't happen. When James called home before they left Seattle, Irene Bergstrom was not happy to hear her oldest son was returning. To Linda the older woman said, "I don't want to see James. I don't want him calling me. I don't want him here."

Although Linda hadn't talked with her in-laws since James's arrest, Chris had said he'd kept them informed. She thought she understood her mother-in-law's hostility, but there was no escaping it—James was coming home.

Of course, James's mother undoubtedly had problems of her own to consider. At least on the surface, things in the Bergstrom household hadn't improved since James and Linda left three years earlier. The previous Thanksgiving, Irene had called Pearland police at 4:09 in the morning to complain that her husband and a crony were drunk and unruly. A squad car was dispatched to the Bergstroms' quiet suburban neighborhood, and officers mediated the quarrel, convincing James C. it was time for bed. Then, just that past April, James C. was charged with driving while intoxicated. In July he pleaded no contest and was sentenced to a year's probation and a four-hundred-dollar fine.

On the phone that afternoon, James nudged Linda as she spoke, urging her to smooth things over. Finally Linda told her mother-in-law, "I'm pregnant. James and I just found out we're having a baby."

"That's great, really great," Irene Bergstrom said sarcastically. "All right," she sighed. "You can come home and stay here until you find a place."

The trip took four days. In her car, alone, Linda had time to think. She was confused and frightened, but at the same time fascinated with what James had done and why. "I began wondering what it was that made someone like James tick, made a man a rapist, and if he could be changed," she said. "I had been raped, and I didn't understand how one person could do that to another. And I felt guilty, as if somehow it was my fault. That I hadn't been a good wife."

Each night in a different motel room, she was forced to confront James in the flesh. At first he was timid, gentle to the point of patronizing. When he tried to touch her and she pulled away, he deferred. "I know you've been through a lot," he said. "I can wait."

But on the last night of the trip, Linda sensed his patience had worn thin. He was fidgety and tense, and grumbled when she closed the bathroom door behind her when she dressed, angry that she didn't want him watching her.

"Can I tie you up?" he demanded that night.

"No," she shouted at him. "Never."

"Linda," he said, "I have needs. I understand you've been through a lot, so I'm not going to force you. But I'm asking you again, can I tie you up?"

"No," Linda said again. "I want you to leave me the hell alone."

Rebuffed, James was furious, and immediately rushed toward her, hurling her against the wall and then onto the bed.

"You're hurting me and you're hurting the baby," she screamed at him. "Haven't you done enough?"

"I could just kill you both," James said as he had so often before, this time grabbing her by the neck.

"Just leave me alone," she screamed. "Can't you understand what you've done?"

"All right, but no closing doors," he demanded, reluctantly backing away. "You're my wife."

Her hands trembling, Linda went in the bathroom and slammed the door. James said nothing.

In the car the next day, she daydreamed about what might happen, how she could get away and start a new life without James. Whenever the reality of her situation crept in, it all seemed hopeless. How would she ever escape him?

Actually these days Linda's thoughts were rarely on herself. The life growing within her was more important to her than anything had ever been. "I was determined that things would be better for my baby," she said later. "I wasn't going to let my child have a life like I'd had. My life may have been a mess, but I was going to protect my baby."

She had no way of knowing that still ahead were even more revelations about the man she had married. Facts waited for her in Houston that, once discovered, would bind her to James Bergstrom. Knowledge that would make it impossible to leave him and lead her to believe the only way she and her baby would be safe was if James Bergstrom was locked away in prison for a very long time.

When they arrived at the Bergstrom house that Saturday, James's mother had been called out of town to a relative's funeral, but James C., Maria, and Adelaide were all there waiting. The house seemed strange to Linda. Adelaide, then just seventeen, and Maria, twenty-two, were dressed as punk rockers all in black, their heads shaved. Even Adelaide's room was painted black and decorated with garbage bags and bizarre sculptures of heads.

Although Linda was certain Chris had kept them informed, no one in James's family spoke of what had happened in Washington, neither his admission to being a voyeur or suspicions that he was a rapist. Instead they asked warmly about his time in the navy. James bragged about the patrols he'd been on, the nuclear sub and the high-powered arsenal it carried. Linda listened in disgust as he entertained them with stories. "James made it sound like he loved the navy," she'd say later. "Like it was the best thing that had ever happened to him."

The following day, Linda went to visit her family. Her mother, brothers, and sisters congregated at the family home to greet her. A few neighbors even made their way over to the Martinez house to welcome her home to Houston. Some teased her about the new physique she'd engineered in the gym.

"You're skinny," Gino laughed when he saw her. "Mom'll have to put a little weight on you."

No one asked Linda why she and James had come home from Washington months early, and she was relieved not to have to explain. When the others finally left, Linda sat in the kitchen with Santos. The house looked much the same, but her mother had aged while she was gone.

"Tell me what happened," Santos said finally. "What happened with James."

Relieved to be able to share it all with someone, Linda talked on, leaving nothing out. When she was finished, she looked at her mother and thought she sensed Santos was having a difficult time believing all she had just heard.

"And guess what," Linda said, tears clouding her eyes. "I'm pregnant."

"No," Santos said.

"Yes. I am."

"Well, maybe you and James can work it out," Santos said, softly. "For the baby's sake, maybe he can go to a doctor and get better."

"I don't know, Mama," Linda answered.

That night, when she returned to the Bergstroms', she found James again regaling his family with stories from the nuclear front. After all she'd been through, listening to James brag about his exploits to his attentive family, a scene that would have seemed normal under other circumstances, struck her as nearly surreal. It was more than Linda could bear. She went to bed.

She slept fitfully, and at about one the following morning awoke and realized her husband wasn't lying beside her. Some sixth sense told her something was wrong. The house seemed too determinedly silent. Linda eased out and walked toward the kitchen. James wasn't there. Nor in the living room. She checked the bathroom. It, too, was empty. She crept back to his bedroom, the one they shared, and waited. Moments later, James shuffled cautiously down the hall toward her, from the direction of his sisters' bedroom.

"What were you doing in your sisters' room?" she demanded.

"I was in the bathroom," he insisted.

"No you weren't," she concluded. "There's something going on here and you're not leveling with me."

"Okay, I was looking at some of their stuff," he said nervously. "They've got a statue in there of a head."

"What?"

"I was just looking, that's all," he answered angrily, before cutting off the argument.

The next morning, James left for Devoe & Raynolds. The company had initially balked at hiring him back, but with his honorable discharge papers in hand, they were required to under union rules. As soon as he'd left, Linda went to find James C. He was in his bedroom, sitting at the computer.

"I'm going to get my stuff and stay at my mother's," she said, crying. "I know James is doing things again and no one is talking. I don't know what to do anymore, but I can't stay here."

"Did he do something here, in this neighborhood?" James C. asked with alarm. "In this house?"

"I don't know," Linda confessed. "I just know he's doing it again. Maybe this is all my fault. Maybe I haven't been a good wife."

"You're not at fault. You've had a hard time, Linda, and there's something you should know," James C. said before calling out to his daughter. "Adelaide, come here."

When she appeared at the door, he ordered, "You need to have a talk with Linda."

"What happened in Washington?" was the first thing Adelaide asked. They were sitting under a tree in a park not far from the Bergstroms' house.

Linda took the newspaper clips from the *Bremerton Sun* out of her purse and handed them to her. "Parkwood rapes suspect arrested," screamed one headline. "Evidence to charge man with rape lacking," read another.

"My brother is a rapist," Adelaide said excitedly.

"He tied the woman up and raped her. He had a gun,"

Linda said sternly, trying to make her understand the seriousness of what James had done. "He has this thing, he was always doing it to me, too. During sex, he always wanted to tie me up and gag me."

Then Adelaide confided that her brother had a long history of such conduct. That for many years he had sexually molested a young girl.

"So this went on before we were married?" Linda asked, stunned.

"Yes," Adelaide assured her. "I used to hear him."

"So this wasn't my fault," Linda sighed with relief.

Linda collected her things and left the Bergstrom house that afternoon and moved in with her mother. She called James at the plant later that day and said only, "I know everything. I know about you. Adelaide told me."

"Let's talk," he said.

"We have nothing to talk about," she answered. "It's over."

"Let me explain," James said.

Linda agreed to meet at a Whataburger, a fast-food hamburger chain known for its orange and white A-frame roofs. It was Linda's idea, because it was public and safe. They sat at a table and Linda looked over at her husband. James was restless.

"Yeah, I used to tie her up," he admitted, fidgeting in his seat. "But I didn't go all the way. I just touched her." Linda listened in amazement as James maintained that while what he had done was wrong, he hadn't really hurt the girl. That she was a child, merely eight at the time it began, didn't appear to enter anywhere into his analysis of what he had done.

"She was just a little kid," Linda protested. "Did your parents know?"

"They found out one night when we had an argument," he admitted. "The night me and you went to that motel together when we were dating."

"The night you said you'd argued about me?" Linda asked. "So that's why they were in such a hurry to get you into the navy and out of the house."

"I've got a problem, Linda," he said with a shrug. "I know that. I'm willing to get help and work hard to get better. I'll go to a doctor, get therapy."

He looked at her, pleading, "I don't want to lose you and the baby. I want to be a family. Stay with me and we can work this out. I can get better."

Linda didn't know what to think. Certainly the Bergstroms hadn't done anything to stop James. Or the navy. If she left him, what would he do? Go out and rape again, most likely. Like that sheriff in Washington had said he would. *Is it possible to change someone?* she wondered. *Can I stop him?*

That night she talked it over again with Santos. "He needs help," Linda's mother told her. "He needs to see doctors to get better. Why didn't his parents send him?"

"They didn't and neither did the navy." Linda shrugged. "The truth is, nobody cares."

"If he agrees to go for help, Linda, maybe you should try," Santos said, sadly.

It was true that Linda no longer loved James, not the man he had become. But she had begun thinking of him as two different men, and she still remembered the old James, funny and gentle. The one who stood outside her house that night in the street and yelled, "I love you, Linda," until her neighbors came to investigate. The man who had looked at her as they drove down the highway and predicted, "Someday I'm going to marry you."

What was she giving up if she waited six months to see if they could work it out? Days passed and Linda examined and reexamined her quandary. She turned it around, looking at it from all sides. No matter how she posed the problem, it continued to look dark. It was like she was a child again, reasoning her way out of her family's cycle of violence. Finally Linda concluded she had only one choice. As she saw it, she could stay with James long enough to see that he got help. Then she could leave knowing she, at least, had attempted to stop him. Linda called James and told him that if he was committed to going to therapy and getting better, she was willing to give it a try.

James was thrilled.

"You won't be sorry," he assured her. "We'll be a family, just like you've always wanted."

Chapter Twenty-Five

At one time or another, we all make some sort of compromise. We convince ourselves to continue in jobs we're weary of, socialize with people we abhor, maintain relationships that no longer thrill us, or stay locked in marriage to a spouse whose touch chills as cold as a scarecrow in winter. Linda had not grown up believing she deserved much from life. Remaining, at least temporarily, with James was a bargain she felt she could make. Yet coming to a decision and living with its consequences are two very different propositions.

In early August, James and Linda Bergstrom moved into the River's Inn Country Villas in Manvel, Texas, not far from Pearland. It was a single street of wood-sided mobile homes painted pale yellow with blue trim, tucked among ranches where snow white egrets on stilt-thin legs trailed bulky grazing cattle. At the driveway's end, the owners lived in their own double-wide trailer.

It was a bucolic setting, peaceful and calm. Connie and Bob Wittstruck had bought it hoping to found a colony where students would live in the trailers and take lessons from Connie, an artist. It was one of those schemes that fail to materialize. Instead their first tenants became James and Linda.

On the surface, the Bergstroms, of course, appeared no different from any young couple awaiting the birth of their first child. James was freshly out of the navy with his honorable discharge in hand. Their furniture arrived from Washington and they settled into the tiny trailer. James drove off to work each afternoon to start the night shift at Devoe. Linda stayed home to care for the household. Yet before long, angry, violent arguments spilled out from unit three into the parking lot, and it became apparent to the Wittstrucks that the young couple was deeply troubled. Still there was no hint of how deep the trouble ran, or the drama slowly unfolding behind closed doors.

"I thought about what my mother had said. If James was willing to go for therapy, I was willing to give it a try," said Linda later. "If he didn't go for counseling, it was pointless. But somehow I needed to stop him from hurting anyone else. I had another plan. I wanted to know what had happened in Kitsap County, everything there was to know about the rape. Things I couldn't have known unless he did it and told me. Because if he wasn't going to get better, I was going to make sure he was caught."

It was a dangerous game Linda played. Each day she prodded James. First she pushed him to go to counseling. As he had in Washington when she'd insisted he register the gun, James agreed but never followed through. Linda tried to maintain calm, fearing that the continual turmoil she was under might harm the baby. But it was no use; they fought constantly. Once he pulled a knife from the kitchen counter and chased her. Another time, he kicked a hole in the bathroom door when she locked herself inside to escape him. After one such argument, the Wittstrucks saw James pursuing Linda as she pulled out of the parking lot in her car. He held on to the door and ran beside her until she gunned the engine and pulled out onto the street.

No matter how she argued and reminded him of his promise to seek treatment, he was intransigent. He would not go to any doctor to discuss what he continued to refer to as "my problem."

"I can't go for counseling, Linda. They'll turn me in," he insisted each time she brought up his promise.

"Doctors don't do that," she scoffed.

"How stupid do you think I am?" he jeered. "That confidentiality bullshit is all talk. They'll tell."

The months ticked by: August, then September. Linda watched the talk shows every time they discussed rape. She wanted to know everything she could about rapists. How they thought, why they did it. She even called the "Geraldo" show one afternoon in New York and talked to an associate producer, begging him to do a segment on treatment for rapists. On "Oprah" she saw a child molester and couldn't help considering how James had molested a young girl. The man on TV had also began victimizing others at an early age.

"What happens if you get out of prison?" Oprah asked the man. "Are you going to do it again?"

"Yeah," he said. "I will."

What Linda heard over and over was how difficult it was to rehabilitate sexual predators. How so few rapists and pedophiles respond to treatment. "It seemed more and more hopeless," she said later.

Still, she had to take action. With no one else to rely on, she began monitoring James herself. One day she drove the distance from Manvel to Devoe and jotted down the time, calculating precisely when James should arrive home from work. Each night she waited, anxiously watching the clock, to hear the car driving on the gravel road to the trailer. Until James was home, she couldn't relax. When he walked inside, she felt the rest of the world was safe. At least she knew on this particular night James Bergstrom wasn't hurting anyone. But there were nights when James was late. Alone in the dark, Linda would peer out the curtains, desperately waiting to see his headlights turn off the road.

"I know how long it takes you to drive home," Linda demanded when he showed up. "Where have you been?"

James always had an excuse. He had to jump a co-worker's car or give someone a ride home. "Why don't you just time me?" he finally suggested. "Write it down, since you're constantly checking on me, anyway."

Linda did. She began a calendar, recording the time he left the apartment for work each afternoon and what time he returned, allowing thirty minutes for the drive to and from Devoe. She insisted he call every evening during his dinner break to be sure he hadn't left the plant. "If he wasn't getting therapy, I was going to watch him," she said later. "I wanted to know what he was doing. I didn't want him to hurt anyone else."

Rather than resist, James relished the attention Linda gave him. In his twisted logic, he viewed it as proof that she still loved him. "We can lick this together," he crowed one afternoon when she wrote down the time he left the house. "You stick with me and we'll do it."

He was less amenable when she pumped him for information, anything she could find out about what had happened in Washington State. "I figured eventually he was either going to get so sick and tired of me asking, he'd tell me, or he'd kill me," Linda explained later.

"Why do you want to know?" James would shout at her at such times. "What does it matter?"

"It matters," Linda insisted. "If I'm going to help you, I need to know. You need to be open with me, if I'm going to stay."

James held back, stone-silent, until one Sunday afternoon when he finally asked, "If I tell you what happened, will you get off my back?"

"Yes," Linda replied. "I need to know. That way, maybe I can get over it."

That afternoon, according to Linda, James told her about Washington State. How it had all started when he accosted women in malls, trying to strike up conversations that would lead to sex. Then he progressed to peeping in windows at the Silverdale Apartments, but that, too, soon failed to satisfy the overwhelming compulsions that drove him. Finally, he said, he'd entered a house through an open window. The woman was asleep in a chair, the television buzzing in the background.

"She was maybe forty," he said, haltingly. "She looked at me and I knew she was still asleep. She probably thought I was part of a dream. I left. She was too old."

James then recounted another house, this one occupied by a young wife and her child. He'd been watching the woman for a long time and felt attracted to her. He knew her schedule and what time she'd be home alone. That morning, he waited until her husband left for work and then slipped in through an unlocked garage door. She was in bed.

"She screamed," he said. "I tied her up and told her to be quiet. That if she cooperated, I wouldn't hurt her."

But the woman fought so uncontrollably, he finally left, running from the house fearing she'd awakened the neighborhood and that police would soon be trailing him.

There were no flashing lights or sirens, no police banging on their door, and the next day James entered again, this time a trailer home off Old Military Road. Inside, a woman applied makeup in the bathroom mirror.

"I had your belt from your white terry cloth robe," James said. "I figured I'd tie her up with it."

Linda felt squeamish remembering how she had looked for that very belt, never dreaming James might have it or what he was doing with it.

"The woman freaked out and I couldn't shut her up," James continued. "I got scared and left."

Then he'd bought the gun.

In a quiet, somber voice, James turned his attention to the actual rape.

"I just picked the house out at random," he said. "I came in through the kitchen window. It was unlocked. The woman inside was about thirty, maybe five foot six inches and a hundred thirty pounds. She was asleep. When she heard me and woke up, I showed her the gun. She said, "How'd you get in?" but I told her not to talk, that if she cooperated, she wouldn't get hurt. I tied up her hands and legs on the water bed. She said her husband was working at PSNS and that he'd be home soon. When I was done, I left out the window."

James didn't cry or say he was sorry. Instead he looked down at his hands, as ashamed as a small boy confessing to shoplifting a candy bar from the neighborhood grocery store.

"What kind of person does something like this, James?" she asked. "What drives you?"

"I've got a problem," he said almost casually. "But I've only done it a few times. I can learn to control it. You're pregnant and we're going to be a family. I'll never do it again. I'd never risk my family that way. Is knowing all of this going to help you? Can we forget it now?"

"Yes," she said. "It's going to help me and the baby."

"From that moment on, I had a clear goal," Linda said later. "I didn't even think about the possibility of changing him. I wanted him caught."

The following Monday afternoon, James left for work as usual, and Linda pulled out the phone numbers she'd kept from Kitsap County. She dialed and a detective answered. Quickly she explained who she was and recited her husband's case number, K89053185. Then she told him everything James had told her the previous weekend, all about the homes he had admitted entering and the night of the rape.

"Now, I couldn't know she had a water bed or what she looked like unless he told me and he did it," Linda said excitedly. "I want to testify against him. I want to help you put him away."

There was silence on the other end of the phone.

"The thing is, Mrs. Bergstrom, you can't testify against him. The law doesn't allow it," the detective said finally. "I appreciate what you're trying to do, but one spouse can't testify against the other. There are laws against it."

Linda thought her heart would stop, lodged as it was in her throat. This was impossible.

"What am I going to do?" she said.

"You're going to have to wait," the Washington detective said glumly. "Wait until he messes up again. These guys always do."

Linda thanked the officer and hung up. She had never felt so alone. Then, just to know she'd done all she could, she dialed the dispatch number for the Houston Police Department. When the operator answered, she told him everything about James, who he was, where he lived, where he worked, what he looked like, the license number of the car, and what had happened in Washington State.

"He could be out raping women," Linda said.

"Who is this?" the dispatcher asked.

"I can't tell you," Linda explained. "I'm afraid of him. If he knew I'd called, he'd kill me."

"Well, we'll keep an eye out for him," the dispatcher said before hanging up.

Then Linda sat back and waited. Waited for something to happen. Waited for the police to knock on the door. Waited for James to come home and say he was being investigated.

She waited, but no one came.

As the days dragged on, Linda grew increasingly despondent. It was obvious no one cared. The navy had done nothing. Washington State couldn't prosecute. *God, if I only knew what Chris did with that gun,* she thought. And apparently, Houston police were ignoring her call as well.

Perhaps the worst toll came from the charade of living together as husband and wife. She hated being in any family or social situations, even taking the step of calling her mother, brothers, and sisters, and pleading with them all not to invite her and James anywhere as a couple. "I just couldn't stand pretending," she said later. "It made me want to scream."

Though her family, for the most part, agreed, James's family was another matter. Thanksgiving came and he insisted they have dinner at his parents'. Linda fumed. She dreaded going to the Bergstroms', even walking into the house knowing what had gone on there for so many years. More and more she blamed them. If they had told her about

James, she never would have married him. It was a house with too many secrets.

When she told James how she felt, he came at her with his fist. Linda arrived at the Bergstroms' that Thanksgiving with an angry black eye rimmed in red, her body covered with bruises. James sat next to her bristling with enthusiasm, acting every inch the devoted son and family man, as Linda ate sullenly beside him, her face stinging from the beating he'd administered. No one even mentioned Linda's injuries or asked how she'd been hurt. She assumed they realized James had beaten her and didn't care.

In fact, James was becoming progressively more violent. She wondered sometimes if it was because in Washington he'd still had something to hide. Now that she knew everything, there was nothing to conceal, not even his fury. The most trivial things could set him off. Once when she was outside washing her car, James bellowed out the window that he wanted her inside, on the couch, watching television with him. She ignored him, until he came outside and kicked the new car's fender, denting it.

"See what you make me do?" James charged, incredulously. "Are you satisfied, you bitch? You can't pay attention to me. Keep paying attention to your new fucking car."

Yet no injustice approached the revulsion she felt every time James touched her. If she shunned him for more than a day or two, he became violent, throwing food around the room or breaking whatever was handy. Eventually she would give in, staring at the corner of the room, thinking about whatever else she could muster while he satiated his appetite. He never seemed to realize or care how far away her spirit was. Of course, James had never liked it when she participated. From the beginning he'd turned off if she moaned or writhed beneath him. He clearly had no need for anything beyond her body.

Although she refused to play his games of bondage, one night he posed her in bra and panties in the shadows in front

of the bathroom mirror. She stared at her reflection, six
months pregnant, her abdomen swollen to the size of a basketball, with James behind her.

"Stand here," he ordered, positioning her in front of the
mirror. "Just like that."

As she watched in horror, he pressed the hot flesh of his
hand over her mouth, until his eyes ignited with excitement.
Her breath quickened and she tried not to reveal the terror that
overwhelmed her as she watched his reflection in the mirror.

"I just knew he must be doing things again," she said
later. "All I could think of was that he was imagining I was
some other woman, maybe someone he saw on the street,
at the store, or someone he watched through a window."

A few days later, Linda peeked into the living room and
discovered James watching an erotic scene in a music video.
Convinced she was right—that he had reverted to his old
habits—Linda prodded James to tell her everything. "I have
to know if I'm going to help you," she argued. After hours of
badgering, he finally admitted later that night that she had
guessed right, that he was again watching through windows
at unsuspecting women.

"If I tell you, you'll leave me," he said.

"No, I won't," she insisted. "I need to know."

James looked at her warily. "I've been doing it on my way
to work, or whenever I get a break," he confessed.

"Show me the houses, James," she said. "I want to see
them."

James and Linda circled quiet residential streets in the
Grand Prix. The homes were in a blue-collar neighborhood
near Devoe & Raynolds where many owners had burglar
bars on the doors and windows. They drove past a small
brick house set back from the street, and James pointed at it.
"This is the place. There's an Oriental woman living there.
She lives with an older man," he puzzled. "I don't know if
he's her boyfriend or her husband."

Linda could see that James enjoyed this confessing. It was
as if he wanted her to share his secrets.

"I'm glad you know," he said, gushing. "There shouldn't ever be anything we don't know about each other, if we're a family."

Disgust overwhelmed her. It was all she could do to keep from screaming at him.

Then he looked at her calmly. "You know, Linda," he bragged, "if I wanted to get into those houses, I could."

"They'd catch you," Linda countered.

"Nobody would ever get me. I'm too good at it to ever slip up again."

The following day, Linda again called the Houston police dispatch number. Again an operator listened to her story.

"I want you to know about this," she said. "If something happens in these neighborhoods, if anything happens to that Oriental woman, you'll know who did it."

Again the dispatcher assured her they would vigilantly watch for any signs James Bergstrom was on the prowl. Again Linda waited and nothing happened.

There'd been friction between Linda and James and their landlords, the Wittstrucks, since they'd moved in, and in early December, James and Linda moved out and into a small apartment a block from the Pearland police station. James busied himself settling in, arranging everything just so in the apartment the way he had once compulsively straightened his room. "It was odd," Adelaide would say later. "It was like the Partridge Family. The couch, the love seat, the towels all folded nicely. Everything perfect. Linda was normal. The baby was a normal thing to do. James loved it."

Linda had little enthusiasm for the pretense, but concentrated on doing what she could to ready things for the baby. They were having money problems, and there was little left to pay for much beyond necessities. James's salary at Devoe was eleven hundred dollars a month, compared to the nearly seventeen hundred dollars a month he had been making in the service. Her car was repossessed that fall, and when she continued to press him to seek counseling, James used their lack of funds as his alibi for not seeking therapy.

"We can't afford it," he'd dismiss every time Linda mentioned it.

"There are clinics, places you can go where they only charge what you can afford," she argued. But he wouldn't.

Linda still planned to leave as soon as she could find a safe way out. More and more, she viewed the situation as hopeless. Then something happened that changed everything, locking her in. As life had done in the past, events made Linda's decision for her. That December, Linda's gynecologist suggested she have an ultrasound to determine precisely when the baby would be due. On her back, as the doctor and technician stood beside her running the wand across her abdomen, Linda watched the screen. There was her child, a moving mass of gray and shadow.

"From the size and development, I'd say the baby's due in mid-February," said the doctor, as the image floated toward them. "Oh look, it's a little girl."

A girl, thought Linda, happily watching the floating image on the screen. *A baby girl.*

James was waiting in the hallway and they drove home from the clinic together. He was bubbling, gushing about their baby girl, but Linda was worried. She kept reconsidering what James had done to his young relative. He'd molested a child, a little girl. "I suddenly realized there was no way of being sure he wouldn't abuse his daughter," she'd say later. "If I got a divorce, as I was still planning to do, how would I know that when he had visitation, he wasn't molesting my baby?"

Linda fought back the panic until James left for work, then she pulled out the yellow pages and flipped to the listings for the myriad of Houston's attorneys. She ran her finger down until she found one who specialized in family law. When the secretary put her through, Linda gulped out everything she could about her situation.

"I can't take a chance he might abuse my daughter," she

told the attorney. "Is there any way I can keep him from having unsupervised visitation?"

"Not unless you can prove he's a danger," the attorney answered. "You'll need something concrete to convince a court to keep him away from his baby. They don't do that without solid evidence."

Linda hung up the phone but quickly redialed, this time the number of the Kitsap County detective she'd spoken with before.

"Can you send me something, anything to show what he did?" she said. "I'm pregnant and I'm going to have a little girl. He molested a little girl. I need proof to keep him away from my daughter."

"Mrs. Bergstrom, I can't do that," he said. "Your husband was never charged with the rape. All we've got is a second-degree trespass. No judge will accept that as a reason to take away his parental rights."

Linda was convinced there had to be some way.

"Then I went to the Bergstroms," she said later. "I told Adelaide and Maria that I was pregnant with a little girl and that I needed their help. I said, 'Please help me keep my baby safe.' I needed them to tell the court what James had done. I had no other evidence. I pleaded with them, 'You can't let this keep going on.'"

James family refused to help her.

"James would have killed us if we'd helped Linda take that baby away from him," Adelaide would say later, dismissing Linda's pleas as unreasonable. "We couldn't do that to our own brother."

Linda didn't know what to do. She was afraid to stay with James and she was afraid to leave him. She felt certain he would hunt her down, maybe kill her and the baby. If not, he'd undoubtedly have unsupervised visitation, and she wouldn't be there to protect her child. Tension built and after one particularly angry argument, she blurted out at James, "You're just a rapist, a damn rapist. And I'm going to tell everyone. I've already told the Houston police. They're going to look out for you and you're going to end up in prison."

To her surprise, James assessed her coldly. He smirked at her and laughed softly.

"Tell the world, Linda," he mocked. "Go ahead and tell the world. I'm not worried about it. No one . . . no one is going to believe you."

Chapter Twenty-Six

At first, Allen Gibson, Caesar, and James Bergstrom's other co-workers had been surprised to see him return to Devoe & Raynolds so soon, months before his four-year enlistment was up. "We thought it was a little odd," mused Gibson. "But hell, James said he had some unused vacation time coming and they gave him an early out. He had an honorable discharge. Why wouldn't we believe him?"

The only one James told a different, vaguely-close-to-the-truth account to was John, whom he worked with on the second floor in the batch-making department, mixing the paste into paint. John was someone James looked up to, a muscular man with a black belt in karate. So one day when John asked again why James would have left to come back to less money at Devoe when he was set to make E-6 and rake in even more navy money, James admitted things hadn't gone all that well in the service.

"There was this woman in our apartment complex, a navy wife, who made some untrue allegations about me," he told his co-worker. "She said I'd been watching her. She didn't have a case and they threw it out, but the navy offered me an early discharge and I took it."

John believed James's account, never considering that there could be more to it. "James just wasn't the type to do anything to anybody," John said later. "I figured some woman probably lied." Yet John, Gibson, and others noticed that the James Bergstrom who returned from Seattle was not the buffoonish and bashful young man they remembered. "He wasn't the same old James when he got back," explained Gibson. "He seemed more serious about things. I thought maybe he'd finally grown up."

The new James talked about Linda and the coming baby as if they were his most compelling concern. James told everyone how he looked forward to being a father. His appearance had even changed; he had assumed a pin-straight military bearing, and he appeared more self-assured, proud, even boastful. James crowed about his navy training in self-defense and the high-powered arsenal of weapons he'd been trained on. It was obvious that he'd begun thinking of himself differently, not as the butt of lunchroom jests but as a trained and potentially deadly force.

Off and on during the workday with John, who, at five feet eleven inches and 190 pounds, towered over him, James practiced karate kicks and punches. "He'd ask me to show him some moves," said John. "I never thought about why he was suddenly interested in learning karate."

Linda knew something was up when she came home from grocery shopping one afternoon and saw James through the living room window, practicing stances and kicks. His foot cut sharply through the air, then jerked downward as he pummeled his fists at an imaginary enemy. She'd already noticed him watching martial arts movies on cable in the afternoons before work. He'd even taped *Bloodsport*, a bloody 1988 movie starring the muscle-bound Jean-Claude Van Damme as Frank Dux, an American major competing in a world-class, to-the-death competition, so he could watch it over and over.

When Linda walked in the house that particular afternoon, James followed her into the kitchen, where she unpacked the groceries. "You know I could kill you and the baby," he said, softly and calmly. "Before anyone even knew, I'd be gone. I could go to Greece and live with my mother's family. I'd just never come back."

Linda tried to ignore him, but she felt as if she'd been on the receiving end of his forceful thrusts, the breath knocked from her lungs.

While they continued to live together, even slept together, the hostility between Linda and James was an open wound, festering and painful. For the most part, she felt trapped and hopeless. Her frustration erupted in small ways, little acts of defiance, like the afternoon she plastered a bright yellow and black Midas Muffler sticker on the Grand Prix's back window.

When James saw it, he demanded, "What's this for?"

"I just wanted you to stand out more," she said mischievously. "So the police won't have any trouble finding you."

Glaring at her, he ripped the sticker off.

Christmas rolled around and James didn't force Linda to accompany him to his parents' house for the holiday. Instead he agreed when she said she preferred remaining home. His only edict was that she was not to leave the house, even to spend the holiday with her own family.

So Linda sat alone in the apartment on Christmas day 1989. She thought of her baby, whom she'd already named Ashley Nicole. And in the early afternoon, she called her mother's home. With her brothers and sisters and their families celebrating in the background, Linda wished her mother a merry Christmas. When Santos begged her to come home for the day, Linda refused, lying that she was on her way to the Bergstroms' to observe the holiday with her husband's family.

It was a new year, 1990, and for Linda nothing had changed. In a futile attempt to get someone to pay attention to James, months earlier she had secretly stopped paying the twenty-five dollars per month he was required to send Kitsap County during his one-year probation. Possibly because of it, an "action memo" arrived from the Kitsap County District Court Probation Services, dated January 4.

Jean Elliott, the probation officer, noted: "The defendant has been absent from Washington State for six months. He has submitted monthly status reports but is still not in treatment. Permission to leave the state was predicated on his willingness to enter and complete counseling. While stating that only finances prevent him from complying, another statement he made suggests he is not being candid. He told me that he would seek pastoral counseling from his neighborhood church on his arrival in Texas. That he would attend such counseling until he could arrange for secular assistance. A review is requested."

Unaware Linda may have played a part in bringing the letter on, James wrote back that he would seek counseling through the church and report back within sixty days.

As she had for months, at home Linda watched his every move. She timed his absences, documented his comings and goings to work. She even noted when he left the apartment to meet Sam, his high school buddy, at the YMCA, where the two of them refereed boys' basketball. While at first James appeared delighted with all the extra attention, as time passed, his patience quickly wore thin. The constant surveillance tugged at him like an animal pulling against the leash.

Linda didn't yet know it, but despite his promises to her, James had already slipped from his precarious grasp on normalcy. As in Washington, he circled malls and shopping centers, looking for women. Once, from a grocery store parking lot, he drove behind a young woman in a gray car miles onto the freeway before giving up and going home. Other times he parked his car in neighborhoods and then jogged blocks away, skulking behind houses. "I tried to figure out which were the bedroom windows," said James later. "And what would be the best way to get inside."

On January 31, 1990, Linda and James went to her gynecologist for another ultrasound. This time Ashley was only weeks away from her due date, and both had a clear glimpse of her.

"Yup, you've got a little girl there," said the doctor.

"Well, you should be happy," James said to Linda. "You always wanted a little girl."

But Linda didn't feel like celebrating. She grew more and more frightened for the child's safety as her due date approached. "I kept thinking about what had happened to me as a child and what James had done to that little girl," she'd say later. "Somewhere this had to stop, and I was going to be sure it stopped with Ashley."

At home, Linda continued to scout for evidence, anything that would stand up in court. She searched James's clothes, looking for tears, grass stains, any sign that he'd been peeping. When she learned Adelaide had revealed James's history to a therapist, Linda prodded at both Adelaide and James for the name of the clinic she'd attended. Adelaide refused, and it wasn't long before James realized why she wanted it.

"Even if you find out, it won't help you get Ashley away from me." He glowered. "That doctor won't help you."

"That's not why I wanted it," Linda replied. "I'm just curious."

"Listen, Linda, give it up," he mocked. "No one in my family is going to help you take Ashley away from me."

Though they had both begun calling her by name, it wasn't until February 16, 1990, that Ashley Nicole Bergstrom made her entrance. James arrived home from work at his regular time, 12:30 A.M., and Linda was ready to leave for the hospital. She'd had labor pains since seven that evening. After James showered, they left for the hospital. At 8:32 that morning Ashley was born, soft and warm with a dark fluff of hair and two squinty hazel eyes surrounded by wrinkles. The doctor handed Ashley to her, and Linda wiped the gooey afterbirth from her new daughter's perfect little body. James, who'd sat beside Linda during the birth, leaned forward and kissed Ashley's cheek. Making contact for the first time, Ashley grabbed her father's finger and clenched it in her miniature fist.

"She's a strong little thing," James laughed. "You know, she looks just like Adelaide."

The nurses took Ashley away, and Linda began crying.

"I've known women who get the baby blues and cry a month or two after they give birth," one nurse teased. "But it's not usually minutes after."

"I'm just so grateful to have her," Linda said. "I wanted her so much."

Of course, Linda was a mass of confusion. There was the happiness of the birth, but it was underlaid with the anguish of past months. Now there was even more uncertainty. Ashley was a real presence, a person who needed her protection. Not to mention all those other women she worried about, the ones who invaded her sleep. In her nightmares the women, like the one James had confessed to raping in Washington, were asleep in their beds, unaware that evil, in the shape of James Bergstrom, sat perched outside their windows. Try as she would, Linda's screams were never loud enough to warn them, as James smiled at her and disappeared inside.

For months she'd carried the weight of James's crimes on her shoulders. She'd worried continually about what he would do when she was in the hospital, not there to watch him. He'd been acting nervous and jumpy, and she knew the constant monitoring ate away at him.

As soon as Ashley was taken away and Linda wheeled into the recovery room, as she suspected he would, James announced he was leaving.

"Why don't you hang out and make sure Ashley's all right?" she asked.

James frowned. "I'm beat and I'm going home," he insisted.

He didn't call that entire day. He never came to the hospital. The woman in the next bed was surrounded by family and friends, flowers and balloons. Linda was alone. The only ones who came to visit her were Gino and Santos, who brought flowers.

Afraid of what he might be up to, Linda tried off and on throughout the day to call James. The phone rang endlessly without an answer. When she finally reached him at ten-thirty that night, she demanded to know where he had been.

"Right here. I unplugged the phone. I was sleepy," he said.

"Sure. I bet," Linda said, wondering if he thought she was stupid enough to believe him. "I'm being released tomorrow."

"Why don't you stay another day?" he asked. "You must be tired."

"No, I'm coming home." Linda didn't mention that she had begged her doctor to release her quickly so she could be home to monitor her husband. "Bring a car seat and get me and the baby early."

James arrived just after ten the following morning with a car seat he'd picked up at Wal-Mart that morning. When the bill was signed and everything in order, the nurse brought the baby. Linda held her gently, but James sauntered ahead, not even pausing to look at or touch Ashley. "I've got a basketball game to referee," James announced. "We've got to get home now."

"Why don't you take the day off?" Linda asked.

"I can't," he insisted. "I need to ref."

In the car, James muttered, "I'm going to be late."

"James, you had all day yesterday to get the car seat. It's not my fault," Linda snapped. "You were probably up to your old tricks."

James swung the back of his hand at her, leaving a hot red slash where he'd slapped her.

"Shut up, you goddamn bitch," he shouted, as Ashley cried. "Quit accusing me of things I haven't done. I'm tired of your shit."

They arrived at the apartment, and James ran inside while Linda balanced the baby and her duffel bag. "I've got to go," he shouted. "I'm going to be late."

"Well, if you're that determined, just go," Linda said, after she'd entered the apartment and carried Ashley into their bedroom. There she stopped short. On the bed was a pair of green warm-ups she'd just bought James, streaked with grass stains and ripped at the knee, as if they'd caught on something.

She laid the baby on the bed and turned toward him. "Now I know what you've been doing," she said. "Why you didn't have time to even visit your new baby in the hospital."

"I caught them on the bed and they tore," he insisted.

"Yeah, right," she answered.

Enraged, James thundered at her. As two-day-old Ashley shrieked, he pummeled Linda. He stripped her of her blouse and bra, ripped off her slacks, and beat her. He only stopped when the phone rang. It was Irene Bergstrom calling to check on her new granddaughter. She cried when she heard Linda screaming and realized what was happening on her granddaughter's first day home. His mother's tears multiplied James's rage, and he threw the phone down and came at Linda.

"Now you've got my mother upset," he shouted, slamming Linda against the wall and slapping her across the face.

"You bitch, always accusing me of something," he bellowed. "I'm sick and tired of your damn accusations," he shrieked, before he turned and ran out.

Years later, James would admit that Linda had guessed right, that he had spent the previous night huddled in the bushes at a house in a rural section of south Houston. He couldn't see anything, but he tore his pants when he climbed over the fence to leave.

Irene Bergstrom stopped in to see her new granddaughter later that day. Linda was dazed, her back bruised from James's blows.

"I'm sorry about the way James acted. He should have stayed home to help you," her mother-in-law offered, admiring Ashley on the bed. "She looks just like Adelaide," Irene Bergstrom whispered, tears running down her cheeks. "Just like James said."

Chapter Twenty-Seven

In his 1992 book *Out of the Shadows*, Patrick Carnes, Ph.D., drew a model with two circles to depict the sexually addictive cycle. The top circle was dominated by a faulty belief system resulting in a delusional thought process that insulates the addict from reality. The second stage: a four-phase addictive system defined by preoccupation, ritualization, sexual compulsivity, and despair. Carnes went on to diagnose levels of sexual addiction. By his early teens with his sexual abuse of his young relative, James Bergstrom fit the profile Carnes labeled level three, the most deviant of actions, including child molestation, incest, and rape.

Perhaps his parents' discovery of his actions interrupted the cycle and sent James Bergstrom temporarily back to a lower level. With the voyeurism in Washington State, he again succumbed to the downward tug of the cycle, and through his fantasies, he may have gained sufficient momentum to return to level three with the alleged attacks and rape.

If so, Bergstrom's arrest undoubtedly was interruption number two. It gave him pause and time to reconsider his actions and their consequences. For a brief interlude, he may have actually believed that he could control his compulsions. But by early 1990, he was again caught in the addictive cycle. His fantasies preoccupied his mind and fed off his renewed voyeurism. But this wasn't the same James

Bergstrom who had peeked at Theresa George at the Silverdale Apartments two years earlier. He'd learned much. He knew the importance of intimidation in the deadly shape of a gun.

Two weeks before Ashley was born, James, under a mandate from Kitsap County, had begun counseling sessions with a priest at a Catholic church not far from Devoe & Raynolds, a tree-shaded parish on a massive complex that encompassed a school and a community hall. The priest was in his fifties, a tall, thin man with white hair, who listened intently as James discussed "my problem." Once a week throughout February, they met for regular sessions. "I told the priest everything," James would later say. "Everything I had done."

At home, Linda had sensed for months that James was worsening. Nervous and agitated, he sat for hours watching television, usually the Discovery channel with its plethora of war and armaments. He especially enjoyed a series titled "Sharks of Steel" on the nation's nuclear submarines and taped it so he could watch it over and over.

Part of Linda was fascinated by James and what he had become. She watched him constantly, trying to understand what drove him. One afternoon as he sat transfixed in front of the television watching a World War II documentary on Hitler, Linda hid in the bedroom, peering at him through the door. As she suspected, as soon she left the room, James flicked the remote control, flipping channels until something caught his eye. It was MTV, and Madonna, scantily clad, pulsated her hips in time to muted music. When Linda entered the room, he flicked the control again, returning to less provocative fare.

In early March, James left as usual for a church counseling session. Linda, as always, marked off the time of his departure on the calendar, 1:00 P.M. She assumed he would return by two-thirty. At three o'clock he still hadn't arrived.

When he finally walked in at three-thirty that afternoon, James looked sweaty and frightened, and hanging from his shirt were strips of duct tape.

"Where have you been?" Linda demanded, patting Ashley, who had just finished a bottle, on the back. "And what's the tape for?"

"I was just fixing something on the car," he answered. Linda didn't believe him. She felt certain she knew what he'd intended to do with the tape. Years later James would admit he had, in fact, accosted a woman that day. James was careful, hesitant to get caught again. When he couldn't easily subdue her, he fled, dismissing the situation as out of control.

"If you don't believe me, call the priest," James bluffed. "I just left there."

After James left for work, Linda did just that.

"No," the priest assured her. "Your husband was here just half an hour. He left a long time ago."

"Father," Linda asked, "I'd like to come in to talk to you."

When she arrived at the church, the priest greeted her and escorted her into an office. "What has James told you about what he's doing?" she asked.

"I can't discuss that, even with his wife," the priest said.

Then Linda told the priest about James, and his history. "I believe James is a rapist," Linda said, finally. "I need to get away from him. He molested a little girl and I'm afraid he'll do the same thing to my daughter."

The priest's eyes narrowed as he assessed Linda.

Later, when she recounted what the priest said next, Linda's voice was thick with anger and she shook her head in disbelief. "He asked me how much James made. When I said about eleven hundred dollars a month, he said, 'It's hard to make money these days. Maybe you should reconsider if you're thinking of leaving your husband.'"

From that day on, Linda stopped attending mass. James went alone. Soon after, the priest released James from counseling. "He told me that I needed professional help," James would say later. "That he wasn't equipped to handle somebody with a problem like mine."

A series of attempted sexual assaults began in the Friendswood area, a small community adjacent to Pearland to the east, in early April 1990. Friendswood wasn't unlike the Parkwood East area in Bremerton: middle-class and principally white, the type of neighborhood where a young, clean-cut white man jogging or driving his car wouldn't attract any undue attention. The first attack occurred in the Forest Bend subdivision. A man in a ski mask and carrying a gun entered an immaculately kept ranch house on a street shaded by live oaks. It was early in the day, and the woman inside was dressing for work. He tried to tie her up, but she cried and fought with him, until he finally turned and left.

Blocks away on April 20, Ann Cook, a stout woman with a short pageboy and big glasses, cared for her children. It was an unusually warm spring day, and she'd been washing clothes in the garage, leaving the overhead door open as she carried baskets back and forth from the house. It was a peaceful neighborhood, bordering a park, the type that feels secluded during the day when most parents are at work, their children in day care or school.

As she carried in a basket of towels, Ann never stopped to consider whether she should lock the door that connected the garage with the house. Inside, her two-and-a-half-year-old daughter sat, legs crossed, in front of the living room television watching "Sesame Street." Ann deposited the towels in the bathroom, then stopped in her son's room to check on him. Just three months old, her new baby boy cooed up at her, kicking his legs and smiling in his crib. He was active for such a young age, and Ann smiled as she murmured comfortingly at him. Then she felt something odd.

"I knew he was there before I even looked up," Ann would say later. "I sensed him."

The man, his face obscured under a white mesh laundry bag, pointed a gun at her. "Stay where you are. Don't move," he ordered.

Hysteria took Ann over. Screaming, she ran toward him.

"Shut up," the man growled, pointing the gun at her head.

But Ann didn't stop. "I was so frightened, I couldn't have if I'd wanted to," she said later.

The man, whom she later identified as James Bergstrom, turned and ran. Fearing he would harm her daughter, Ann followed behind, shouting, "Get out of my house," until he disappeared out the door and through the garage. In all, it was less than a minute since she'd first noticed him, but Ann would remember it forever. She ran back inside, locked all the doors, and called the police. As they had in Washington, the police were there quickly, but the man in the mesh mask had disappeared. They dusted the back door, the garage, and the bedroom door for fingerprints, but found nothing.

The following week, Ann's husband erected a six-foot fence around the yard. Years later, she would still shudder at the unexpected creek of a floorboard or the flutter of a tree's shadow against the window at night.

For Linda and James, Sundays were nearly always the same. The afternoons were spent at home, where James meticulously cleaned their apartment and then methodically washed and detailed his car. About 8:00 P.M. they usually drove to the Bergstroms'. She knew James was eager to give his parents the impression he'd buried his past and was a changed man. Once they arrived, James disappeared into the seclusion of his parents' bedroom with his father. Linda sat in the living room with Irene Bergstrom watching a chronically green and grainy television. She always marveled that though James C. fixed other people's televisions to make extra money, the one in his living room was impossible to watch. Of course, she knew that in the bedroom James watched a new set James C. reserved for himself.

As the hours passed, Linda counted off the flickering minutes on the VCR until enough time had lapsed for her to remind James it was time to leave.

After one such Sunday, James drove home. Linda sat in back, and Ashley slept in her car seat in the Grand Prix's front passenger seat. When they pulled into the parking lot of their Pearland apartment, Linda stepped out of the car and reached in to unbuckle Ashley, when something clanked to the floor. Linda glimpsed down at a pair of metal handcuffs. Rage flooded through her.

"What's this?" she demanded.

"They're old," James said.

"Bullshit," she screamed. "The cops in Washington searched the car. These weren't there. They're new."

Then she bent over and ran her hand under the front seat and pulled out a rope.

"You did it in Washington and you're doing it again," she screamed at him.

James lunged at her, trying to grab them, but she pulled them away.

"Don't make a scene," he ordered. "Let's go inside."

Inside the house, Linda took the handcuffs and rope, and threw them under the bed, hidden by the dust ruffle.

"What are you going to do?" James asked, putting Ashley into bed.

"Get rid of them," she said.

Linda didn't know what to do with the evidence she'd found. On the surface, it probably wasn't enough to get James arrested. In fact, she had no proof he had done anything illegal with the handcuffs or the rope. Though if it wasn't enough to get James caught, she reasoned, it might be enough to persuade the Bergstroms they had to help her get their granddaughter safely away from James.

The next day, Linda tucked the evidence into a large pocket in the back of Ashley's car seat and told James she was taking the baby to see his mother. When she arrived, she suggested Irene Bergstrom come outside. As her mother-in-law watched, Linda reached into the back pocket.

"I want you to see something. Your son is sick. You think you can control him? See this?" she said, dangling the hand-cuffs and rope before her mother-in-law. "He's doing it again. Does this prove to you that he's doing it? That we need to turn him in?"

Irene Bergstrom appeared panicked. "Oh my God," she said. "Leave these here so I can show his father."

Linda left the Bergstroms' and drove Ashley to her older sister's house in Galveston. Mary listened as Linda re-counted the weekend's find and her morning with her mother-in-law.

"Linda, that was the dumbest thing you could have done. They're not going to do anything," Mary scoffed. "Why are you there with him? Why don't you get out?"

"You're not in my position," Linda cried, fearing Mary was right. "It's easier said than done. Do I just disappear and hope he never finds me? If I stay in Houston, how do I pro-tect Ashley? Do you think I love him and that that's why I'm there? I hate him."

"Linda, he could kill you," Mary pleaded.

"I know that," she said. "But I've got to hold on. One day he'll mess up and they'll get him. I have to make sure that happens. It's the only way Ashley and I will ever be free."

Later that week, Irene Bergstrom called James and said his father wanted to talk with him. James returned to the apartment late at night after the meeting. Linda waited up, eager to know what was discussed. James wouldn't tell her. Years later, James would say his father asked him if he was doing the things Linda alleged—if he was a rapist.

"I told him no," James would say years later with a shrug. "I couldn't admit to him what I was doing."

Still, a few days after the family conference, Maria called James with the telephone number for counseling at Belle Park Hospital. He threw it to the side.

"I'm not going," he told Linda. "Why should I tell them the truth? They'll just have me locked up."

"If you don't get counseling, I'm going to tell the police," Linda threatened. "I'm going to tell them about the stuff I found in your car."

"Tell them," James laughed. "No one will believe you. They'll just think you're lying against me. You're just a damn liar."

The Bergstroms never mentioned the handcuffs or rope to Linda again. It was as if nothing had ever happened.

Linda made her third anonymous call to the Houston police dispatch number the following week. Every time she called, someone new answered the phone. This time she gave sketchy details about the past, then identified James and told of the handcuffs and rope. "I told the dispatcher James was doing it again and that they had to watch out for him," she said. "The guy who answered the phone said he'd file a report and they'd be on the lookout." As James predicted, nothing further happened.

When Linda told her mother what she had found and that the Bergstroms had done nothing and were still refusing to help her gain sole custody of Ashley, Santos found it difficult to believe they could turn such a blind eye. As the months had passed, Santos's concern for Linda had grown. Once, Linda came to her admitting she was afraid to sleep, terrified James would kill both her and Ashley in the night.

"I worry about you," Santos said. "You're always upset and you don't even go to church anymore. You need your faith."

"I don't know if I believe in God anymore," Linda confessed. "God? Is there a God? If there's a God, why am I going through this? I'm in hell already."

That night Santos called Linda to check on her. Linda answered the phone, but in the background, James raged, demanding she hang up and sit beside him on the couch. Linda finally gave in. "Mama, I can't talk now," she said, and hung up.

Santos paced her living room, until in desperation she called her youngest daughter, Alice, and asked her to call Linda to be sure she was all right. Alice did as she was asked, but as with her mother's call, James's screaming ended the conversation.

After one particularly violent argument, Linda fled with Ashley to Gino's house, knowing it would be a place James would be afraid to search for them. She slept on the couch that night, the phone ringing often with James asking Gino or his wife, Benita, if they knew where Linda had gone.

"Lily, why don't you divorce him?" Gino asked her that night.

"I can't," Linda cried. "No one believes me. Not even the police. I can't let him get Ashley. I just can't risk it."

Linda returned home to James.

Days later, Santos called Gino, fretting about Linda and James. "I'm worried about Lily," she said. "I think he might hurt her."

"Do you believe James is doing all these things?" Gino asked.

"Yes, I do," Santos answered. "At first I wasn't sure, but now I do."

In May, Santos Martinez suffered a minor stroke. When Linda saw her mother, her skin was pallid and one side of her face drooped so she couldn't close her eye. The doctor had chastised Santos about stress and told her she'd have to calm down or she could have a major stroke and be permanently paralyzed. Linda worried that she was responsible, that her mother's concern for her had brought the stroke on.

That day Linda vowed that though her mother was the only one who truly believed in her, she would never again confide in her. "I didn't want to be responsible for her death," Linda said later. "I knew she worried about me, and I just couldn't take the chance that anything else would happen."

Chapter Twenty-Eight

It was obvious that James Bergstrom had reverted back to his old ways. Later there would be questions asked. Why were there no rapes with his MO reported in Houston's southern suburbs during the summer of 1990? Police would acknowledge that Bergstrom's arrest had made him paranoid and compulsively careful. "He was watching his tail, leaving if anything got out of hand," assessed one investigator. They would also label it "unlikely" that he was inactive during that period. Instead they dismissed the interruption as the reality of rape; studies show as few as 16 percent of victims report their assault to police. It wasn't that Bergstrom was inactive, they'd theorize. It was that his victims weren't reporting.

Linda had no doubt where her husband's interests were that summer. She rocked Ashley in the bedroom on the white rocker that had been passed down through her family. Once, decades earlier, Linda's grandmother had soothed her children to sleep on that very rocker. Now Linda sang to Ashley, caressing the baby's sweet, warm forehead. In the living room she heard James flicking channels on the remote control. She knew what he was looking for, something in which a scantily clad woman danced or was pictured in danger. Maybe the actress cowered in a corner, the camera lens focusing through the eyes of an attacker.

Despite everything, Linda continued to do what she could to stop him. At eleven A.M. on Monday, July 30, she made an appointment for him to talk to a therapist at Belle Park Hospital. When he refused to go, Linda went instead. The doctor listened sympathetically as Linda detailed James's history and her fears, sobbing so hard at times that she had to stop to compose herself. In the end, the doctor said there was nothing he could do to help.

"You can't do this for him," he said. "Your husband has to want the help and come in here himself."

"What am I going to do?" Linda pleaded.

"Get a lawyer," advised the doctor.

"I've already talked to a lawyer. He can't do anything for me," Linda said resentfully. "Is a lawyer going to help me get away from him? Can a lawyer keep my daughter safe?"

Never far from her thoughts were the other women, the ones in her dreams. She sometimes heard their screams in her nightmares, felt their fear as a masked stranger with a gun descended on them. To help them, she agreed when James continued to badger her to play the game.

"If you let me do it to you, I won't have to do it to anyone else," he insisted.

"Promise?" she asked.

"Yeah," he said. "I won't risk losing my family, but I've got these urges I have to satisfy."

Every time he knotted the bindings on Linda's arms and legs, tying her to the bed, panic throbbed through her. Each time, sometimes as often as twice a week, she endured it. It never felt like lovemaking. Always it felt like rape.

Helpless to change her situation, Linda tried to make what accommodations she could to live as normal a life as possible. To gain some time for herself, she initiated separate days out, alternating days when she and James would be free to do what they wanted for an afternoon. Always James was with his friends, Sam and Eddie. At one point she even called Sam and explained the situation. "We have to watch

James," Linda told him. "Or he's going to hurt someone else and end up in prison."

Although she sensed Sam didn't believe her, he agreed, saying, "I'll do what I can to keep him out of trouble." From that day on, when the two friends got together, Linda would call before James left the house to say he was on his way, and Sam would telephone as soon as James left him, alerting Linda that until he arrived home, he was unaccounted for.

It was on October 7, 1990—a Sunday and Linda's day out—that James Bergstrom first came to the attention of the Pearland police. Linda had made plans to go out shopping with friends, and James and Sam were scheduled to baby-sit for Ashley. To her surprise, Sam stopped by briefly, urging James to hurry to meet him at the YMCA—Sam's basketball team was scheduled to play, and he wanted James to substitute for an absent player. Linda blew up, insisting James and his friend live up to the bargain and relieve her from her child-care duties for the afternoon.

"It'll only be for a couple of hours," she said.

"You're not going," James announced. "I've got other plans."

The phone rang and it was Irene Bergstrom. She could hear the screaming in the background.

"I want to go play ball with Sam, and Linda wants to go with her friends. There's no one to watch Ashley," he said, bitterly. "That fucking bitch wants to tell me what to do. I'm sick and tired of it. She's trying to control my life."

Linda could tell from the sound of James's voice that his mother was agreeing with him.

"If you people raised James right, this wouldn't be going on," she shouted.

James waved the phone in front of her, and Linda could hear Irene Bergstrom screaming and crying. His eyes widened and fixed on her, lit up with excitement.

"You hurt my mother, you bitch."

Ashley was on the floor shrieking as James paced the room, seizing every piece of glass and crystal he could find, smashing it against the walls. Frightened, Linda picked up a ceramic pot. Warily she came at James, who circled her in a karate stance. Then, instantly, he kicked her in the abdomen, knocking her backward, the pot falling from her hands. "You want to control my life?" he shrieked. "You fucking bitch."

"Don't come near me," she ordered, running toward the cordless phone. James grabbed it before she could and threw it. It slammed into Linda's abdomen but rebounded, striking Ashley in the head. The baby's wails renewed, now from physical pain.

Linda fled to the kitchen and grabbed a knife, backing cautiously away from James. Again he drew near her, knees bent, hands extended, like a scene out of the karate movies he loved to watch. With a lightning-quick blow, he kicked the knife from her grasp. Fearing that this time he might hold true to his threats and kill both her and the baby, Linda ran to the bedroom and punched 911 on the phone. As James crept into the room, screaming and bellowing at her, Linda left the handset dangling.

The call came in to 911 operators, and the automatic tracking system indicated it originated at unit number 158 at 3340 East Walnut in Pearland. As operators listened, James Bergstrom pushed Linda against a wall and pressed his hands against her throat, applying pressure until she gasped for air. All the time he screamed, "You want to control me? You think you can?"

"You're strangling me," Linda whispered, vainly struggling to pry his hands from her neck. "Stop."

Suddenly there was a knock at the door.

"The police," she choked out. "I called."

"You say everything is all right," James ordered as he released her.

The Pearland officers already had guns drawn when Linda opened the door. One grabbed James and ordered him outside. Linda ran to pick up Ashley, sobbing on the floor, surrounded by broken glass.

When Santos arrived at her daughter's apartment, Linda was bruised and battered. The baby was quieted, but the floor was covered with jagged shards of glass. They drove to the Pearland police station, where James had already been taken, and waited in the hallway until police were ready to take Linda's statement. Linda was weeping, her hands shaking, her face and body a patchwork of bruises. Before long, Irene Bergstrom appeared and sat down next to Linda.

"What have you told them?" James's mother demanded.

"I haven't gone in yet," Linda said. "I'm still waiting."

"Are you going to tell them everything?" Irene demanded.

"Yes," said Linda. "I am. There are too many secrets."

A few minutes later, Linda was called into an interview room with a large glass window and given forms and a pen to write her account of that afternoon's blowup. "My hands were shaking so hard, I could barely hold the pen," Linda remembered later. "I was nearly hysterical."

Then, according to Linda, she walked over to where an officer sat at a nearby desk.

"Is there anything I can do to keep him here?" Linda beseeched him.

"We'll do our best," the cop said, sympathetically assessing her.

"Listen, this guy sexually molested a little girl and committed a rape in Washington State. He's been peeping in houses here," Linda told him, her words tumbling over each other in her urgency to make the officer understand. "In fact, he took me to see the houses. And I know he's raping again, here in Houston. I've found stuff in the car."

"What kind of stuff?"

"Rope and handcuffs."

Linda watched as the officer's demeanor changed. Although he'd seemed genuinely compassionate about her bruises, he now appeared openly doubtful.

"You mean like these?" he asked, holding up the handcuffs he pulled from his belt, waving them in her face.

"Yeah, like those."

To Linda's dismay, the officer snickered at her.

"Lady, you can buy handcuffs like these at K Mart," he said, ruefully. "That doesn't prove anything."

Linda felt her mind reeling, the officer's words hitting as hard as her husband's blows had that afternoon.

"Then I went and got my mother and left," said Linda later. "I was like, 'Forget it, I'm out of here.'"

Santos, who'd heard the exchange, asked Linda in the car, "Why don't they listen? Why won't they help you?"

"I don't understand why they don't believe me," Linda answered, exhausted, the reality of another defeat overtaking her.

Unbeknownst to Linda, Santos had called Gino, and while they were at the Pearland Police Department, her brothers and sisters had moved her belongings out of the apartment she'd shared with James. Linda drove to her mother's, convinced that whatever it took, she would not spend another night living with James Bergstrom. She simply couldn't go back.

"Could Ashley and I stay here and live with you?" Linda asked her mother.

"As long as you want," Santos assured her.

When Gino arrived that night, Linda told him again about all her suspicions and that she was sure James was a rapist.

"I can't believe the police didn't believe me," she said. "It seems like they'll have to catch him in the act before they'll believe it."

But Gino was having his own difficulties believing. After all the years Gino had worked with James, he found Linda's allegations hard to accept. "I didn't think she was lying to me. I knew she believed she told the truth," Gino said, later. "But I thought there had to be some mistake."

James was charged with assault and endangering a child, but the next day he'd made bail and was on the phone calling Santos, looking for Linda. When Linda finally agreed to talk to him, she immediately brought up her intention to file for divorce. Rather than shouting and protesting as she expected, James was ice-cold, calm and in control.

"I'm going to give you your divorce. I'll even pay for it," he sneered. "But I'm going to fight you for custody of Ashley. If I can't get that, I'll have her on the weekends. And, Linda, remember you won't be here to watch her."

Dazed, Linda hung up the phone and walked back in the living room, where Santos waited. She thought about all that had happened. If she fought James for Ashley, who would win? There was no reason to assume a judge in a custody battle would find her story any more believable than the Pearland police officer had that afternoon.

She looked at her mother and said, "I'm going back."

Two days later she agreed to drop all charges.

Chapter Twenty-Nine

After that October blowup, James and Linda moved out of the Pearland apartments and into Painter's Mill, a sprawling two-story, beige brick-and-siding complex just off Interstate 45, the main north-south artery that runs through Houston toward Dallas to the north and Galveston to the south. That winter, on February 7, 1991, a thirty-eight-year-old mother of two was unloading groceries into her clean-scrubbed Friendswood ranch house, just a few miles from the home where Ann Cook had been attacked the previous year. It was a clear winter day when a ski-masked man followed Sarah Williamson through the door. He held a gun to her head, but Williamson, like Cook, screamed and cried out, shouting that her husband was on his way home. The man turned and ran. It was the third attack by a ski-masked assailant in a quiet Friendswood neighborhood in the past year.

Ashley's first birthday was the following week, and Linda threw a party. Irene Bergstrom had wanted to have it at her house, but Linda, still upset that they continued to refuse to help her, insisted she'd rather do it herself. The Bergstroms didn't come, but most of Linda's family gathered in the small apartment. There were streamers, balloons, and a cake covered with pink frosting and decorated with a delicate rocking horse.

A few days later, an exterminator sprayed the apartments

in their complex for insects. Linda placed Ashley on her back sucking on a bottle on the living room couch as the man unsuccessfully pumped the sprayer holding the pesticide. It appeared jammed, and he pumped harder and harder, attempting to force the poison into the nozzle and out of the sprayer. When it kicked in, it was with a punch that sent insecticide splattering across the room, the couch, and Ashley. The baby cried, and Linda whisked her up and carried her to the kitchen sink, where she doused her tiny body in water to wash off the poison. When Ashley continued to sob, Linda called her pediatrician, who suggested she bring the baby in. Linda called James at work, and he rushed home to take them. After an examination, the pediatrician advised Linda and James that Ashley would have to be watched to determine if there was any permanent damage from the chemical spray.

Linda continued to worry about Ashley, and a few months later she picked up the yellow pages and flipped as she had once before through the listings for attorneys to look into bringing a civil suit against the exterminator. This time she called Reynaldo Ramirez, who practiced in a two-lawyer office not far from Pearland.

Over the summer, Linda and Ramirez talked on a few occasions. The attorney recommended Linda document what she could, and Linda wrote out an account of the accident and photographed James holding a tape measure to show the distance between the baby and the sprayer.

James didn't want to help. Furious with Linda, he charged she was making trouble, and in the photographs she snapped that day, he glared into the camera with a quiet, dangerous aloofness. Linda knew why he wanted no part of anything that shone a spotlight on him. The apartment, his family, the cocoon he had so carefully spun around himself, were there, after all, to foster an air of normalcy. Anything that focused attention on him made James nervous.

Spring passed and Houston's hot, humid summer moved in. Since the day she'd found the rope and handcuffs, Linda methodically checked James's clothes for clues and conducted random searches of the Grand Prix. Some days she even removed the backseat to check behind it. In the complex's parking lot one stifling August afternoon, on a hunch, Linda announced to James that she was going to search the car.

"Go ahead," he said. "I haven't been doing anything."

As James glared at her, she worked her way through the car, the front seat, the backseat, even under the hood. Her heart quickened when, in the trunk, she discovered a thin nylon rope and, under the spare tire, a ski mask and a gun, crudely constructed from pipe. James grabbed for them, and they began a tug-of-war in the parking lot. His wiry strength overpowering her, James wrenched his rape kit from Linda's hands and announced, "I'm gonna throw these out," and ran toward the Dumpster.

"You're a damn rapist," she shouted, chasing after him. "I'm going to go call the police."

James glanced up and saw a man watching from an apartment balcony. A woman carrying in groceries in the parking lot turned and stared at him. "Here," he said, nervously. "Take them. They won't believe you. This doesn't prove anything."

Linda ran upstairs and threw the things into a box in Ashley's closet. James never asked what happened to them. Later he would say he never believed Linda would take them to the police. The next day, Linda transferred them to a brown paper grocery bag and drove to her mother's house.

"Don't even look inside this, Mama," she begged, as she gave Santos the bag. "Put it on a shelf and keep it for me, please."

"Are you all right, Lily?" Santos asked. "What is this? What's wrong?"

"Everything's fine," Linda insisted. "I just need to have you keep this for me, in case I need it later. Please don't worry about me."

A few days later, Linda called Ramirez when James was at work. This time she was interested in discussing, not a suit against the exterminator, but another matter: her husband. "She told me all about him," Ramirez would say later. "What happened in Washington and what she figured he was doing in Houston. I'd been in criminal law, a public defender for a while, and what she said seemed true. It sounded right."

Linda worked her way to the all-important question. "What about Ashley?" she asked. "If I leave him, is there any way I can keep him away from her?"

To Linda's dismay, Ramirez confirmed what the first attorney she'd consulted had told her nearly a year earlier.

"It's difficult to take a parent's rights away on a mere allegation," he advised her. "Without proof of molestation or a dangerous past history, absolutely not. That's the law."

When Linda said she had proof, that she'd removed a ski mask, rope, and pipe gun from the car's trunk, Ramirez asked, "Did you touch them?"

"Sure, when I took them out."

"Then they won't work," Ramirez assessed. "They've got your fingerprints all over them. His attorney will claim they were planted. Next time don't touch them. Let the police be the ones to remove them from the car. In the meantime, call them and let them know what's happening so they can be on the lookout."

"I've already done that," Linda said bitterly. "But I don't think they're taking it seriously."

"I know a cop on the force in Baytown," Ramirez offered. "I can give him a call."

Linda agreed, and Ramirez called Baytown police that afternoon. The officer took down the information. Ramirez never heard any more about the case, but years later it would appear Baytown was one of the Houston suburbs Bergstrom missed on his marathon of terror.

"The thing I'd always remember about Linda was how hard she was trying to do the right thing for her baby,"

Ramirez would say later. "She seemed to have no concerns for herself, only that the little girl was safe."

It was just after nine on May 6, 1991, a Monday morning, in a house off I-45's Scarsdale exit south of Houston. Kimberly Greenmen, who'd once dreamed of being a model, sat at the kitchen table in her rented ranch house, paying bills. Her mechanic husband, whom she'd kissed good-bye as he left for work half an hour earlier, had given her two hundred dollars that morning, and she had a little extra, money she'd earned decorating wreaths with dried flowers and selling them to friends and neighbors for their front doors. She divided the money, piling enough to cover the electric bill here, the gas bill there, money for food in another stack. Kim, at twenty-six a willowy woman with shaggy brown hair and the air of a cowgirl, felt happy. Later that day she planned to buy money orders to mail, and then for another month the family would be solvent, paid up and current.

It was a quiet morning. Annie, her five-year-old, attended kindergarten at the neighborhood elementary school. Two-year-old Jenny sat near her mother in the kitchen, under a child's folding table, drawing on an old oilskin tablecloth Kim had hung against the wall. It was her answer to Jenny's artistic bent, which favored vertical surfaces, like freshly painted walls. Kim smiled down at her daughter. Maybe it was due to a tough pregnancy, three months on her back, but her younger daughter, blond with a slightly upturned nose, was a timid child and never ventured far from her sight.

Somewhere in the recesses of her mind, Kim thought she heard the gate into the fenced backyard open. She looked up and saw no one. The family's two white Siberian huskies lumbered unconcerned at the far end of the fenced-in yard. The dogs were so docile, the family often joked that if they were ever robbed, the two dogs would lick the burglar to death. Kim wondered if the electric or gas meter reader had come for another look. *One bill not paid yet and another on the way,* she thought. *Oh well, that's life.*

At first Kim thought she was imagining it all, like some kind of mesmerizing daydream. Later she'd remember hearing the door between the house and garage open. She glanced up and the first thing she saw was the gun, long-barreled and black. Next it was the man in the light blue pants and dark blue striped shirt, and a strange-looking green ski mask. Always she'd remember the green ski mask.

"Get down on your knees," the man ordered.

"Take the money," Kim said, pointing at her neat piles.

"I don't want it," the man growled, pointing the gun at her chest. "Lay down on the floor and I won't hurt you."

"I've got my daughter here," Kim pleaded.

"Lay down," he ordered again, his voice politely cold.

Following orders, Kim lay down. Flat on her stomach, she looked over and saw Jenny scrunched against the wall under the table, panic plainly visible in her innocent blue eyes.

James Bergstrom grabbed an orange towel off the table and covered Kim's head. Then he pulled out sections of thin nylon rope from his white athletic sock and tied her hands behind her, wrists together.

"Get up," he ordered. "Let's go," he said, pointing down the hall. Grabbing her from behind, he pushed her toward the master bedroom. It occurred to Kim that the man knew her house, including where the bedrooms were. Later she'd learn James Bergstrom had watched her off and on for weeks.

In the bedroom, Bergstrom pushed her onto the bed. When he pulled out a cloth to gag her, Kim protested. "Please don't," she said. "I won't scream. I wouldn't risk having my little girl hurt."

Reluctantly James threw the gag on the floor. Instead he pulled a pillow from the bed and placed it over her eyes.

"Put your legs through your arms," he ordered her.

Kim tried, but the bindings were too tight.

"I can't," she said.

Bergstrom frowned. He turned her around on her stomach and untied her hands. He undressed her, tugging at her shorts until they fell to the floor. Ripping her T-shirt over her head. He flipped her again and this time tied her wrists, arms spread, to the bed frame. While he did the same to her legs, Kim looked up at the headboard. Behind it, she knew, was the .44 Magnum handgun her husband kept for protection. It was so close. So close yet unobtainable, useless.

Bergstrom replaced the pillow across her eyes. Kim shivered as he ran his hands over her. *It's just a dream,* she told herself. *I'll wake up in the kitchen, paying the bills. Everything will be fine. I'll just fix dinner and drive to school to pick up Annie.*

But it did happen. Later Kim would estimate Bergstrom spent forty-five minutes in her house, toying with her as she lay naked and trussed to the bed frame. She could see just barely under the edge of the pillow. Something inside her died when, as James Bergstrom entered her and moved above her, she wondered if her two-year-old was watching from the hallway.

Bergstrom didn't ejaculate. It wasn't the point. In fact, years later, he would say it wasn't the sex at all. "It was having the woman there, tied up," he'd say. "It was the control thing."

When he was finished acting out his fantasies on her, James Bergstrom untied her and ordered her to stay in the bed and count to one hundred. Fearful that now that he was done with her, he might kill her, Kim Greenmen counted: "One, two, three, four . . ." She thought about the gun. So close. "But I couldn't risk it," she said later. "I couldn't take a chance that I'd make him angry and he'd hurt my daughter."

She heard the garage door close, and Kim jumped up and ran to the kitchen. When she saw Jenny, rolled in a fetal position under the little table, where she'd played so happily just an hour earlier, Kim scooped her toddler into her arms.

When police and Kim's husband arrived, she was down

the block, at the home of friends. She trembled and cried, clutching her baby close to her chest and refusing to release her. That night Kim Greenmen tried to sleep, but she was afraid to close her eyes.

The following day, her husband tried to convince her to go to her mother's house, but Kim refused. Instead she dropped Annie at school, Jenny at a neighbor's house, and after he left for work, she took out the .44 Magnum and loaded it. Hour after hour, she sat on the living room floor, back to a wall, and watched the doors. She listened for every creak, any noise, the rustle of the trees. "I thought he'd be back," she'd say later. "I was waiting for him. I wanted him dead."

Six months after the rape, Kim left her husband, saying simply, "I can't be married anymore." She took jobs waitressing and traveled. In a box her mother found a note in Kim's handwriting, scribbled on a sheet of paper: "Will I ever be able to sleep in my own bed again? Make love to my own husband? What does he think of me now?"

Eleven days later on a cloudy afternoon, a ski-masked man attacked again. This time the intended victim lived in a quiet residential street in Clear Lake, a suburb that surrounds the Johnson Space Center. She was lucky. Her dog chased him away.

But on May twentieth, James Bergstrom was in a quiet subdivision just across the highway from where, exactly two weeks earlier, he had raped Kimberly Greenmen. He knew why he was there. Weeks earlier he'd singled out Cindy McKenzie, an attractive, twenty-something saleswoman with flowing black curls and long red fingernails.

Bergstrom had stalked her for days. He knew what car she drove and the one driven by the man she lived with. He knew on this particular morning that she was home alone. When it started to rain, Bergstrom, dressed in his jogging garb, smiled as he eased his way through the garage toward the door that led into the house. Rain was a good cover, he knew. It would disguise the noise he'd make entering the house. James wasn't worried. He had lots of time. Unbeknownst to Linda, he'd taken a vacation day from work.

That particular morning, Cindy was in the bedroom. Dressed in a T-shirt and silk boxer shorts, she packed for a business trip to Corpus Christi. Her suitcase lay open on the bedroom floor and her clothes were stacked around her. When she looked up, James Bergstrom, everything but his eyes and mouth concealed behind a ski mask, walked into the room.

"Get on the bed, facedown," he ordered, pointing a gun at her.

"Please don't hurt me," she begged.

Bergstrom made her strip, then took his time tying her arms and legs to her four-poster bed with shoestrings he'd brought with him. Once she was secured, he played with her, fondling her breasts for what seemed like forever. Revulsion welling up inside McKenzie, she stared at him, trying to remember every detail. It made Bergstrom nervous. In a jerk of the wrist, he delivered a threat, the gun barrel thrust ominously between her legs. Then he laid an empty pillow case over her eyes.

When James Bergstrom had finished with Cindy McKenzie, he peered down at her and smiled.

"Is there anything you'd like me to do?" he asked politely.

McKenzie shook her head. "No. Just leave," she whispered.

At the bedroom door, Bergstrom turned to her one more time.

"Who left the garage door open?" he asked.

"My fiancé," she answered.

"Tell him to keep it locked in the future," Bergstrom suggested blandly before he turned and left.

Chapter Thirty

Living with James Bergstrom took an incredible toll on Linda. She had nightmares constantly. Always, there was the silhouette of an unidentified woman and the distant James with the cold eyes. James, too, often awoke shivering in the night, his body coated with sweat. Much later, he would admit that he had his own bad dreams, nightmares in which he'd been caught.

At home, James demanded continual attention. When she signed up for a class at a local professional school, hoping to get certified to work as a medical aide, James tore up her books and destroyed her homework, even taking the light bulbs from lamps so she couldn't see to study at night, just as her father had done to her as a child when he turned off the electricity. Instead, James ordered her to sit next to him while he watched military shows on cable television. If she moved, if she ignored him, he'd become enraged, yelling, "I owe you, bitch." Linda grew to believe James Bergstrom kept a tally of her supposed sins and used them as justification for his own monstrous deeds.

Despite everything, Linda hadn't given up. She kept trying to stop him. She not only monitored his whereabouts, but put him on a strict allowance, hoping he wouldn't have gas money to use to circle neighborhoods, stalking victims. She'd noticed how quickly the Grand Prix guzzled fuel. One day the tank would be nearly full, the next almost empty. Once when he'd stopped at a convenience store to buy milk,

Linda searched the inside of the car, knowing he wouldn't have had time to hide anything. She discovered forty-five dollars hidden in the Grand Prix's fuse box.

"What's this?" she demanded when he returned.

"It's not mine. It's Sam's. Go ahead and ask him."

"I guess you're up to no good again," Linda said, bitterly.

"You and your damn allegations," James shouted back. "I'm not doing anything wrong."

Later Linda would learn James stole small amounts of money from some of his victims.

There were other signs. James had no vacation left that summer; he'd taken it scattered throughout the year, days Linda assumed he'd worked when he actually jogged through neighborhoods in search of potential victims. It hadn't escaped her notice that he increasingly arrived home late at night, always blaming his tardiness on a flat tire or some minor mechanical problem with the Grand Prix.

That summer James was promoted to a daytime slot in Devoe & Raynolds' lab, where technicians monitored quality control: the paint's weight, viscosity, color, and texture. Linda didn't know, but the lab was a perfect cover for James. Now that he worked on salary, no one watched his comings and goings. Often he'd arrive at work later than his eight A.M. starting time. In the afternoons, he returned home well past his four-thirty quitting time. Sometimes he called ahead. Other times he didn't, like the afternoon Linda saw him drive past their apartment complex around five. Instead of turning in the parking lot, James kept driving, continuing east on Edgebrook Drive. It was nearly half an hour later when James returned home, announcing he had just gotten off work.

"No you didn't," Linda confronted him. "I saw you drive past a long time ago."

As he had on so many other occasions, James answered her with profanity and his fist.

Though he still denied he had returned to his old ways, it was like an unspoken acknowledgment between them. Once he came in the bedroom as she folded baby clothes. Ashley napped peacefully in her crib.

"Why are you doing this to Ashley and me, James?" she pleaded. "Why don't you just let us go?"

"Because I love you and we're a family," he told her.

"Why don't you do what other men do? Just go out and hire a prostitute. At least that way you won't be hurting anyone."

James laughed at her. "Is that what you think I want? Someone I have to pay?" he asked. "I don't want to catch some damn disease. Prostitutes give it easy; that's their job."

It's that they aren't struggling and afraid, Linda thought.

One afternoon during a particularly vitriolic argument, James grabbed Ashley and ran from the apartment. Dangling the baby like a paper sack, he jumped into the Grand Prix. "You'll never see her again," he shouted as Linda ran after him.

"What do you mean?" she yelled. "Where are you taking her?"

"I'll hurt her," he yelled. "You'll never see her again." He gunned the engine, swerving the car from side to side as she tried to jump in front of it, blocking his exit.

"She's just a baby, leave her alone," Linda begged. "She has nothing to do with this."

James gunned the engine again, coming at her, then swerving to the side.

"Call the police," Linda screamed at neighbors who'd collected outside, watching the show in the parking lot. "Please call the police."

James looked frightened when he heard the word "police." The door popped open and he handed Linda her daughter, then he squealed out of the parking lot as Linda watched the exhaust from the Grand Prix curl out into the street.

That September, Linda thought the stress would drive her mad. She called a local women's help line, who referred her to the University of Houston—Clear Lake Psychological Services. Linda spent an hour-long session recounting the horror of the past four years. The counselor listened sympathetically and then suggested she call the police or a lawyer.

"I've already done that." Linda shrugged. "It didn't help."

For the most part, Linda sat by helplessly as the charade continued. When they were home alone, James had little time for Ashley, ignoring the toddler as she ambled around the apartment, playing with her toys. More often than not he noticed her only when she cried or got in his way. But when there was an audience, Linda watched James transformed into the perfect father, concerned and loving, fawningly showing her off to his friends and family.

Linda wasn't surprised, then, when on Halloween 1991, her twenty-eighth birthday, James insisted they bring Ashley to the Bergstroms' house to trick-or-treat in the Pearland neighborhood in which he'd grown up. Linda dressed the toddler as an adorable black cat with whiskers, a long tail, and an orange plastic pumpkin to hold her candy. James, as she knew he would, insisted on carrying his daughter to the front doors of his childhood neighbors. As each door swung open, he held her up like a badge of honor, shouting, "Trick or treat," and grinning proudly. A disgusted Linda stayed in the background, taking pictures of Ashley, including one, at James's insistence, in his arms.

"They were in their own place," explained Adelaide later. "He could hide out. He could hide the craziness. He could hide his hitting her, his weird delusions about sex and women. So he acted really nice when he came over. But you could tell, it wasn't real."

In hindsight, by the fall of 1991, it was obvious James Bergstrom had learned his lessons well in Washington State. He did everything he could not to repeat old mistakes. Instead of concentrating his attacks in a single jurisdiction, he jumped boundaries between Houston, Clear Lake, and

Friendswood. Each was patrolled by a different agency with no communal data bank, so no one realized there was a pattern developing, a ski-masked assailant who tied his victims up. No one had yet discovered a serial rapist worked the southern boundaries of Houston.

He also changed his appearance. In Bremerton, the Parkwood East rapist had worn a signature red ski mask. In Houston, Bergstrom destroyed his masks after every attack, making new ones by crudely cutting them from the arms of discarded sweatshirts and sweaters. "I didn't want them to figure out that one guy was doing all of them," James would later explain. Then, in November, James made another change. He left behind the single-family homes and the morning attacks and turned his attention to the myriad of apartments that border Houston's freeways and clutter the high-tech corridor near the Johnson Space Center, where mission control monitored shuttle flights. "I figured that in the single-family homes, women would be home alone during the day while their husbands worked," he'd explain later. "But in the apartments, I knew I'd find single women alone at night."

On November 11, 1991, Jesse Neal, a twenty-year-old waitress in a Mexican restaurant, was hitching a ride home with a friend. Just after midnight the two women drove into the parking lot of a Gulf Freeway apartment complex where Neal was apartment-sitting to care for another friend's dog. Neal invited her friend upstairs to the apartment. As the two women walked the short distance from the parking lot, neither noticed a man lurking in the shadows.

James Bergstrom was in a desperate mood. He'd combed the streets and freeways for hours, searching for a victim. For the last fifteen minutes, he'd been jogging through this particular complex, looking in windows and watching as tenants arrived home for the night. Now he waited in the darkness between two of the complex's buildings. He had a hunch the blond woman's friend wouldn't linger for very long, that she'd soon be alone. As he'd hoped, Neal's friend paused for less than ten minutes. Then Jesse, a short, supple woman with wispy auburn hair, walked her to the door and let the small dog she was caring for out one last time before bed. When she opened the door to call the dog back in for the night, James Bergstrom, in a yellow ski mask, pushed his way past her.

Before Neal had a chance to scream, Bergstrom slapped his hand over her mouth and poised a hunting knife with a curved blade a breath from her neck.

"Do as you're told and don't make any noise," he ordered.

With shoelaces, James Bergstrom tied Neal's hands behind her and pushed her toward the bedroom. Jesse had the stereo on, soft rock, and Bergstrom turned it off. In a deliberate, steady manner, he pushed a hodgepodge of clothes off the bed and forced her down onto it, turning off the lights. The knife still inches from her neck, he dropped his gray sweatpants, then ripped open the brightly colored uniform Neal hadn't had time to change out of.

"Why are you doing this?" she pleaded.

"I have a sexual problem." Bergstrom shrugged coldly. "You should have locked your doors."

The tender indentations the shoelaces etched into Jesse Neal's wrists were still visible two days later when Detective Robert Tonry of the Harris County Sheriff's Department picked her up at her apartment and drove her to his office for questioning.

They talked little in the car, Tonry careful to wait until Neal was in an interrogation room where he had a tape recorder and could take notes. So they discussed the little things people do when they've been thrown uncomfortably together. They were both immigrants to Texas from New York: Neal had moved to Houston from Queens just that summer; Tonry had relocated from Staten Island nine years earlier.

"Do you ever get used to summers? The heat and humidity?" she asked.

"Nah, still bugs me," he admitted.

Tonry had once been in the air force, military police. At the sheriff's department he handled what were designated as crimes against persons: murder, kidnapping, and rape. A detective for three years, he liked it better than anything else he'd ever done. In a sense, rape cases were the hardest; working with the victims could be as tricky as walking a high wire between gaining evidence and facts to pursue the case, and doing the victim even greater psychological harm. Afterward, many of the victims were wracked with self-doubt. Those who hadn't fought back wondered if they should have. Those who did and were beaten for their efforts wondered why they hadn't just given in. Tonry never second-guessed a victim. Especially with a gun to her head or, like Neal, with a knife to her throat, as far as he was concerned, if a woman lived through a rape, she'd done the right thing.

On the surface, Tonry didn't look like the kind of cop who could put rape victims at enough ease to talk about what was often the most private pain of their lives. In his early thirties, he was a bulky man, muscular, his short-sleeved shirt straining over hardened biceps. But his brown eyes, under thick, dark eyebrows, were warm and understanding.

Since he investigated five to ten rape cases a month, Tonry had learned how not to approach the victims. There was no blustering interrogation. He talked in soft, hushed tones, not pushing until he sensed a woman was ready to tell her story. He'd seen a wide range of emotions from the victims. Some were hysterical, others angry. Jesse Neal appeared neither, rather hurt and disappointed. She was quiet but polite. Only when they were seated in an empty office did Neal's composure crack. Then the confusion and pain dripped out in her tears. She couldn't figure out why this stranger had done it, or why he had done it to her.

"Tell me everything about what happened," Tonry asked. "Don't worry if there are things you can't remember."

"Well," she said, "I had just gotten home from work . . ."

Tonry listened to every word, formulating questions for when she eventually stopped talking on her own. Neal went on for a long time, leaving nothing out: not the dog, the yellow ski mask, or the man's curious remark about having a "sexual problem."

"I had my tip money on the dresser," she finally finished. "There was a bunch there, but he took only twenty dollars of it. Isn't that odd? Why didn't he just take it all? Take it all and leave me alone?"

Tonry knew the guy, whoever he was, wasn't there for the money. That had been incidental.

When it came to a description, Neal was sketchy. "I couldn't see much because of the mask," she explained. But she said the man was white, probably in his twenties, and thin. "He had a jogger's build," she told him, wringing her hands as she had throughout the interview. "I bet the guy runs."

Tonry remembered a security guard had spotted a man jogging near the complex in gray sweatpants the night Neal was raped. The detective made a mental note to bring the guard in later that day to work with one of the police artists.

After Neal left, Tonry asked around and found out there'd been other, similar assaults in the general area in the last year: principally, two rapes within two miles of Neal's apartment just that last May—a mom at home with her two-year-old daughter, and a saleswoman who'd been home packing for a trip.

When Tonry compared the three cases, there were a lot of similarities. All the rapists were described in similar terms: five feet eight inches, white, slim, twenty-something. All had worn ski masks and tied their victims. That was unusual, but far from unheard-of. Approximately 10 percent of Tonry's rape cases included some form of bondage. But there were also differences: The ski masks were all different colors, sometimes green, white, now yellow. The time of

day was different, the women in May in the morning, Neal
at night. And the others had been in single-family homes.
Neal lived in an apartment. The other women had been assaulted by a guy with a gun. Neal's assailant had a hunting
knife. All or none of it could be important. It might be the
same guy or maybe it wasn't. The thing with rapists is that
they usually settled into a pattern, finding one method that
worked and repeating it. *If this is the same guy,* Tonry decided, *he's damn smart.*

Five days later at seven-thirty in the evening there was
another attack, this one at an apartment complex on Bay
Area Boulevard. Tonry got the file and investigated. The
thirty-six-year-old white woman had been accosted as she
got out of the car. The ski-masked man put his hand over her
mouth and carried a knife, long, thin, with a curved blade,
just like the man who'd raped Neal. "But this time the
woman had enough warning to hit the guy in the balls and
he went running off," Tonry said later. "I figured it might be
connected."

In none of the cases had the rapist left any physical evidence. No fingerprints, hair, or semen. Tonry figured he had
a serial rapist but no clues. The files took up residence on his
desk as the detective put out the word that he had a composite of a man—a charcoal sketch with a long, thin face and
dark eyes—who might be a rapist, a rapist who wore a ski
mask and tied his victims up. Two deputies who worked the
area called and asked to see it. Tonry sent copies, but neither
was able to tie the man in the drawing to any of their cases.
The charcoal sketch then joined others that papered the
walls of the offices Tonry shared with his fellow detectives.
Another face with an unknown name.

On a Sunday night two weeks after Jesse Neal was raped,
James Bergstrom circulated through the streets of Clear
Lake, a Houston suburb south of where he'd committed three
rapes in eighteen months. He drove up and down Clear Lake
Boulevard and Bay Area Boulevard, scouting the myriad

apartment complexes surrounding the Johnson Space Center. In the Grand Prix, Bergstrom was nearly invisible behind tinted windows. Inside the car, rap music thundered. When he hunted, Bergstrom liked the beat. It helped his concentration, built up his machismo. Other kinds of music distracted him. "The rap music made my blood rush," he'd say later. "It enhanced my wanting to do stuff."

At just before ten, Bergstrom maneuvered through the traffic on Bay Area Boulevard when he saw a dark blue 1985 Mustang. He was frustrated. He'd been driving for hours. If something didn't happen soon, he'd have to go home, his urges unspent. Bergstrom turned off the car radio. He wanted to be totally committed, thinking about what he was doing. No distractions. No mistakes. He pulled into the parking lot of the University Green Apartments right behind the Mustang and then drove a short distance and parked just in time to see a beautiful young woman with soft, dark brown hair and a Christie Brinkley figure get out of her car.

Andrea Hoggen usually hated walking the short distance from the parking lot to her first-floor apartment. The shadows from the high patio fences and hedges spooked her. But this Sunday night she hadn't considered the possibility of evil lurking in the bushes. It was a week before her twenty-first birthday and she'd just come from watching football with friends. The green-eyed computer programmer wanted to call her boyfriend and then take a long bath and sleep. Tomorrow was a workday. She would never remember hearing footsteps behind her as she walked briskly toward her front door.

As he trailed her, Bergstrom became flustered. He'd arrived too late and was cutting it too close. He would have preferred to be in position, ready to pounce. When the woman thrust her key into the lock, he awkwardly rushed toward her. As the door opened, James Bergstrom pushed Hoggen into her apartment and shadowed her inside.

At first, Andrea thought it was a friend playing a joke on her. The only light in the room was the reflection off a lighted clock and the few beams from an outside lamp that streamed in through her patio door, but as her eyes adjusted, she distinctly saw a man pointing a gun at her. He was wearing a maroon ski-type mask, but there was something wrong with it. It looked odd. Andrea's terrier, Sylvia, charged at the stranger, growling and nipping at the man's ankles, until the stranger kicked her away.

Bergstrom was nervous. He was usually so careful. In his rush to get inside the apartment, he'd yanked the mask over his head and it was askew, the back hanging over his eyes. But he wanted her and he moved up behind her, putting the gun to her head.

"Be quiet," he ordered as he slipped his free hand over her mouth. "I have a gun."

Then he pushed her to the floor, and Andrea Hoggen crumpled on the floor. Not wanting to see him, as if it would make him disappear, she covered her face with a comforter her grandmother had made that she kept folded next to the couch.

"Is anyone else coming?" Bergstrom asked, trying to secure the chain lock Andrea's father had just installed a few weeks earlier. The lock had never lined up quite right, and Andrea had developed a trick to lock it. Bergstrom, all nervous thumbs, fumbled.

"Yeah, my brother was following me in his car," Andrea lied, Sylvia snarling and barking. "He stopped for gas. He ought to be here any minute."

James Bergstrom sized up the apartment. One bedroom, he figured. Feminine. The girl was lying. He kept fumbling with the lock.

"If your brother is coming, what's taking so long?"

"He's coming. You'll see. You better just take my purse and go," Andrea pleaded. Inside she was praying, *Please, God, don't let it be messy. If he's going to kill me, don't let my mother find my body.*

Andrea peeked up from under the quilt and saw the man standing above her had taken off his ski mask. For the briefest second, she saw his face, long, thin, dark eyes, angular, before he readjusted the mask to cover his face.

James Bergstrom sensed something was wrong. He looked down at Andrea and thought, *She saw me.* The door still wasn't locking and the little dog yapped louder than ever. He turned and left. Andrea jumped up, shaking. She'd been preparing herself to die. Now she locked the door, flipped on the lights, and called her mother. Police were called. A report was filed. But this time the jurisdiction was HPD's, and no one knew about Tonry's sketch on the wall at the Harris County Sheriff's Department.

James Bergstrom went directly home that Sunday night. He was frightened. It was a close call. He waited for the doorbell to ring. For someone to shout, "Police. Open up." He promised himself that this time he'd come too close, he was taking too many chances. He had to stop. "But when nothing happened, I figured nobody even cared," James said later. "I guess it was a week or so, and I was out stalking again."

Chapter Thirty-One

In the fall of 1991, doctors scheduled Gino's wife, Benita Martinez, for a battery of medical tests. In preparation, she was instructed not to sleep during the twenty-four hours before the tests began. So the night before her appointment, Linda brought Ashley and stayed overnight to help her stay awake. Benita, a wide woman with short, dark hair who worked as a department store clerk, had known Linda since 1986, when she first dated Gino. Early on, Benita had written her sister-in-law off as unfriendly. In the past two years since she and James had returned from Washington State, Gino had often invited them to their small condo. The Bergstroms rarely showed up. Usually Linda would call, urging her brother to not invite them again. "This isn't a real marriage. We're not a real family," she explained. "Please don't push this. I can't stand to go anywhere with him."

Over the years, Benita had heard stories about James Bergstrom through the Martinez family grapevine. Though Linda had sometimes used their condominium, cheerily decorated with everything from cat pillows to cat pictures, as a safe house, somewhere to run to hide from James, Benita tended to discount much of what her sister-in-law said. After all, Gino had known James for nearly a decade from work and liked him. He always described James as shy and timid, not the kind of man likely to terrorize his wife or anyone else.

Yet on the night they spent together, for the first time Linda opened up to Benita, confessing to her about Washington State and the telltale signs she'd discovered that convinced her that her husband continued to stalk women and rape them. Linda seemed sincere and desperately unhappy. Before long, Benita believed her.

"What are you going to do?" she asked, incredulously. "Can't you turn him in?"

Linda then detailed the incident with the Pearland police and her calls to HPD, ending with what she'd learned about James and the little girl he'd molested and what the two attorneys had advised her about the impossibility of keeping Ashley from James if they divorced.

"I hate to just leave. I'd have to hide out forever," Linda said. "James would kill both Ashley and me if he ever found us. I figure I'm safe enough till Ashley gets older. I don't think he'll abuse her when she's still a baby. But if something doesn't happen, it'll get to the point where I'll just have to leave. Then I'll have to run and pray that he never finds me."

The last day of November, James came home angry, swearing that the car had been broken into. The radio was stolen and the steering column gutted where would-be thieves had tried to hot-wire it.

"Good job, Linda," he seethed. "Thanks for leaving it unlocked."

Certain she had locked the car the night before, Linda went out to look, James glowering behind. On the driver's side of the Grand Prix, Linda found the window scratched as if something metal had been inserted to pop the lock.

"I told you I locked it," she insisted, pointing to the evidence.

To James, her proof didn't appear to matter. He was angry. Linda wasn't surprised. She had come to believe James used his anger as fuel. "I owe you one, bitch," he seethed.

"Owe me what?" Linda asked, but in her heart she feared

she knew, and that some unsuspecting woman would suffer for his unjust accusations against her.

Wary that he'd be on the prowl, Linda wasn't surprised when later that week, on Thursday, December 5, 1991, James announced he had plans to spend the evening with his high school buddy Sam. Months earlier, the arrangement Linda had made with James's friend had deteriorated, when Sam accused her of lying about James. Convinced Linda was playing some sort of bizarre game, Sam no longer called when James arrived at or left his apartment. Linda knew James. She knew he'd take advantage of any opening. She'd sensed for months that James used the ruse of a night out with Sam as a way to escape her Argus-eyed scrutiny. The way James prepared to leave that night, brusque and nervous, Linda felt certain he planned a solitary pursuit.

"Why don't you stay home," she prodded as he slipped on a jacket and headed for the door.

"Sam's expecting me," he insisted on his way out the door. "Don't wait up."

All night long, Linda waited. She paced the living room, fidgeted endlessly in front of the television, tried to read but couldn't concentrate. No matter how she attempted to distract herself, she couldn't escape the premonition that haunted that night. It was like her nightmares; somewhere someone was screaming in fright, and she couldn't stop it. She fell asleep praying, *Please let it be tonight that he gets caught. Please make this end.*

At one A.M. the following morning the phone in the Bergstroms' apartment rang. Linda, groggy from sleep, answered. It was James. He'd been arrested.

Convinced that authorities had finally caught up with him, Linda listened in disbelief as James told her he was in the county jail on a minor traffic violation, failure to signal a turn. They'd brought him in simply because he'd left his wallet, with his driver's license, car title, and proof of insurance, at home. The cops had noticed the broken steering column and booked him, suspicious that the car may have been stolen.

Linda doubted James was telling the truth. When she continued to question him, he put an officer on the phone who assured her that her husband had, indeed, told her the truth.

Disappointed, Linda listened as James gave orders: "Call my mother and have her bring you. I need bail money. The car was towed to the county impound lot. But don't go get it," he ordered. "I'll do that when you get me out of here."

Irene Bergstrom had to work, but at six the following morning Maria picked Linda up at the apartment and drove to the bank, where she withdrew two hundred dollars for a deposit on James's two-thousand-dollar bail. Then they drove into the acres of marbled and mirrored skyscrapers that comprise downtown Houston. At the Harris County Jail, Linda posted bond, and a clerk informed her James would be released later that day. Moody throughout the day, Maria, Linda sensed, was anxious to leave.

"Why don't I just drop you off at your car?" she suggested.

In the web of red tape required to free James from jail, much of the day had passed. It was nearly four P.M. when Maria drove away, leaving Linda at the county impound lot, where a burly attendant wanted $75.73 to pay off towing charges.

"By the way," Linda asked the man, "where was he picked up?"

"Checking up on your husband, huh?" said the attendant.

"Not really," she answered. "Not for the reasons you think."

The thick-necked man leafed through the Grand Prix's papers with fat, oil-stained hands. "It looks like he was off Dixie Farm Road about 12:01 this morning," he said. "They pulled him over at a gas station."

Just after midnight, alone, a deserted road surrounded by subdivisions. *I knew it. He was out stalking again,* Linda thought. *Why else would he be out there?*

The attendant pulled up the car and left it running. As Linda climbed inside, she glanced at the passenger seat. Her eyes trailed downward to the floor and fixed on a pile of James's belongings. For just the briefest second it didn't click that what she saw were two ski masks, duct tape, a glove, and a rope. "Oh shit," she muttered, stepping harder on the gas to get home as soon as possible. She ran red lights and stop signs all the way home. Ramirez's words kept replaying in her mind: "Whatever you do, don't touch anything."

She pulled into the apartment parking lot and locked the car, then sprinted upstairs. Hands shaking and heart pounding, she dialed the by-now-familiar number for Houston Police Department's dispatch. When a woman answered, she shouted, "I need an officer now. My husband is a rapist and there's evidence in the car."

"Is this that same woman who's been calling?" the woman who answered asked, sounding a bit perturbed.

"Yes, it is. And I'm telling you there's evidence in the car. You need to get someone out here now, before my husband gets home, or he'll destroy it. I just bailed him out of the county jail. Can you stop his release?"

"Not if you paid the bail," the woman said.

"Listen, you've got to help me," Linda pleaded.

"I'll see what I can do."

Half an hour passed with no sign of the police. Linda was frantic. She called dispatch again, yelling into the phone that she needed help. "Please, please, I'm begging," she cried. "I need someone out here now."

When she hung up, the phone rang. It was James calling from the county jail. "Why'd you get the car?" he demanded.

"Maria was tired. The police called," she lied. "They're on their way out to look at it."

"Why?"

"Because of the stuff in the front seat. Someone filed a report."

"Don't let them."

"Why? Did you do something?"

"No," he shouted. "But I don't want them in my stuff. Get in the car now and come pick me up. Now!"

"No. How am I supposed to stop them?" she said. "You know, James, I'm not Bonnie and you're not Clyde."

Linda slammed down the receiver, and almost instantly it rang again.

"Officer Dawson here, HPD," a man's voice said. "I'm at the apartment gate. I need to get in."

Linda pressed the button to open the complex's security gates, then ran outside, just in time to spot a white HPD van pulling into the parking lot. She flagged it down.

Officer L. L. "Lee" Dawson, a thirteen-year veteran of HPD, had worked CSU, the crime scene unit, for five years. In his van, he carried everything necessary to fingerprint, photograph, and document physical evidence. More often than not, Dawson, a husky man with graying hair and wire-rimmed glasses, worked murder cases, sometimes when the only link tying a suspect to the crime was minute traces of fabric, a hair, or a single fingerprint. Dawson saw the petite woman with the dark hair running toward him as he got out of the van.

"I want this stuff out of my car," she was shouting. "My husband's a rapist and this is his stuff."

"How do you know?" Dawson said, looking inside at the pile of paraphernalia on the front-seat floor of the brown Grand Prix.

"I know," Linda persisted. "I've tried to tell everyone. I tried to tell the cops in Pearland and I've been calling dispatch for almost two years. You've got to believe me." Then she started talking about everything, from Washington State to the duct tape James had worn home on his shirt from a "church visit" to the handcuffs she'd given to his mother.

"Well, when the guys who pulled him over last night saw this stuff in the car, they thought he might be robbing convenience stores," Dawson said skeptically. "That's why they brought him down to the jail. But they did a search and it didn't match anything."

Dawson looked carefully at the woman. Her hands were shaking and she appeared on the verge of tears. "Is it possible he's just hiring prostitutes?" he asked. "That he likes to tie them up?"

"No, he's a rapist," Linda shouted, the anger and fear welling up inside her. "He's confessed to me and I just know he's doing it again."

Finally Dawson believed her. This woman was too frightened—terrified was a better description. She was pleading for help. Every time he mentioned the husband, she trembled. It didn't feel like a wife just trying to get her husband in hot water. "All right," he said. "I'll bag this stuff and take it in."

Linda signed a consent form, and Dawson carefully removed and bagged each item separately in clear plastic zip-top bags, labeling each and sealing it with HPD evidence tape. Both the masks appeared odd. When Dawson looked closer he realized they were homemade: The maroon one had eyes cut into a regular knit cap; the yellow one was a section cut from the sleeve of a medium-weight, yellow knit shirt, eyes cut and the top stapled shut.

"Have you got any photos?" he asked.

"Sure. I'll be right back."

Linda ran upstairs and retrieved two photographs, including one taken just that Halloween. James, the proud father, played it up for the camera, smiling broadly as he held Ashley in her cat costume. Outside she handed them to the officer.

"Look at this," he said, holding up a long, black, military-style handgun. "I found it in the trunk."

"Is that real?" Linda asked.

"No," Dawson answered, inspecting the gun. "It's a pellet gun. But it looks enough like a .45-caliber semiautomatic to scare the hell out of anyone. It's as convincing as the real thing." Dawson took his own weapon from his holster and held them side by side. "From a distance or in low light, they'd look identical. Even I couldn't tell the difference."

"What am I going to tell James when he gets home? He'll kill me if he finds out I called," she said as Dawson got ready to leave. "Maybe I can say this was all HPD's idea? If James calls, will they tell him the guy from the impound lot told you about this stuff and you came out to get it on your own?"

"Okay," Dawson assured her. "Don't worry. We won't tell him you called. If he asks, tell him we think he's robbing convenience stores or something and that we took this stuff to investigate. Don't mention rape."

Dawson pulled a card out of his pocket and wrote something down. "Here's my phone number and the number for the department's sex crimes unit," he said. "Call them on Monday morning. Tell them I suggested it."

Linda took the numbers and Dawson left. When James arrived, he was distraught, asking question after question about why the officer had come and what the officer had said.

"He said they were curious about why you had the stuff in the car," Linda said with what she hoped was a casual shrug. "They thought that you might be robbing Stop-n-Gos."

"I'm not doing that," James insisted.

"Yeah," she answered. "That's what I told them. Then there's nothing to worry about, is there?"

Throughout the weekend, James continued to badger Linda. Like a train circling on a track, he'd rush past her, shouting out questions. "What did they want? What did they say? What do they want the stuff for?" he asked over and over, incessantly through the day and into the night. Even in the bathroom he pursued her, shouting in to her as she sought a few minutes of solace in the shower. "I can't believe he didn't tell you why they needed the stuff. What did they say they were going to do with it?" he demanded. "You're not telling me everything."

He prowled through the apartment, grabbing her by the arm and pointing to the cabinet that housed the air-conditioning unit high on the bathroom wall.

"If the police come for me, I'm going to hide up there," he said, sternly. "You tell them I'm not here. They'll never find me."

"No, I'm not going to do that," she answered, shaking her head. "I won't. If you have nothing to worry about, why are you acting like this?"

By Sunday night, Linda was drained. Ashley had fallen asleep on a blanket on the living room floor, and she walked toward the bedroom to change for bed. James followed immediately behind her.

"We have unfinished business," he demanded, pointing at the bed.

She'd been deflecting his demands for sex for days and knew that if she continued, he'd subject her to an angry outburst that would awaken the baby, so, exhausted, she undressed and lay down on the bed. Her heart sank when he pulled out long strands of shoestrings knotted together.

"No," she said, instinctively wary. "Not that."

Grinning, James jumped on top of her on the bed, pinning her shoulders beneath his knees and binding her wrists so tightly to the bed frame, her hands ached. Then he grabbed one of her leg warmers, anchoring it around her mouth.

Terror filled her. She kicked violently, adrenaline pumping, as he seized her legs, attempting to control her long enough to finish anchoring her to the bed. Always before, James would have stopped if she'd fought back so aggressively. But when she saw his face, she knew he had no intention of stopping. There, looking down at her, she recognized the cold, distant, detached James. *He's going to kill me,* she thought. Her heart throbbed and her hands grew numb as she pulled against the bindings. She kicked harder, dislodging the gag by pushing against it with her shoulder.

"James, stop," she cried out. "Please stop."

He laughed, grinning maniacally at her. Instead of stopping, he came at her with renewed relish, pushing her hair atop her head to get it out of the way, then cinching the gag more firmly into her mouth. Then he yanked the shoestrings binding her arms. He tightened the knots until a piercing pain shot from her wrist into the length of each finger. He gazed blankly down at her and laughed, grinning as if he'd just sunk the winning basket during a high school basketball game. Instantly he returned to the task at hand, tying her legs.

He looks like he's in a trance, she thought, the dread within her growing. *My God, he is going to kill me.* In desperation, she kicked harder, pushing at the gag wedged in her mouth. Tears ran down her cheeks as she nudged it, finally edging it loose.

"Please, James," she shouted, crying. "Please stop. You're hurting me."

Her husband's back turned toward her, Linda saw James pause, his shoulders sag, then he sat back on his haunches and shook his head. His hands flew to his forehead and he cradled his skull as if in pain. When he turned to her, it was the old James.

"I'm sorry," he sobbed, fumbling to loosen the bindings on her hands. "I'm so sorry."

"Cut them off," she cried. "Please."

He returned with a scissors and snipped the shoestrings, releasing her hands, which had turned a bright bluish purple. "I didn't mean to hurt you," he said, stroking the deep crevices the shoestrings left behind. "I'm sorry. I'm so sorry."

Then, before she could object, he pushed her down and mounted her. Oblivious to her pain, he satisfied himself before quickly rolling over and falling immediately to sleep.

On Monday morning, as soon as James left for work, Linda retrieved the telephone number Officer Dawson had given her and called HPD sex crimes. The woman who answered the phone listened intently as Linda explained everything, including what had happened in Washington State and the evidence she'd turned over to Dawson just the previous Friday.

"Mrs. Bergstrom," said the woman, matter-of-factly, "I appreciate your call. One of our detectives will get back with you."

Linda hung up the phone convinced that she would never hear from any detective at HPD. She was certain this was simply another dead end. But just in case they took her seriously, at 3:55 P.M. Linda called the Kitsap County Sheriff's Department one more time. Detective Jim Pendergast got on the phone. Linda reminded him of her husband's case, then filled him in on what had happened since their return to Houston. "Then she asked me if there was any way she could testify against her husband," Pendergast, a laid-back man with soft brown hair and a full mustache, remembered later. "I told her I didn't think so, but I'd be happy if she gave my name and number to the Houston detective when they called her."

After he hung up the phone, Pendergast walked to the opposite side of the county building and cornered Ione George, an assistant prosecutor. He gave a synopsis of the Bergstrom case and then asked if there was any way Linda Bergstrom would be able to testify against James. As he suspected, the attorney said no. Pendergast knew that meant that unless Houston came through, there was no way to touch James Bergstrom.

That day at Devoe & Raynolds, Allen Gibson and a few of his other co-workers wanted to know why James hadn't been in on the previous Friday. They'd noticed his tendency to arrive late and leave early, but it was unusual for Bergstrom not to come in at all.

"James, where have you been?" asked Gibson.

"Jail," James answered. "I was out with friends and when I was riding home, I got pulled over by a cop for not signaling. They took me in because I left my proof of insurance at home. The thing is, I had some stuff in the car and they took it. A wool cap and some other stuff. They said they thought I was robbing convenience stores."

Gibson laughed. "Well, young 'un, I guess if I was you, I'd probably grow a beard and a mustache. Sounds to me like they think you look like somebody they're after."

Caesar, who was listening in, elbowed James. "Yeah, they must figure they've got a live one, huh?"

A few days later at work, both Gibson and Caesar laughed again at Bergstrom when they noticed the shadow of a embryonic beard and mustache.

"Now, why's he doing that?" Gibson whispered to Caesar.

"Guess we must have really shook him up," Caesar chuckled. "You know James."

The two men walked apart, laughing once again. After all, they both believed that for all James Bergstrom's eccentricity, he was completely harmless.

Daniel, Linda's youngest brother, and his wife stopped at Devoe a few days later. Gino, who was home sick, had asked them to pick up his payroll check. At the spur of the moment, Linda's former protector decided to drop in on his brother-in-law. He asked the woman at the desk to page James, and a few minutes later Daniel noticed him peeking through a nearby window, obviously checking to see who waited for him.

When the door opened, James wore his lab attire, a blue cotton lab coat and a white hard hat. He seemed friendly, but Daniel sensed a fearfulness about him.

In the parking lot, Daniel, who'd moved to Virginia years earlier and knew nothing of Linda's situation, turned to his wife and speculated, "You know, the way James was acting, you'd think he was afraid we were the cops. I don't know what he's up to, but that guy's scared."

Chapter Thirty-Two

"Mrs. Bergstrom," a man with an East Texas drawl said over the phone, "I'm Sergeant Rusty Gallier, with HPD sex crimes."

Though only days had passed since she'd spoken with the woman officer, Linda was surprised. She'd already written the call off as another useless exercise.

"I'd like to go over some information with you if you've got a little time," Gallier said, immediately launching into a list of items James had pawned in the past year, including jewelry and a television set.

"I know about all those things," Linda said, losing patience. "They are ours. They're not stolen. My husband isn't a burglar, he's a rapist."

"We just need to rule everything else out," Gallier cautioned her. Later, he'd characterize their conversation as his mode of "feeling" out the case. He needed to know if Linda was honest. There could be any number of explanations for a wife making allegations against her husband. Perhaps it was all part of an elaborate maneuver to smear his name and win a nasty custody battle. "Now, tell me why you think he's a rapist."

For the second time that week, Linda told her story. When she was finished, she recited Detective Jim Pendergast's phone number at the Kitsap County Sheriff's Department. "He can tell you I'm not lying," Linda pleaded urgently. "But I need to know, can I remain anonymous? If James finds out I'm helping you—if he ever finds out I turned him in—he'll kill me."

"Sure," said Gallier, who sensed this wife might be telling the truth. "No problem. Listen, next time I need to talk to you, I'll have one of the women in the office make the call and ask for Susan. If he's there, you call back later."

"Great," Linda said. "And thanks."

Linda hung up the phone in shock. For the first time, someone believed her. Something was finally happening and the misery was going to end.

Meanwhile, Gallier put through a call to Pendergast in Washington State. "We've got a woman here making some pretty tough accusations against her husband," Gallier said.

"Linda Bergstrom?"

"Yeah."

"Believe her," Pendergast advised. "That woman knows who she's married to."

Gallier would later admit curiosity drew him to the Bergstrom case. When the report of Linda's phone interview circulated through the sex crimes unit, he hurriedly volunteered to take it on. "This wasn't a run-of-the-mill case. Usually we have a crime and we have to find the crook," he said. "This was the reverse. We had the crook and we needed to find the crime."

It'd been a busy week for Gallier. He'd just helped crack a celebrated Houston case, that of Gary Wayne Sheppard, a thirty-one-year-old chemical plant worker nicknamed the Ritzy Rapist. Gallier was on television news reports after the arrest of the stalker rapist who targeted rich society women, cutting their pictures from newspapers and keeping a detailed diary of his intentions. The scrapbook contained home addresses and phone numbers, along with Sheppard's notations like, "I want her."

Sheppard earned his nickname when police searched Sheppard's home and found women's lingerie: 122 pairs of panties, 24 bras, 37 teddies, 48 camisoles, 6 corsets, 57 slips, gloves, binoculars, a hunting knife, and a .357 Magnum revolver. Sheppard was eventually tried and convicted of only one rape, that of a woman whom he'd forced to wear a white bustier.

Rusty Gallier had grown up in Woodville. "So far back in East Texas, you have to pipe sunlight in," Gallier would say. "If you blink, you miss the one red light in town." At six feet three inches and with the body of a football player, Gallier cast an imposing presence. But at thirty-eight years old, his face was boyish, round cheeks under soft brown hair. On the surface, Gallier displayed a jovial, fun-loving exterior, soft-spoken but with a slight twinkle in his eye.

All he was certain of when he graduated from high school was that he didn't want to be a sheet metal worker like his dad. Instead he followed a friend to HPD in January 1973, beginning as a traffic cop. Once he'd been assigned to homicide. "It was my Cajun heritage that kept me out of it," he said. "Cajuns don't like dead bodies."

Gallier's favorite story about his short stint in homicide recounted a night he answered a call to a hospital to investigate a possible murder. A man's body lay on a table where emergency workers had unsuccessfully attempted to revive him. Everyone else left the room to take statements as Gallier photographed the wounds. Uncovering the corpse, he untied the jaw to get a better view of a neck wound, then straddled the lifeless form, high up on the examining table. To his astonishment, through the camera lens, he saw the cadaver slowly sit up, eyes open. The dead man looked at him. In Gallier's urgency to flee, he fell from the table, bringing the body down with him. When Gallier ran from the examination room shouting, "He's alive, he's alive," the dead man's mother fell to her knees crying, "Praise the Lord."

Of course, the man was dead, his untimely rising merely a postmortem contraction. HPD's hierarchy quickly reassigned Gallier from homicide to sex crimes, and on the day he spoke with Linda, he'd been there for twelve years, an unusually long time. Gallier had watched other officers come and go. Throughout the department, sex crimes was known as a tough place to work.

Over the years, Gallier came to divide his fellow officers into three groups: those who wanted to save the victims; those who wanted to catch the bad guys; those who wanted to do both. Gallier judged himself a number two. He wanted to catch the bad guys. Emotionally, the others were too hard to handle for very long. "Lots of guys get emotionally involved with the victims and take their work home at night," he said. "There's a high burnout rate. I like getting into the minds of the rapists. I don't have a degree and I can't write a book on the psychology of rapists, but I've learned a lot about how they think. What I do best is get a confession. I'm good at it."

In Gallier's experience, all rapists display two qualities: a self-centered, selfish ego that has no empathy for anyone else, and an abnormal way of relieving stress through sex. "I don't hate the rapists," Gallier explained. "But there's only one place for them—prison. You've got to get them there and keep them there."

To accomplish that, Gallier tried to get deep into a rapist's psyche to understand how he chose his victims. "When you've got a sixteen-year-old boy raping an eighty-year-old woman, that's a clue. Maybe the first woman the boy saw nude was his grandmother. Maybe he attached a sexual connotation to it," Gallier said. "If I know why a rapist is doing it, chances are I can get him to talk."

With Pendergast's assurance and his gut feeling, Gallier decided Linda Bergstrom had probably told him the truth. Now he just had to prove it. That wouldn't be easy. Searching for crimes James Bergstrom might be guilty of would be as hard as finding a hill in south Houston's flat terrain. That year alone, HPD had handled 1639 reported sex crimes, including 922 rapes. To start, Sergeant Bill Dunn, the unit's crime analysis expert, ran a computer search for Gallier on all rape and attempted rape cases within Houston's city limits that fit Bergstrom's MO by punching "rapist/white/gun/duct tape/ski mask/rope" into the computer. The database pulled up literally hundreds of possible leads. Then the officers narrowed the search to an area within ten miles of the Bergstroms' south Harris County apartment. Still, when Gallier sat down to review files, he had a conference table a foot high in possibilities.

Yet the table was not piled as high as it would have been if all the possibilities were listed in the data bank Dunn accessed for Gallier that afternoon. HPD computers only covered crimes within its jurisdiction. Gallier wouldn't find out until much later about rapes and attempted rapes outside Houston. "We just don't get that kind of information," Gallier would explain later. "A community like Friendswood? For all we know about what's going on there, it might as well be France."

That afternoon, Gallier spent hours weeding through the HPD unsolved sexual assault cases. He began a pile of possibilities, rapes and attempted rapes that fit Bergstrom's style. Some he'd put to the side would later prove to be Bergstrom's, like the rapes of Kimberly Greenmen, the mother of the two-year-old, and Cindy McKenzie, the saleswoman, because his instincts didn't immediately single them out as probables. Gallier didn't yet understand how cagey Bergstrom had become after Washington State. He expected this rapist to act like others he'd investigated, attacking in the same area, the same way, the same time of day. That Bergstrom jumped from one area to another, in and out of jurisdictions, and varied not only his ski masks but his mode of attack and weapon, were possibilities Gallier was not yet ready to consider.

After hours of weeding through cases, Gallier settled on three possibles, all unsuccessful rape attempts within the past two months clustered in the Clear Lake area near the Johnson Space Center. It was something Pendergast had mentioned to him that drew Gallier to the conclusion these cases especially fit Bergstrom's MO. "The guy's really careful, almost paranoid," Pendergast had told him. "He runs if he can't manage the woman, if she fights back too much. No control of the situation and he's out of there."

Of course, since Bergstrom carried a weapon—in Washington he'd owned a nine-millimeter Beretta—the decision of whether or not to fight was a difficult call for any woman. Many experts had cautioned for decades that fighting an armed rapist was foolhardy, only likely to incite more violence, and that the smartest course was always to give in. It was a judgment call often made while staring down the barrel of a gun. But in each of the cases Gallier pulled that afternoon, the women had fought back and the rapist had run.

On closer inspection, one of the three cases stood out. In that attack, the intended victim saw her assailant's face. Gallier pulled the phone number out of the folder and put in a call to Andrea Hoggen.

Andrea Hoggen arrived with her mother at Rusty Gallier's office in HPD headquarters the next morning, nearly a month after the night of her assault. "I'm not sure I'll be able to remember his face," she said. "I've been trying to forget him."

"Just give it a try," Gallier urged.

On his desk, Gallier fanned out eight photos of men, all white, all about the same age, all with dark hair. "Take your time," he suggested. "Give them a good looking over."

Hoggen assessed the photo lineup and barely hesitated. There may have been more photos there, but she saw only one—James Bergstrom's.

"That's him," she said, contemptuously pointing at the photo. "That's the guy right there."

"Bingo," said Gallier. "We've got him."

Chapter Thirty-Three

In the rush from Hoggen's unequivocal identification, Gallier had a woman officer in the unit telephone Linda Bergstrom.

"Is Susan there?" the woman asked.

"This is Linda. My husband's not here," she said. "I can talk."

Since she'd last spoken with Gallier, Linda felt as if she were living in a bubble that could burst at any moment. One minute she was thrilled; the next, frightened about what lay ahead. Deciding she needed to do what she could to help, she'd searched James's clothes every night after he went to bed for evidence, anything that might tie him to a rape. She'd uncovered nothing.

Convinced he must be hiding something behind it, she even stripped off the sheet James had meticulously arranged as a bedroom curtain. He'd hung it while mouthing epithets, when Linda, weary of carrying on the charade of being a real family, defiantly refused to decorate the apartment or buy a curtain for the window. Over the last year, Linda had suffered more than one beating when his makeshift curtain appeared out of place. "He was obsessive about it," Linda said later. "I was sure that meant he had something there." She found nothing. The drape, it appeared, was merely another manifestation of her husband's compulsiveness.

When days passed with no word from Gallier, she sank back into doubt. Why hope when she'd been disappointed so often in the past? It was almost too much to expose herself to any more frustration. "Any news?" she asked excitedly when Gallier's familiar voice said, "Hello."

"We've got a positive identification in an attempted sexual assault," he told her. "We're going to pick him up at work this Friday, the twentieth."

"Thank God," Linda sighed, untold weight slipping from her shoulders.

Friday morning, December 20, 1991, arrived, and Linda dropped James at work. She did her best to act as if nothing unusual were about to happen, but feared James was becoming suspicious when she insisted on keeping the car that day.

"Why do you want it?" he demanded.

"To do a little shopping," she lied.

She couldn't tell him it was so she wouldn't have to bail it out of the impound lot when he was arrested later that afternoon.

The minutes clicked off the clock. In the apartment, Linda paced, nervously watching Ashley, sometimes trying to lose herself in a talk show or soap opera. At noon, she called James at the plant. He answered the phone, and she knew Gallier hadn't yet come. She expected the phone to ring all afternoon, James with his one phone call. But it didn't. It was unusually quiet. Finally, at nearly 5:00 P.M., the phone rang.

"Aren't you going to pick me up from work?" James demanded, angrily. "I suppose you forgot about coming for me."

Gallier never called Linda to say the arrest had been called off. In fact, it would be months before she heard from Sergeant Rusty Gallier again.

For a short time, Gallier thought he'd been lucky, that the Bergstrom case would be one of the rare ones that fell together quickly and easily. He had a positive ID from Andrea Hoggen. All that remained was to file charges. But when he approached an assistant DA with the file, he was turned down flat. There was no way to use Hoggen's case to file anything other than a misdemeanor trespass charge, he was told. Bergstrom hadn't threatened the girl with rape. There was no evidence he intended to do any more to her than he did that night. No way to prove attempted sexual assault.

That put Gallier in an untenable position. "I could have gone in and filed on Andrea Hoggen's case immediately. We had him on that," he'd explain later. "But it would have been nothing. He would have been out on the street again in less than twenty-four hours, and we would have blown any element of surprise. Or we could wait, risk having more women hurt, and try to get him on a more serious charge."

When Hoggen called to check on the progress of the case later that week, Gallier was unable to give any guarantees.

"We haven't been able to arrest him," he told her. "We're going to try to group your case with others. Is that okay?"

"Sure, anything to keep him in jail," she said. "Just let me know what you want me to do."

"We think this guy may be responsible for other attacks. We want to get him good," said Gallier. "Put him away for a long time."

Hoggen didn't mention to Gallier the nightmares she'd had since that day in his office when she'd again seen James Bergstrom's face. In them, Bergstrom chased her and she ran and ran until she awoke, shaking and bathed in perspiration. There wasn't a day that passed without her fearfully considering the reality that he was still on the streets, free to do whatever he wished. Any unexpected sound frightened her. One night, a friend came to her door after dark. Andrea Hoggen, afraid to answer, hid in her bedroom closet.

As Gallier saw it, his only hope was to tie Bergstrom to another case, one in which he'd actually attempted or committed a rape. That way he might be able to group the cases on a warrant and show intention in Hoggen's case. He put out feelers, including notices to other agencies in the area describing Bergstrom as a possible suspect in skimask rapes, especially those involving bondage. When no one called with any leads, Gallier asked around and found a SWAT unit with enough manpower and overtime to keep an occasional eye out for Bergstrom.

For the veteran cop, it was maddening. "Pendergast was right. Bergstrom was careful to the extent of being paranoid," he said later. "I was worried. If he didn't get careless, he might just get away."

PART FOUR

PART FOUR

Chapter Thirty-Four

Depression had toyed with Linda Bergstrom over the years, but it never clenched her in its heavy fist more than after Rusty Gallier failed to arrest James Bergstrom that December 1991 afternoon. She had never come so close or been so sorely disappointed. Perhaps if Gallier had contacted her to explain he had not given up on the case, she might have reacted differently. Later he would label it "against his instincts" to let a wife know any more about an investigation into her husband. "She might have changed her mind and decided not to cooperate," he said. "Maybe she'd even tip him off. Linda'd shot straight with us, but I didn't figure I could take the chance."

To Linda, Gallier's silence felt like abandonment. "I knew there was nothing I could do," she'd say later. "It was out of my hands. I did everything I could to help James realize it had to stop, but you can't help somebody like that. No one else appeared to care. Not James's family, the navy, the police, no one. It was hopeless."

Going through the daily motions of living continued to extract a higher and higher toll. James, as ever, was obsessively demanding. Determined to control her every move, at night he held a fold of her nightgown so he would know if she left the bed. Once, in a fit of unexplained anger, he exploded when she carried groceries into the apartment, throwing food against the walls until they were as splattered as a painter's drop cloth. Linda guessed part of his frustration built from her refusal to play his games of bondage since the night in which she'd so feared he would kill her.

After all, she'd grown certain that James had continued to rape and that her sacrifice had protected no one. "Nothing I'd done or tried to do had stopped him," she'd say later. Any sex with James was repugnant enough. It was always demeaning and humiliating. In his latest trick, he'd taken to mimicking a drill instructor. "Get into the bedroom and assume the position," he'd order, meaning flat on her back, naked, with her legs spread. Sometimes when he demanded sex, she could successfully distract him, but before long he insisted on his "rights." To keep the peace and not upset Ashley, who sobbed through every one of their arguments, Linda eventually gave in. Those endless minutes she endured staring at a corner of the ceiling while he moved on top of her would live with her forever. She felt humiliated, used, and powerless. "Sometimes I wanted to cry, but I'd try to wipe the tears away and wait until he fell asleep before I cried," Linda would recount later. "Or he'd get mad and then things would only get worse."

That December, Linda knew she had to make changes. It had been more than two years since their return from Washington State, and she had to find a way out of the marriage. The first step was to gain some independence. Answering an advertisement in a free weekly paper, she applied for a day position caring for Colt Hargraves, a sandy-haired twenty-nine-year-old quadriplegic. Hargraves, paralyzed from the shoulders down, interviewed Linda in his Clear Lake area home. During the interview, Linda recounted how she had "always wanted to be a nurse," and that she had once taken classes in hopes of becoming a medical assistant.

"Why didn't you finish?" he asked.

Linda fought the memory of James destroying her books so she couldn't study. "It just didn't work out," she said.

Despite what he sensed was a sadness about her, Hargraves liked what he saw in Linda. She seemed straightforward, concerned, and enthusiastic. When he offered her two hundred dollars a week and asked if she could start the following Monday, Linda Bergstrom jumped at it.

Colt Hargraves, once a six-foot, two-hundred-pound, hot-shot, barrel-racer working the rodeo circuit, had been dealt a paralyzing blow by the boot of a honkey-tonk bouncer six years earlier. "I had an attitude," he'd say later. "I was kind of a bad-ass." The night Colt mouthed off to the brawny bouncer, he was ejected to the parking lot, his jacket jerked over his elbows, shoved on the ground, and kicked as if he were a gunnysack of grain. "The last thing I remember is laying on my back and I saw a big boot coming toward me," said Hargraves. "I turned my head and somebody kicked me in the back of the head with a big old cowboy boot."

After three and a half months in intensive care, Hargraves was transferred to a rehabilitation center. But the damage was permanent. Immobilized except through a mechanized chin-operated wheelchair, Hargraves sued the bar and won a hefty settlement.

With the money, Hargraves bought a home, a pick-up truck, and a sports car. But he was forever unable to move anything but his head, and he shrank down to 150 pounds. "I need people round the clock to be my right and left arms and both my legs," Hargraves said to Linda the afternoon he hired her. "I basically need you to do everything for me."

Hargraves fancied himself a good judge of character. After years of depending on others, he'd had a few bad experiences with aides who hadn't worked out. He tended to watch people carefully and assess. What he saw in Linda was someone who worked hard and who genuinely seemed to care.

For Linda, Hargraves was a godsend. She found a motherly woman who ran a small day care out of her home to care for Ashley, and barely flinched when James complained bitterly about her long hours and absence from the apartment. After paying for day care, the money wasn't enough to matter, but her job represented freedom, and Linda grabbed it.

In mid-January, Detective Robert Tonry of the Harris County Sheriff's Department learned through a constable who worked his district that a Sergeant Rusty Gallier in HPD sex crimes was asking questions about a ski-masked rapist who liked to tie his victims up. Tonry, remembering Jesse Neal, the waitress who'd been raped the past November, called Gallier. On the phone, Gallier filled him in on Linda Bergstrom and her allegations against her husband.

The next day in Gallier's third-floor office at HPD headquarters, he and Tonry compared notes. The detective briefed Gallier on his cases. He'd brought along four files: the ones on the rapes of Kimberly Greenmen, Cindy McKenzie, and Jesse Neal, and one on a similar attempted rape, along with the composite sketch made from the security guard's description of the man he'd seen jogging just before Neal's rape. When it was his turn, Gallier detailed the cluster of three attempted rapes in Clear Lake. They compared Tonry's charcoal sketch to the photo Linda had supplied. They looked similar, both admitted, but were far from identical. In the sketch, the man with the long face wore glasses. Bergstrom didn't. It could be the same man. But that Bergstrom was responsible for all of the attacks seemed like a long shot.

"We tried to get prints at the waitress's apartment," Tonry said. "He turned off the stereo, and we thought we might get something off the button, but it was too smudged to help."

In fact, there was no physical evidence to tie Bergstrom to any of the cases. No fingerprints, fibers, hair, or semen. In all three rape cases, the rapist hadn't ejaculated. Of course, that wasn't unusual. Gallier knew that rape was less about sex than violence and control. "If you filled a room with rapists and, on a scale of one to ten, had them place the actual importance of the intercourse, it would be about a two and a half," Gallier estimated later. "It's not sex, but the thrill of having a woman he can totally control."

Mentally Gallier wrote off the McKenzie and Greenmen rapes as probably not Bergstrom's. His gut told him the MO was too different from the Andrea Hoggen assault, one in which he already had an identification. But Gallier still figured between them they were looking at one rape and a least four attempts. "If this is the same guy, he's being damn careful," Gallier said to Tonry that afternoon. "No telling how many rapes he's done."

Tonry left HPD that afternoon convinced there was a good chance "James Bergstrom was my guy." But he had no way to prove it. After poring over the files, neither of the two officers had discovered a way to build a case against the former navy man for anything but the trespass of Andrea Hoggen's residence.

"We agreed we were going to keep in touch and keep our eyes open for Bergstrom," Tonry said.

According to Gallier, a week later the head of the SWAT unit that had agreed to keep an eye on Bergstrom called sex crimes. "They had to pull off of it," Gallier said later. "They had no luck and they couldn't justify it any longer."

Although disappointed, Gallier wasn't surprised. He'd expected the call. HPD had been in a budget crunch and short-staffed for the past five years. They didn't have the money to keep the surveillance up forever on his hunch that Bergstrom would strike again. And Gallier had more than thirty other active cases on his plate, too many to devote all his time and attention to James Bergstrom. To do what he could, he called the constables and HPD stations that covered Houston's southern fringes and cautioned them to be on the lookout for anyone fitting Bergstrom's description or rapes with his MO.

At work, James Bergstrom looked more and more anxious. He complained constantly to co-workers about the police and how they'd taken his "stuff" from the car and refused to return it.

"That doesn't sound right to me," Gibson told him one afternoon. "Seems like you ought to be able to get it back, James. What do they need it for?"

"Damn if I know," Bergstrom said.

Gibson had grown used to Bergstrom's bad moods and complaining. In the past weeks, he'd griped often, not only about the police, but about Linda. If you listened to James, his wife was a cold woman who prudishly refused to sleep with him.

"Is she frigid?" Gibson asked one day.

"I don't know, but sometimes I have to force her to have sex," Bergstrom insisted. "If she doesn't come around, I'll have to start getting it someplace else."

"Well, James," said Gibson, "you've got a baby now. It won't do that baby any good if you divorce."

"I don't know how much more I can take," James answered with a shrug. "If I should stay with her or not."

Gibson suggested James rent an X-rated movie and drop Ashley at his mother's, "so you two can heat it up."

"Oh, Linda's not into that stuff. She wouldn't watch it," James insisted, playing the victim. Then, ironically, he brought up lingerie, something Linda repeatedly tried to wear, much to his displeasure. "She won't even wear the lingerie I buy for her."

Gibson nodded sympathetically.

Since Linda's car had been repossessed shortly after they returned to Houston and they were down to just the Grand Prix, mornings were hectic at the Bergstroms' apartment. Each day on her way to work, Linda dropped James at Devoe, and Ashley at the sitter's. In Hargraves's view, Linda was working out well, but he had concerns. She was conscientious, yet often preoccupied and depressed. As efficient as she tried to be, constant phone calls from her husband interrupted the day. Even from across the room, Colt could hear James Bergstrom cursing.

"What's wrong with him?" Colt asked Linda after one such call.

"James is just that way," she answered.

Then one afternoon in January, Linda arrived at work as usual, but a few hours into the day, became tense and temperamental to the point Colt feared she might collapse in tears.

"Okay, what's wrong?" he asked. "I need to know what's going on."

"I forgot my purse at home, and James didn't go in to work today," Linda told him. "And there's something in there—if my husband sees it . . . well, it could really be bad."

"What?"

"A phone number for a cop," Linda admitted. "A cop in Houston's sex crimes unit."

Hargraves looked at her for answers, and Linda gulped hard and started talking. Tears lined her cheeks. As she had to so many others—from James's family to the police, a doctor, a priest, a therapist, and two lawyers—Linda confided in Hargraves. It wasn't hard. Her new boss was sympathetic, and from the beginning seemed to believe her. "You see, I know James, and I know he'll go through my wallet," Linda explained. "If he finds that number, he'll know I'm trying to turn him in. He'll kill me. Maybe even the baby. He's threatened to often enough."

As Hargraves listened, Linda called home. A calm and collected James answered the phone.

"Something wrong?" he asked.

"Yeah," she said. "I forgot my purse."

"I know," James said. "I went through it. From the sound of your voice, it seems like you've got something to hide."

"No," she said, "I was just worried I'd lost it."

Relieved, Linda explained to Hargraves that everything seemed to be all right.

"Well, maybe you'd better leave early anyway," he suggested. "Get home before he decides to take another look."

When Linda arrived home that afternoon, she found James, as usual, staring at the television. She walked into the bedroom, where she found her purse on the closet floor. Everything inside was out of place, and it was easy to see he'd rifled through it. Hands shaking, she opened her wallet and searched through one of its small compartments. Inside she found Gallier's telephone number, just as she'd left it on a folded card tucked between her credit cards. *Thank God,* she thought. *If he'd found it, I'd be dead right now.*

After that day, Linda talked openly with Hargraves about her almost seven years of marriage to James Bergstrom, her fear of him and her fears for Ashley. "I had a hard time believing her, especially when she said she'd told the police and they didn't believe her," Hargraves would say later. "But I told her whatever I could do to help her, I'd be happy to do."

Before long, Linda and Colt began idling away afternoons hatching plans for Linda to escape. Often they were at the lake, sitting in his sports car looking out at the water. Downstream, Clear Lake, ringed with expensive houses, emptied into Galveston Bay and the Gulf of Mexico, but here it was brackish and calm.

"I'll set you up in a place," Hargraves offered on one such afternoon. "Until you could get away from him."

"Thanks," Linda said. "That's really kind. But what I'd really like is for him to get caught. I hate to think about what he's doing to those women. He has to stop. And it would be hell having to spend my life hiding out and watching over my shoulder for him."

How she could help police move in on James Bergstrom was a puzzle that had dominated Linda's thoughts for the past two years. Since Gallier's apparent abandonment, she'd concluded the only way James would ever be arrested and stopped was if he was actually caught in the act. Often she thought back to Washington State and how James had successfully eluded police for months before becoming careless. In Linda's mind, the determining factor had been that she had bought the car—the blue Precis that was later repossessed. When

James had the Grand Prix at his disposal and she was distracted with her work at the day-care center, he'd attacked at such a rate that the police increased their efforts and eventually caught him. As painful as the thought of turning James loose and unhampered to terrorize other women was, Linda had grown to believe it was the only way he would ever be stopped.

So when Colt Hargraves asked Linda one afternoon, "Is there anything I can do to at least make things a little easier for you?" she didn't hesitate.

"I could use a car," she said. "At least that might get him off my back. Now he's always yelling at me about working and taking the Grand Prix."

Colt hesitated for only a minute. "I tell you what," he said. "I'll buy you a car. Hell, I've got plenty of money. Someday you can pay me back."

"Really?" Linda asked.

"Yeah, let's do it."

No one had ever been that kind to her before, and Linda began crying.

"None of that," Hargraves said, laughing.

At the end of January, Colt Hargraves paid ninety-five-hundred dollars to buy Linda Bergstrom a used two-door car.

Now they'll get him, Linda thought on the day they picked it up. *I know James is just going to lose it and make a mistake.*

When James asked, "What'd you have to do to earn that?" Linda told him that Hargraves had just wanted to be sure she'd arrive at work on time. "It's a company car," she said. "He's sick of hearing you yelling on the phone." James didn't press the point. Perhaps he was already fantasizing about the future—with Linda preoccupied and total access to the Grand Prix, there would be nothing to stop him.

Chapter Thirty-Five

By February 1992, fantasy ruled James Bergstrom's life. The dark urges controlled every desire. When he wasn't stalking, he was fantasizing about it as he meticulously constructed ski masks from the sleeves of old shirts. Exactingly he cut the eyes, trying it on over and over, slicing off slivers at a time, calculating how to make the openings just wide enough to see through without exposing any of his face. "I was always thinking about doing it," he'd say later. "I thought about it constantly. I couldn't help myself. It was more important than anything else. Once Linda stopped watching me, I blamed it on her. She didn't care enough, so I was teaching her a lesson. Sometimes I would drive around or jog for hours looking for the right opportunity. I'd be so tired, but that was a relief, because it meant I was too tired to do anything and I could go home."

On February 7 a woman in her mid-forties was attacked as she got out of her car in front of her Clear Lake apartment complex. The assailant wore sweats and a ski mask, and, as in the two November 1991 cases, carried a hunting knife. It was two-thirty in the afternoon in broad daylight, and when the woman screamed her son's name, the man ran. The file landed on Detective Robert Tonry's desk. He now had at least one rape he and Gallier suspected Bergstrom of—that of Jesse Neal, the waitress—and five attempted rapes, and nothing solid tying the ex-submariner to any of them. Tonry called Gallier, who told him he'd circulated Bergstrom's description and MO to HPD patrols working Houston's southern limits. "We'll get him," Gallier said, hopefully. "He can't continue to be this careful."

In mid-February, Bergstrom's high school basketball buddy, Eddie Smith, was home one morning after working the night in the parts department of a plant near the Johnson Space Center. He sat in the dark, drapes pulled, in his small, second-floor apartment, considering sleeping the afternoon away when he heard a frantic banging on his door. Smith, assuming it was his girlfriend angry with him again, ignored it and sat on the couch waiting for the commotion to stop. Moments passed. Smith heard someone leap from his doorway, over the five-foot gap between his porch and balcony. Smith stood up. Whoever it was had just jumped the balcony's railing. "I was thinking, man, that can't be her," Smith said later.

Before he had time to react, Smith heard the patio-style door slide open and saw the curtains part. "This real scary-looking face came at me," Smith said later. "The guy looked like an animal, a wolf."

Suddenly Smith recognized the man.

"James, what're you doing?" he demanded.

"Oh, I'm sorry," Bergstrom said, his expression softening. "I just wanted to see if you had time for a swim."

James apologized until Smith finally told him to shut up. "Just don't do it again," he said. "You looked so damn weird, if I'd had a gun, I would have shot you."

Before James left, he talked Smith into lending him a pair of shorts and T-shirt, ostensibly to change into after his swim. Later James would admit that he was on the run. He'd circled back to the Grand Prix after stalking an apartment complex and noticed a squad car with two cops parked suspiciously nearby. The clothes Smith lent him were a precaution. He changed into them before returning to the car, in case someone had spotted him circulating through the complex, looking in windows.

Bergstrom had sensed for weeks that he was being watched. Sometimes he'd drive down the street and notice a squad car pull up behind him and follow for a few blocks. He talked often to Linda about wanting to paint the Grand Prix white, but she—certain it was to hide from police—wouldn't hear of it.

James wasn't the only Bergstrom who caught the eye of the authorities that February. On the eighth, James C., drunk and disagreeable, chased his wife and youngest daughter around the house until Adelaide took refuge in her locked bedroom. Flushed with liquor, he got a gun and shot through the door, the bullet's ricochet barely missing his daughter. The two women eventually escaped through windows, and police were called. Pearland's SWAT team moved in for a three-hour standoff, before James C. relinquished his gun to police. Arrested, he was later allowed to plead to a misdemeanor and sentenced to two years' probation. As part of his plea bargain, he agreed to attend counseling for alcoholism.

The following week, Linda, James, and the Martinez family went to the Bergstroms' as planned for Ashley's second birthday party. Linda decorated with purple streamers and bought a cake topped with Sesame Street characters. Afterward Irene Bergstrom walked her to the car. "People in the neighborhood think we're crazy," the older woman told her, shrugging. "Last week we had the police here, now it's a party." Then Irene Bergstrom leaned closer to her and whispered, "You know, what you're going through isn't half of what I've been through. But I don't complain. And I don't take it outside the family."

Irene Bergstrom, of course, couldn't imagine what Linda went through when she was alone with James. "I was there for one reason, to get him caught," she said later. "I was on a mission. He wanted to get close to me, and I would never let him. Never. I never let him know who I was or what I was thinking anymore."

Though they'd grown increasingly apart, James continued to watch her every move, wiping her lipstick or makeup off on his shirtsleeve when she went out shopping with a friend. She looked for small opportunities to strike back. When they drove together, she wore headphones and listened to tapes because she couldn't stand the sound of his voice. Once when they drove past a county jail, she taunted, "That's where you're going to end up, James. Someday it'll be your home."

"You make me this way," he'd barked at her one night when she pulled away from his touch. "Do I have to spend my life fighting you for some goddamn sex? You goddamn bitch. If you don't give it to me, I'll rape you." Like on so many other nights, James pushed her on the bed and tore at her clothes. When it was over, Linda's eye was swollen and her lip bleeding.

Months later, he would confess to Linda that at times he dreamed about doing just that, entering their apartment as he had so many others, his face hidden and holding a gun. He daydreamed about the expression on her face when he, an anonymous stranger, raped her.

As weeks passed without his arrest, Linda began envisioning James as invincible, a predator who could never be stopped. He sometimes startled her with his quickness, like the afternoon they locked themselves out of their apartment complex's security gates. James easily swung over the wrought-iron fence that surrounded the grounds, as gracefully as a house cat mounts a kitchen counter. Another night she returned home from Colt's late with Ashley and was certain she saw James pull in behind her, but by the time she ran upstairs, he was already undressed and in bed.

"Where have you been?" she asked.

"I was here all night," James said, feigning a yawn. "I went to bed early."

Linda went downstairs with James trailing behind her. She put her hand on the hood of his car. It was hot.

"I told you I can do anything, Linda," he said, smiling smugly. "I can get into a house while the family is there and they don't even see me. I'm just so fast."

It was Santos who thought there was something strange about the way James always called her house when Linda was on her way over. "It's like he's checking on you," Linda's mother speculated. "You call him back when you get here and he knows he's safe. I bet he's up to something."

On a hunch one afternoon, Linda left her mother's house right after James's call and returned to Painter's Mill to discover her husband eating an apple and talking with a teenage girl on a nearby balcony. Linda knew the girl was moving out of the complex in a few days. *I bet he's trying to find out where she's moving to,* she thought. *He wants to know how to find her.*

"You don't know who you're talking to," she shouted up at them. "This guy's stalking you. He's a rapist."

"Then why are you with him?" the girl said, contemptuously.

"Because I can't prove it yet," Linda answered, James's eyes boring into her. "But when I do, I'll be out of his life, that's a guarantee."

"He wouldn't hurt me," the girl scoffed.

"Don't count on that," Linda advised.

There were two more reported attacks by ski-masked intruders near Clear Lake that month, but they never made their way to Rusty Gallier's desk. They were hasty, desperate strikes. One of the women splashed a bottle of bleach to fend off her assailant. In both cases, the women successfully fought their assailant off. *Bergstrom again,* Gallier might have thought had he known. He might have taken some comfort. At least on the surface, it looked promising. If it was James, he was becoming increasingly careless.

"The first time a guy goes out and rapes, he's so careful. Everything's got to be right," Gallier would say later. "Then, after he does it, he runs home and waits for the police to kick the door in. When it doesn't happen, he gets bolder. As time goes by—more rapes and he's not caught—he gets bolder and bolder and bolder, to where he'll do it next door."

James Bergstrom did just that.

February 22, 1992, started out pretty much like any other day for twenty-nine-year-old Maggie Heller as she walked back and forth from her second-floor apartment to the complex's laundry room. Taking advantage of a Saturday afternoon, Heller was catching up on her household chores. A quiet woman with pale red hair and a lanky figure, Heller didn't lock her apartment door. After all, she was just walking around the corner, less than one hundred feet away from her front door.

James Bergstrom watched from the parking lot. Months earlier, Bergstrom would never have been bold enough to stalk a victim in the apartment complex directly adjacent to the one in which he lived. But he'd gone so long without getting caught, it had become nearly habit now, nothing to worry about. His methods were even changing. Instead of acting as a jogger, he'd taken to canvassing parking lots in his white hard hat from work, toting a clipboard and acting official, as if he were an inspector searching for a certain apartment.

Maggie noticed the dark-haired man in the hard hat and approached him.

"Can I help you find someone?" she asked.

"No," Bergstrom said, thinking the woman seemed friendly. "I'm fine."

Heller walked away, and James scurried to his car. Thinking about what he would do to the friendly woman he'd just met, Bergstrom pulled on warm-ups and stuffed a ski mask and gun under his arm. Then he watched until Heller trudged down the stairs toward the laundry, carrying a plastic basket loaded with clothes. When she turned the corner, James made his move, walking casually toward her apartment and up the stairs.

Inside, he pulled on the ski mask and assessed the apartment. One bedroom, small, feminine. She probably lived alone. He stepped quietly into the bathroom and peered out toward the kitchen, waiting. When Maggie returned she headed for the kitchen, turned on the faucet, and ran the water in the sink. She reached into the cabinet and pulled out a glass. Heller had the glass of water to her lips when a ski-masked man lunged out at her from the apartment's recesses, brandishing a gun.

Maggie Heller froze and screamed. Bergstrom grabbed her by the arms and yanked her hands behind her, then forced her toward the bedroom.

"Do what I say and I won't hurt you," he ordered in an eerily calm voice, overpowering her until she fell face down onto the bed.

"Take your blouse off."

Heller did and felt the cold metal of the gun pressed against her back.

Then the man turned her over, tying her hands to the bed frame. He pulled off her jeans but left on her underpants, tied her ankles down and groped between her legs, fondling her.

"Do you like that?" he asked.

"Don't hurt me," she implored him.

James took off his sweats and ripped off her underpants.

"Do you use birth control?" he asked.

"No, I'm a Christian," Heller said, sadly.

"I'm a Christian, too," Bergstrom said, grinning as he climbed on top of her.

The next day, Maggie Heller was seated in Rusty Gallier's office, crying. "She put her whole soul and emotions, everything into my hands," he'd say later. "It was like, here I give myself to you, do something."

Gallier, of course, immediately suspected the rapist, who had stayed in the apartment fondling and talking to Heller for nearly an hour was James Bergstrom. Although an HPD crime scene unit had combed the apartment for evidence, they'd come up empty. At the hospital, nurses used a rape kit to take samples, but as in the other cases, the rapist left behind no semen or hair. Not knowing Heller had talked to an unmasked Bergstrom moments before the attack, Gallier decided against showing her a photo lineup. Since she insisted her rapist was masked and she would be unable to identify him, he feared it would only torment her further. "You just don't do it when you've got a case like that," he'd say later. "The woman can't identify him. All I'd be doing is giving her six faces to haunt her dreams. She'd be sure one of them was her rapist."

Gallier sensed how deeply Heller suffered. "I don't usually take these cases home with me, but this one I couldn't shake," he'd say later. "I knew it had to be Bergstrom. I wanted to get him." He complained so bitterly to his coworkers of Bergstrom's protective paranoia that the office joke became "Why doesn't somebody go over and just shoot the asshole and be done with him?"

Maggie Heller entered a psychiatric hospital just days after her rape. She spent five weeks there. "I just couldn't seem to function," she'd say later. "I couldn't forget what had happened."

The Monday after Heller's rape, James returned home from work and found a notice from Painter's Mill management on his doorknob. "There is a rapist working the area," it read, then mentioned that one rape had taken place just the Saturday before in the adjacent complex. James's eyes widened as he read the description of the man: five foot eight to ten inches, dark hair, dark eyes, thin.

James shredded the paper into confetti and threw it into the complex Dumpster. When Linda arrived home that evening, she found no warning that a woman had been raped within shouting distance of her front door.

Chapter Thirty-Six

In March, Linda visited Colt Hargraves in the hospital, where doctors scheduled tests for his annual examination. But Linda's health, not his, monopolized the afternoon's conversation. Hargraves had worried about Linda for months. He'd grown to view her as a friend, and it was difficult to sit by and helplessly watch as she deteriorated in front of him. Always skittish, she constantly seemed on edge, sometimes to the point that she lost her temper or cried over the smallest things. And she was drinking. It had become unusual to see Linda Bergstrom when she wasn't raising a small bottle of white wine to her lips. She kept Hargraves's refrigerator, her car, sometimes even her purse, stocked with ten-ounce bottles of Sutter Home White.

Hargraves didn't know how to feel about the way she was changing. Had he been wrong to trust her? His faith in Linda hadn't come without challenge. His mother, once she learned her son had bought his new aide a car, told him almost daily that he was being used. "You're letting this one take you for a ride," she'd say. "There hasn't been anything in the papers about any rapist on the loose."

In the hospital room, Hargraves echoed his mother's words to Linda.

Please believe in me, she thought. *Not you, too.*

All she said out loud was, "I'm telling the truth." Then, "I've got to leave."

"You're going to drink," he scolded.

"Yeah, I am," she admitted. "Why not? Ashley's with the sitter. I don't care anymore. It's the only way I can relax and not think about it. It takes the pressure off for a little while. If this is my life, I've got to do something to cope."

Yet no anesthetic was strong enough to drown out the guilt that haunted Linda, that of freeing James on an unsuspecting world. It ate away inside her, spawning horrific nightmares. In desperation during one argument, she scratched her husband's face, etching bloody lines from forehead to chin. "I wanted people to see it," she'd say later. "I would have liked to put a red *R* for rapist on his forehead. I wanted people to know what he was."

At work, James explained away the scratches claiming three teenagers jumped him at his apartment complex's Coke machine.

"James," Allen Gibson cautioned when he heard James's tale. "Kids these days, you don't know they weren't armed. You better be careful."

"Maybe so," James said.

Gibson had noticed a change in James. His absences from work had become increasingly frequent. Many of the hourly workers at Devoe knew Bergstrom habitually arrived late or left early, if he came in at all. "I'd ask where James was and one of the guys would say he wasn't coming in today," Gibson would say later. "It got so it was routine. When he was there, he was in a world of his own. His body was there, but his mind wasn't. James didn't want to shoot the bull no more."

Gibson wrote Bergstrom's detachment off to problems at home. Later he would remember other things: that he'd heard of a rape in the apartment complex next to the one the Bergstroms lived in on Edgebrook; and the day one of the men in the plant said he'd seen James running out of an apartment complex, not the one where he lived. When

Gibson mentioned it to him, James claimed he'd been playing tennis with a friend.

Since Maggie Heller's rape, opportunities had dried up for Bergstrom, making him increasingly frantic. "I watched the papers and there weren't any articles about the rape," he said later. "But everybody seemed more cautious. Doors were locked. Garage doors weren't up. The women around the apartments seemed more cautious. I figured I had to come up with another way to get inside."

In early March, Linda noticed a hard hat and sunglasses in the Grand Prix's backseat.

"What's that for?" she asked.

"It's from work." James shrugged, innocently. "I just forgot to put it away."

Later she'd learn the truth. That like the ski masks, duct tape, rope, and guns she'd found, a hard hat, clipboard, vial, and sunglasses were now part of her husband's rape kit.

Chapter Thirty-Seven

At 3:30 P.M. on March 16, 1992, Sandy Colyard gossiped on her portable phone with a friend in the living room of her Friendswood apartment, a ten-minute drive from the Clear Lake strip Bergstrom had stalked for the previous five months. A fourth grade teacher, the twenty-three-year-old Colyard had slept in on the first day of spring break. Just out of the shower, she felt her wet hair tickling her neck, so as she paced the room, she ran her fingers through thick, dark curls.

Colyard had looked forward to this leisure for months. She'd had a tough spring semester with a particularly unruly class. "I really needed this R and R," she told her girlfriend on the phone. Then she went on to detail her week's plans. Her boyfriend, a student at the University of Texas, was in town, and after a few days of rest, they were considering a short trip, maybe to the Texas hill country if the bluebonnets were blooming.

"Hold on a sec," Colyard said, when she heard a knock at the door. "I'll be right back."

When she opened the first-floor apartment door, there stood a man in a hard hat and sunglasses, carrying a clipboard and a test tube.

"There's a problem with the water. I'm here to check it," James Bergstrom said. "It'll just take a minute."

Colyard's immediate reaction was suspicion.

"You got a note from the apartment manager last week

saying we were coming," Bergstrom persisted when she didn't let him in.

In the past, Colyard had missed notices on the exterminator and the maintenance man. *Maybe I just didn't see it again,* she thought.

"Okay," she said. "Come on in."

James Bergstrom walked in and headed toward the bathroom as Colyard picked up the phone. Her friend, who had heard everything, chastised her. "You shouldn't just let someone you don't know in your apartment," she said. "Stay on the phone until he leaves so I know you're okay."

Colyard did just that, watching suspiciously as Bergstrom left the bathroom to draw a water sample from the kitchen. Two vials of water in his hand, he let himself out the door.

"He's gone and I'm fine," Colyard told her friend as she locked the front door behind him. "Thanks, but I've got to go."

In the bathroom with the hair dryer buzzing, she never heard James Bergstrom jump the six-foot barrier surrounding her patio. She never heard the scraping of the patio door as he eased it open. She never realized he was there until she saw a man in a ski mask staring back at her in the mirror. Bergstrom quickly grabbed her neck with his left arm. *It's not really happening,* Colyard thought as she stared in the mirror at her own face shadowed by a stranger holding a gun to her head.

"Do exactly what I say and I won't hurt you," the man ordered.

Immediately Colyard recognized the voice as that of the water tester.

"Lay down," he ordered.

Lying face down in the hallway, Colyard winced when the stranger jerked her hands behind her. In a process that seemed to take forever, he meticulously tied her wrists together behind her back with long black shoelaces. A throbbing pain shot through her hands into her fingers as he yanked on the bindings to test them.

"Please don't hurt me," she said, in a voice so frightened, it sounded like it came from someone else.

"I won't if you do what I say," he said, clutching her by the arm and hoisting her to her feet.

Is he going to kill me? she wondered. When he pushed her toward the bedroom, she knew exactly what he intended for her. *My God, he's going to rape me.*

The stranger shoved her harder in the direction of the bedroom, but this time, incensed, Colyard lunged, hitting him in the chest with her shoulder. Bergstrom abruptly stopped and stared at Colyard. Later he would say he had the unshakable impression that she recognized him as the water tester. She sensed immediately that something had changed.

"All I want is money," Bergstrom hastily demanded, shyly looking away from her.

"I've got two dollars in my purse," she said, no longer frightened. "Take it and leave. My brother should be here any minute."

"I want your money," he said, again.

"Then take it and leave," she shouted. "Get out of here."

Colyard, hands still bound behind her, followed her would-be rapist into the living room, screaming at him to get out.

"Calm down," Bergstrom ordered her, as he grabbed the money from the purse. "I'm going to put you in the bathroom. I don't want you following me."

"Okay," said Colyard. "Just get out."

Bergstrom closed the door on Colyard, and a moment later she heard the front door squeak and slam shut. She turned her back to the bathroom door and strained against her bindings until she grasped the doorknob, turning until it swung open. Then she rushed out, eager to call for help. When she reached the living room, there was the water tester, mask off, getting ready to flee. Bergstrom ran out the door, Colyard chasing him and shouting for help. When she spotted the apartment's maintenance man, she ran toward him, turning so he could see the bindings on her wrists. "Don't let him get away," she shouted. "Look what that guy did to me."

Once she was certain the other man was in pursuit, Colyard rushed to the manager's office, kicked at the door until someone opened it, and screamed, "Call the police. Now."

Within minutes, the apartment lot was flooded with squad cars. Officers took Colyard's statement and that of the maintenance man who'd failed to catch Bergstrom as he fled from the scene. Among those present at Colyard's that afternoon was Detective Frank Fidelibus, a twelve-year veteran of the Friendswood police force. He took one look at the square-type knot in the shoelaces the apartment manager had cut from Colyard's wrists and said, "You know, I'd be willing to bet this guy's been in the navy."

The next morning, Frank Fidelibus, slight, dark-haired, with a manicured mustache and beard and wire-rimmed aviator glasses, started making inquiries. First he called the water department and confirmed that no testers were working in the area of Sandy Colyard's apartment that day or in previous months. Then he asked around the office and learned there had been two similar attacks in Friendswood subdivisions, also unsuccessful, in the spring of 1990 and another in February 1991. When Fidelibus checked with the Harris County Sheriff's Department, someone mentioned they, too, had a detective investigating a series of sexual assaults in Houston's southern rim.

"Tonry here," the detective said when he answered the line.

"I'm Frank Fidelibus, detective, Friendswood," the other man said. "I understand you're looking into some rapes. A guy who likes to tie women up?"

"Yeah," Tonry said. "I sure am."

The following day, Tonry and Fidelibus met at Friends-wood's police headquarters. In Frank's office, they compared files. Tonry explained everything he knew about Bergstrom and the rapes he was already suspected of.

"This guy's wife's been trying to turn him in," Tonry went on, telling him about Sergeant Rusty Gallier at HPD and detailing Gallier's talks with Linda, and Bergstrom's history in Washington State.

"I don't know. This Colyard case is different than the ones you and Gallier have. This time the guy posed as a water tester," Fidelibus said, stroking his dark beard. "I think Bergstrom could be my guy, but do you think he's done them all?"

"Beats me," Tonry said. "But I've gotta say, I think he could have done my cases, too."

"Well, those knots he used on Colyard," Fidelibus went on. "I'm a boater and I'd swear this guy's been on a boat. The navy thing fits. Let's map it out."

Fidelibus grabbed a yellow legal pad from his desk and made up a grid. On the left he listed the names of his four victims, including Ann Cook and Sandy Colyard, and Ton-ry's three, including Jesse Neal, the waitress. Across the top he listed different categories: date, time, place, means of entry, ski mask color, material used to tie victim up, type of weapon, what said, what he did to each victim.

As with Gallier's examination months earlier, there were differences and similarities, but both officers' gut instincts told them Bergstrom was responsible for the majority if not all of their cases.

"Have we got a picture?" Fidelibus asked.

"Gallier's got one."

"Well, I'm gonna send for one. Then we can stop guess-ing," Fidelibus said, picking up the phone and dialing the Texas Department of Public Safety for a copy of Bergstrom's driver's license photo.

"It'll be here tomorrow," he told Tonry when he hung up. "Then we'll know for sure."

When the photo arrived via Federal Express the following morning, Fidelibus called Sandy Colyard and made arrangements to meet her at her apartment at noon.

"Take your time," Fidelibus told her as he arranged the eight photos on a table. "We're in no hurry."

Fidelibus stole a glance at her wrists and saw that, though it had been four days since the attack, the red, tender ridges from the shoelaces were still plainly visible. He knew the knots Bergstrom used were designed to tighten, cutting deeper into the skin if she fought against him.

"This is him," Colyard shouted almost instantly. "I know it's him."

Colyard held photo number six—James Bergstrom.

"Sure?" he asked.

"Positive," Colyard answered. "Absolutely positive."

Chapter Thirty-Eight

On Friday, March 20, 1992—four days after the attack on Sandy Colyard—Friendswood detective Frank Fidelibus and Harris County detective Robert Tonry drove to HPD headquarters on the outskirts of downtown Houston for a meeting with Sergeant Rusty Gallier. When they arrived, Gallier led them into an empty office. Each man carried an armful of files.

"You think Bergstrom could be responsible for all of these?" asked Gallier, whose cases included Maggie Heller's rape.

"Tonry and I mapped ours out yesterday," Fidelibus said, pulling out his yellow legal pad. "Let's add yours."

To the bottom of their existing list, Fidelibus added the names and data on the rape of Maggie Heller, the attack on Andrea Hoggen, and two unsuccessful attempts in the Clear Lake area. The completed list included two rapes and seven attempted sexual assaults. Then Fidelibus drew a map plotting all the cases and noting the date of each. One thing showed up quickly: The attacks were all clustered on Interstate 45, fanning out into Clear Lake and Friendswood. Except for the two cases in which victims had identified Bergstrom, no evidence linked him to any of the crimes.

"The MO was all over the place," Gallier would say later. "We all thought he was the one who did ours—not theirs. It just didn't seem like it could all be the same guy. Usually rapists settle into a pattern of what's worked for them and they keep repeating it. We had cases where he walked in through unlocked doors, others where he followed women and forced himself in; now he was posing as a water tester."

"If this is all him, the guy's damn smart," Fidelibus said that afternoon, echoing sentiments Tonry and Gallier had expressed months earlier.

"This could be the same guy," Tonry postulated.

Gallier agreed, but he wasn't optimistic. He'd already reviewed the new Friendswood case—Sandy Colyard's—with an assistant DA. As in Hoggen's case, according to Gallier, the prosecutors couldn't charge Bergstrom with attempted rape because he'd never told Colyard what he intended to do to her. The most they could come up with was a burglary charge for the two dollars Bergstrom lifted from her purse on his way out of the apartment. The prosecutor could go with burglary, a second-degree felony with a sentencing range of two to twenty years. Since Bergstrom had no other felony convictions, a judge would undoubtedly give him probation or a two-year sentence. With good time in jail, Bergstrom probably wouldn't serve more than a few months, and any advantage they had from the element of surprise would be gone.

"We're sitting here with possible rapes," Gallier stressed after reviewing the situation. "If we move in now, we may stop him for a little while, but we'll have blown the bigger cases and he'll be out in no time."

"But we can't just keep letting this go on," Fidelibus argued.

"What say we wait until the end of the month?" Gallier asked. "If we don't have more on him by then, we group what we've got together and go into the DA's office and see if we can't convince them to package these cases based on his MO."

All three officers knew it was a weak case. None of them liked the bargain, but it was the best they had.

"Let's do it," Tonry said, and Fidelibus nodded in agreement.

Chapter Thirty-Nine

Linda Bergstrom would always remember March 1992 as a nightmare. It began the morning she blew her hair dry in the bathroom only to have Ashley sidle up next to her. She playfully squeezed her daughter in her arms, tickling her soft, round belly, then placed the child with her wispy fawn-colored curls on the vanity next to her. In the past, the toddler would have mischievously giggled, inspecting herself and robustly slapping the mirror with her soft little palms, squealing in delight at her own reflection. This afternoon, to Linda's horror, Ashley solemnly posed staring into the mirror, one tiny hand with its perfect fingers ominously cupped across her mouth like a gag, just as James had positioned Linda during so many of his sex games.

Could she have seen James do this to me? Linda wondered.

The next day, when Ashley's baby-sitter reported the two-year-old acted strangely, Linda's translation of Ashley's actions took on a more dire interpretation. "She's crying every time I change her diaper," explained the matronly woman. "As soon as I start to take her diaper off, she just sobs. I don't know what's wrong, but she's upset about something."

Dread overwhelmed Linda, who drove directly to the pediatrician's office. Once inside the examining room, she told the physician about James, his history including his molestation of a little girl, the baby-sitter's concerns, and Ashley's chilling play in front of the mirror. "I never thought he'd do anything to her when she was so small," Linda cried. "My God, she's a baby."

"Let's not jump to conclusions," the doctor warned. "Let's just take a look."

Linda sat nervously fidgeting in a chair as the woman examined her daughter. *I watched her. I did everything I could. This just couldn't have happened,* she thought, pain and guilt rushing through her body like adrenaline. *Not my baby.*

When the examination was over, the doctor sat down with Linda. As Ashley played at their feet, she said she'd found no physical signs that James had sexually abused his daughter. "But that doesn't necessarily mean it didn't happen," the doctor cautioned. "I suggest we set Ashley up for play therapy with a psychologist."

"If they think he's done anything, will I be able to get Ashley away from him?" Linda asked, fighting back tears.

"It's possible, but it's hard," the doctor admitted. "With a child so young, when there's no physical evidence. She's too young to testify. But don't worry about that now. Let's just wait and see."

Linda, however, was no longer willing to wait and see. She'd done that for more than two years, and what had it accomplished? She was sure there were still more victims—now maybe even her own daughter. All her good intentions to protect everyone else had accomplished nothing. In fact, she was no closer to safely escaping James than she had been when they first arrived back in Houston.

She had to find some way to protect her daughter.

On the drive home, Linda thought back, remembering how Maria had threatened a few weeks earlier to report her and James to Children's Protective Services, because they'd argued in front of Ashley one night at the Bergstroms'. It gave her an idea.

When James arrived home that night, Linda told him about her trip to the pediatrician, but said that she'd been ordered to take her there by CPS. "Someone called in an anonymous tip about you and that little girl and what happened in Washington State," she said. "They're going to check Ashley randomly to make sure you aren't abusing her."

Then she told him the doctor had prescribed play therapy, during which a psychiatrist would watch Ashley and interpret her actions to determine if she expressed the type of sexual overtones often displayed by children who have been sexually abused.

James became incensed. Assuming, as Linda knew he would, that his sisters were behind it, he picked up the phone and called Adelaide and Maria, demanding to know if they'd been the ones who had phoned in the anonymous tip. Startled, both James's sisters denied any involvement. From that day on, Linda noticed James kept his distance from Ashley. He shunned her to the point of not picking her up or holding her on his lap, obviously afraid to be close to her.

For the meantime, her lie seemed to be having its intended effect, keeping James at arm's length from Ashley. But she knew at best it was a Band-Aid on a problem that would surely fester. In her heart Linda knew she no longer had any choice. There was nothing left to consider. Despite the risks, she had to take Ashley and flee. If that meant hiding out, moving to a strange city away from her family to start over on her own, then that's what she had to do.

The following day, Linda called Colt and asked him if he was still willing to help her escape. "Sure," he said. "Just tell me what you need."

"A place to stay until I can get away from him."

"You've got it."

Then Linda called her younger sister, Alice, and asked her to get the family together for Saturday, March 28, James had plans to spend the day with Sam McDonald, and while they were out, Linda's family would have time to move her belongings and Ashley's.

"I need to get away from him as soon as possible," she

told her sister. "If James ever finds me and Ashley, he'll kill both of us."

When Linda hung up the phone, she made a vow—no more drinking. Not a drop. Ashley needed her vigilance. From now on, she would think only of her daughter until they were both safe.

Chapter Forty

On Sunday night, March 22, a ski-masked intruder stalked the University Green Apartments on Bay Area Boulevard, the same complex where Andrea Hoggen had been attacked just three months earlier. Later the two women would speculate that the man who attacked them had picked them out at a nearby Laundromat where they'd washed clothes earlier that evening. Neither heard the interloper jump the fence and slide open their patio door. When he entered, he flashed a gun. Then he tied them, one at a time.

"Two," the man mused as he slipped a knotted nylon stocking around the last woman's wrist, pushing her into a chair. He ripped at one woman's clothes, as they both realized the stranger was not after their money.

"Don't fight. I won't hurt you," the stranger ordered.

But the women were unmanageable, wildly shouting and screaming.

"Please leave us," one pleaded as the other wailed.

The would-be rapist was nervous. There'd been so much commotion, surely someone had heard it. He turned and ran, leaving the two women crying out for help.

After calling 911, the apartment manager dialed the phone number for another of his tenants, Sergeant Charles Dunn, who worked burglary and theft in HPD's Clear Lake substation. A brotherly-looking man with blond hair and a full reddish mustache, Dunn had recently moved into the apartments after separating from his wife. His landlord's description of the night's events piqued Dunn's interest. Before hanging up, he assured the man he'd look over the file on the case the next morning.

At the Clear Lake substation that Monday, Dunn pulled the file on the attempted rapes of the night before and dropped in to consult the officers in crime analysis. "A guy with a ski mask and a gun isn't a onetime rapist," Dunn told them. "I bet we've got a serial rapist here. Run a check on ski mask, bondage, white male, rape, and attempted rape for me."

Later that day, Dunn got the news: There were clusters of similar incidents throughout the area, and one of his counterparts at HPD sex crimes, Sergeant Rusty Gallier, had phoned in a request for information on all such cases. Dunn dialed Gallier's number at headquarters.

"I don't want to step on anybody's toes," he said, when Gallier answered, "but I've got an attempted rape here with bondage. I hear you're working on a similar case."

Gallier filled Dunn in on Bergstrom and the string of rapes he was suspected of. "You think the two women can identify him?" he asked.

"It's doubtful," Dunn admitted. "They were pretty shook up. We had a hard time even taking statements. And the guy had something like a ski mask on."

"Like a ski mask?"

"Yeah," said Dunn. "They said it looked funny. It was real long and the eyes were cut out."

"That fits," said Gallier. "Bergstrom makes his. Some of the other women have reported the same thing, and the two we picked up from his wife in December were hacked out of a knit hat and a shirtsleeve."

The following day, Dunn hooked up with Gallier at the Harris County District Attorney's Office, where they met with an assistant DA. They detailed the cases, as Gallier had in the past, but added the new one. There was still no real evidence tying Bergstrom to anything beyond the attacks on Andrea Hoggen and Sandy Colyard. "Get me some more

IDs," the prosecutor suggested. "We can package enough cases, maybe we'll have something."

"Well, hell," said Dunn to Gallier. "I can afford a little overtime. Let's go out and see if we can't get them some."

Gallier was doubtful but frustrated enough to give anything a try.

On Thursday, March 26, four days after the attacks on the two women, Dunn and Gallier began their rounds. It took most of the day, but they tracked down one after another of the women who'd filed the complaints. Each time it was an emotional moment as the women eyed the photo spread and relived their attacks. The two men finished up at 9:00 P.M. with nothing to show for their efforts. Not one additional victim was able to pick Bergstrom from the lineup. They agreed the following day, with or without new evidence, they would arrest Bergstrom. It was a weak case, but it was all they had. Gallier and Dunn went home frustrated and bitter. It had been a disappointing day.

They wouldn't discover until the next day that Bergstrom, too, had been on the prowl that very afternoon, and that another young woman, this one a seventeen-year-old high school student, had joined his list of victims.

"I'd been driving around looking for someone and I saw her outside the apartment," Bergstrom would say later. "She was pretty, short with curly blond hair."

With his hard hat, sunglasses, clipboard, and test tubes, a smiling James Bergstrom knocked on the door of the Clear Lake-area town house apartment Jenny Karr shared with her family.

"I'm here to test the water," he said. "It'll just take a minute."

The high school senior let him in.

Bergstrom was nervous and frustrated; later he'd describe himself as "out of control." He knew he was growing careless when he didn't even bother to return to the car to change, instead pulling on his ski mask in the girl's bathroom. "I'd been doing it for so long, I figured no one even cared," he said later. "Maybe none of the women were even reporting."

Jenny froze when Bergstrom came at her, knocking her down on the living room floor and tying her hands behind her. He pushed her up the stairs to a second-floor bedroom and attempted to rip her clothes off. She fought as he retied her hands, this time to a bed.

"You're really getting me pissed off," he growled through clenched teeth. "You don't stop, I'm going to have to kill you."

"You might as well kill me then," the feisty Karr shouted, kicking hard with her still free legs. "Because I'm sure not going to let you rape me."

When she heard Bergstrom unzipping his pants, Jenny twisted and kicked so violently, she threw him off balance enough to grab the gun's barrel.

"You're just going to have to shoot me," she screamed.

Bergstrom gathered his things and ran from the room. He could still hear her screaming for help as he slammed the front door.

It was Sergeant Dunn who hand-carried the photo lineup to Clear Lake High School the next morning. A message was sent to pull Jenny out of her English class. When she arrived at the principal's office, Dunn was impressed with the teenager's composure. She glanced down at the photo spread and flinched. Dunn knew immediately she recognized Bergstrom. "He told me he was going to kill me," Jenny said, pointing at Bergstrom's photo. "I told him he was going to have to. I wasn't going to let him rape me."

Dunn called Gallier at home. It was his day off. "I think we've got him," Dunn said. "This girl ID'd him."

"Finally," Gallier hissed, knowing the difference in this case was that Bergstrom had gone far enough to show intent.

Dunn drove Jenny downtown, where she recounted her story to Gallier. Under questioning, the girl held up well.

More than anything, she was angry. But every time she recounted Bergstrom's threat to kill her, she cried.

"Jenny, Sergeant Dunn is going to take you home," Gallier finally told her. "You've done well. I think you may have corralled this guy for us."

Chapter Forty-One

Tonry was working a homicide investigation that Friday afternoon when Fidelibus, Gallier, and Dunn met in an HPD conference room to compare files one last time. Their best bet, they decided, was to package the two cases in which they had ID and could easily prove intent—Jenny Karr as an attempted sexual assault and Sandy Colyard's case as a burglary. With Bergstrom still free, they wanted to do the bare minimum to get a felony warrant as quickly as possible. "We wanted to catch Bergstrom at work because we knew as soon as he got off, he'd be out looking for more victims," Dunn explained later. "We needed to get him before he had the opportunity to hurt anyone else. This guy had been loose for too long."

Dunn called the assistant DA he and Gallier had consulted the day before. "It sounds like you've got a case," the prosecutor told him. "Get your stuff together and let's go." Fidelibus and Gallier headed to the criminal courts building to get the arrest warrant; Dunn left to pick up another officer in Clear Lake to set up surveillance on Bergstrom, anxious to move in as soon as they received the go-ahead.

At the courthouse, Gallier and Fidelibus sought out the assistant DA. They handed him the Karr and Colyard files and then held their breath. No one wanted a holdup when they were so close.

To their relief, the prosecutor smiled up at them. "I think you've got enough for your warrant, gentlemen," he said. "Let's go see a judge."

As Fidelibus and Gallier talked to the judge, Dunn drove to Devoe & Raynolds with HPD Sergeant Victor Rodriguez in an unmarked squad car. The afternoon had dwindled away and it was nearly 4:30 P.M., Bergstrom's quitting time, when the call finally came in on the police radio from Gallier.

"The ink's not even dry yet, but we've got the warrant on both counts," Gallier beamed. "Pick him up and let's rope him in."

"You guys took long enough," Dunn laughed. "Let's get him."

Dunn entered Devoe & Raynolds' main office just after four that afternoon, flashed his badge to the glassed-in receptionist, and said, "I'm Sergeant Charles Dunn, HPD, and I'd like to talk to James Bergstrom."

Surprised that a police officer would be asking for James, the woman stuck her head into a nearby office, and a supervisor came out and shook Dunn's hand.

"I hear you're looking for James Bergstrom," the man said. "Is there a problem? What do you want him for?"

"I can't tell you that," Dunn replied. "We'd just like a few words with him."

The supervisor told the receptionist to call James to the office. As he waited, Dunn saw workers in lab coats walking past the office. Word had spread quickly through the plant that the police were up front asking questions about James. Curious, the men scanned Dunn's face for a clue. Dunn stared back, assessing not the workers but what they wore: white hard hats—just like the one Bergstrom had on in at least two of the assaults.

"Bergstrom's already left for the day," the supervisor finally returned to tell Dunn. "Can't you give me some idea why you're here?"

"No," the officer snapped. "But thanks anyway."

All Dunn could do now was head for James and Linda's apartment at Painter's Mill and wait. "It was just crazy. I was beside myself," he'd say later. "I knew he was out stalking someone else, and there was nothing I could do."

Actually James Bergstrom had been gone from Devoe & Raynolds for nearly an hour when Dunn entered the plant. Gino noticed he'd left when at 3:00 P.M. Allen Gibson asked if his brother-in-law had gone home sick again.

"Gee, I don't know," Gino shrugged. "Could have."

"He's already missed two days this week." Gibson frowned. "He'd better watch it or someone will start noticing."

Getting in trouble at work was the last concern on James Bergstrom's mind that afternoon. As he had for months, he thought of nothing but leaving the plant and getting out on the streets in his car. When he wasn't stalking, he envisioned himself behind the wheel, rap music pounding, watching. He was the hunter stalking his prey. He enjoyed knowing that the women went about their lives as unaware of him as of a growing cancer. The element of surprise made the process more exciting. In James Bergstrom's mind his quarry had long since stopped being individuals, women with children, husbands or boyfriends, family and friends. To him, they were barely human. He'd never hunted wild animals, but Bergstrom was sure this was how it felt.

Dunn was getting nervous. He and Rodriguez sat in their unmarked car outside the Bergstroms' apartment waiting for their target to drive into the parking lot for more than an hour. The longer he waited, the more Dunn worried. Always in the back of his mind was the unspoken fear that as they sat idly by, Bergstrom attacked another victim. Another life damaged. *He'd threatened to kill that last girl,* Dunn thought. *Maybe this time he'll be desperate enough to do it.*

Gallier called twice to say he and Fidelibus were stuck in rush-hour traffic but on their way with the warrant.

"Have you got him yet?" he asked.

"Not yet," Dunn said.

"He'll be there," Gallier assured him. There was no reason to believe Bergstrom had any idea about what was about to go down. Gallier anxiously anticipated, not Bergstrom's possible escape, but what would happen once they had him under arrest. There was still no evidence tying him to any of the actual rapes. Though Karr's case established intent and they could use it to package the cases, arguing Bergstrom had used a similar MO, it was at best a weak case, one easily dismantled by a competent defense attorney.

"Get me a good confession and we can put this guy away for a long time," the prosecutor had urged as the two officers ran from the courthouse. "Without it, he'll be out in no time."

As they drove down the freeway, Gallier wondered how Bergstrom would respond. He thought about the role-playing he and Fidelibus would both have to do to convince him to confess. "We couldn't go up there angry and treat him like a disease. We basically had to think like a rapist thinks. We had to convince him that we understood him," said Gallier. "We had to tell him that he was right, and that women are bitches and that they aren't good for anything other than a piece of ass."

Just after 5:30 P.M., Dunn recognized a brown Grand Prix with Bergstrom's license plate number pull into the apartment complex parking lot. James drove past the two men in the unmarked car without noticing them. He was distracted, tired and frustrated. The afternoon had panned dry. When he'd found no likely victims, he'd tired of the game and driven past Eddie Smith's apartment to see if his friend was home. When he wasn't, Bergstrom decided to return to his apartment at Painter's Mill to wait for his wife and daughter.

As James pulled into his parking space, Dunn maneuvered the unmarked squad car in behind him, parking him in. Both officers, guns drawn, approached Bergstrom from opposite sides of the car. "Get out. Hands up," Dunn shouted, holding out his badge. "Police."

Bergstrom stepped out, his hands in the air. "What's this all about?" he asked calmly.

Dunn looked down into the car and noticed a hard hat, clipboard, and test tube in the front passenger seat. "There are charges and a warrant on the way. Attempted sexual assault," Dunn snapped, handcuffing Bergstrom's wrists in front of him. "You have the right to remain silent . . ."

When he finished reading him his rights, Bergstrom immediately waived his right to an attorney. "I don't know what you're talking about." He shrugged, avoiding Dunn's steady gaze. "I haven't done anything."

"Mr. Bergstrom," Dunn said, "you're no longer in Washington State, and this time it won't end up the same way."

James appeared stunned, as if Dunn had slapped him.

"I've got this problem," Bergstrom said, suddenly humbled. "I need help."

"That's obvious," said Dunn, handing him a consent-to-search form for the car as Rodriguez radioed Gallier and Fidelibus that they had Bergstrom in custody.

"Should I sign this?" Bergstrom asked.

"You can cooperate or we can do this the hard way and get a search warrant," Dunn said. "It's up to you."

Bergstrom hesitated, then signed the form. As Dunn watched his prisoner, Rodriguez searched the car. From the trunk, he pulled out a ski mask and a gun. At first Dunn thought the handgun was real, but on closer inspection he realized it was a convincing copy. Then Dunn ordered Bergstrom into the backseat of his squad car. "I knew how important that confession was," he'd say later. "I didn't want to do anything to start him talking and risk fouling it up."

Gallier and Fidelibus pulled into Painter's Mill ten minutes after Bergstrom's arrest. They quickly picked Dunn's car out of the parking lot, and as they drove up, Gallier rolled down his window and Dunn filled the two detectives in on what had transpired. Then Gallier walked over to meet the man he'd been hunting for nearly three months.

"I just wanted to walk up and give him a hug and a thank you for the seventeen-year-old. The timing was phenomenal. Without her, we'd have gone ahead and filed and had practically nothing," Gallier would say later. "But I couldn't be cocky. I needed a confession. I treated him like he was just my little friend."

"James," Gallier said as he opened the car door and helped Bergstrom out of the backseat. "I'm Sergeant Rusty Gallier with the Houston Police Department."

"Yeah, I recognize you," Bergstrom said.

"Recognize me?"

"Yeah," he explained. "I saw you on television last fall with that rapist, the one with all the lingerie. I used to watch all those reports to see how the other guys got caught."

Gallier smiled.

"I know it looks bad, but keep your chin up," he said, downplaying Bergstrom's problems as he always did when he needed to get a suspect to talk. "At least you didn't kill anybody."

Bergstrom nodded in agreement.

Gallier touched Bergstrom on the arm, making physical contact. It was a ploy he used often with rapists. "I'm going to read you your rights again, James," he said, his voice dripping with concern. "You listen carefully. But remember, you're not that different from me or any other man. Lots of us have thought about doing what you did. You have the right to . . ."

When Gallier finished, Bergstrom again declined his right to an attorney. Gallier recorded the reading and his refusal in his notes. If he got a confession, all this would be paramount when Bergstrom's defense attorney, as they all did, fought to keep his client's confession from the jury's ears.

"We'd like you to sign a consent to search the apartment, James," Gallier said next.

"I don't know," Bergstrom said.

"James, we've been watching you for months," Gallier said. "We can do this the hard way or the easy way. What's it going to be?"

"Let's do it the easy way," Bergstrom said.

"Great." Gallier smiled. "Now, why don't you sign this and then take us in the apartment. Show us the clothes you wore when you did these things."

Upstairs Bergstrom pulled out nearly everything he owned. All his shirts and warm-ups. "All this, James?" Gallier asked.

"Yeah," said Bergstrom. "I think you'll need it all."

When they were finished in the apartment, Dunn loaded Bergstrom into the back of his car and drove him toward the Clear Lake Substation, where Fidelibus and Gallier planned to begin the interrogation.

Though Dunn attempted to change the subject, Bergstrom kept trying to confess in the car. "I've got this problem. It's all I think about, twenty-four hours a day," he said. "If I cooperate, will I get help?"

"Listen," Dunn said. "I don't know what'll happen. I'm not Monty Hall and I can't make a deal."

At the substation, Dunn deposited Bergstrom in a glassed-in conference room.

"Want a Coke, James?" Gallier asked when he arrived.

"Sure," he said. "Can I call my wife?"

"Of course," Gallier said. "Go right ahead."

James dialed the apartment, and when Linda didn't answer, he left a message on the answering machine.

For the third time that afternoon, Gallier again read Bergstrom his Miranda rights and again James declined.

"So now, James," said Gallier, with the niceties out of the way. "I think we need to have a little talk to find out what's going on here." Gallier sensed Bergstrom would open up easily. This obsession had ruled his life, and yet he hadn't spoken of it with anyone. Not even his best friends at the paint company knew what he was doing. "Then all of a sudden, I come along and I tell him I understand about him," said Gallier later. "It's a psychological game. Once you understand that, you don't have to play by the rules. You handle enough cases, you can tell a rapist more about himself than he knows. I never coerce them. You've got to be careful not to cross that line. Do I lie to them and tell them what they've done isn't so bad? Sure I lie. It's not against the law to lie to a rapist."

To James, Gallier said, "I think you should know something. I understand what you did. A lot of guys think about it. I have fantasies, too. I've always wondered what it was like to take a shoestring and put a mask on so that nobody would know. To tie the woman's hands. Feel her arms shivering. I tie the knot tight," Gallier said, watching James's eyes glaze over as he slipped into his fantasy world. "The only difference between you and me is that you had the balls to go out and do it."

Fidelibus sat at a typewriter and hit the keys with a steady clack clack as Gallier and James talked. Gallier began the conversation with the attacks he was most certain of, a triangle where the top consisted of those cases in which they had identification.

"Let's start with that little blond Clear Lake girl you did yesterday," Gallier said.

"I knew she saw my face," Bergstrom said. "I noticed her when she was coming home . . ."

Gallier listened attentively, rearing up angrily against Bergstrom each time he strayed from the facts.

"You're not playing straight with me, James," Gallier said, fuming if his account didn't ring true. "I thought we understood each other, but you're not telling the truth."

Carefully Bergstrom backtracked, correcting everything, apologizing over and over. In a few short hours, Gallier had taught his prisoner to need his approval, and he wanted him to know that he couldn't be fooled.

Before long, Bergstrom admitted all three attacks in which the officers had ID: Sandy Colyard, Andrea Hoggen, and Jenny Karr. Carefully Gallier worked the questioning around until Bergstrom admitted his intention was to rape each of the women. Always in the back of Gallier's mind was what the prosecution would need when the case entered a courtroom.

Then, as he saw the lines of black ink collecting on Fidelibus's typewriter, Gallier turned the conversation to a less certain subject—the rape of Maggie Heller.

"That's the woman on Edgebrook Drive," Gallier prompted.

"Yeah, I remember her," Bergstrom piped in. "The woman who was washing clothes . . ."

At 7:30 P.M. Linda arrived home with Ashley. She'd made it a point for weeks to stay away as much as possible, giving James ample room to trap himself. But now she walked in and found the apartment in chaos. Kitchen drawers were open and emptied onto the floor; in the bedroom, clothes were scattered about. To Linda it could only mean one thing: Somehow James had learned that she'd made plans to run the next morning, leaving him and all the pain behind. She was terrified. She half expected him to jump out at her from a closet, his fists clenched, the veins in his neck protruding in anger. Then she saw the message light flashing on the answering machine. She hit the button.

"Linda, it's me," said her husband's voice. "Please call."

Linda dialed the number James had left on the machine, her heart pounding against her eardrums.

"Clear Lake Substation," a voice asked.

"Is James Bergstrom there?" she asked, trying not to become hopeful. "This is his wife.'

"I've been arrested," James said when he answered. "Can you bring Ashley here? This may be the last time I get to hold her. Things got out of hand. You'll never know how bad."

Finally, Linda thought. *It's over.*

It was 8:45 P.M. when Linda entered the Clear Lake Substation. Ashley on her hip, Linda found James seated with two men in the conference room.

"Are you Linda?" Frank Fidelibus asked, walking out to meet her.

"Yeah," she said. "What's going on?"

"Rusty's got him talking pretty good," he said. "Come on in."

The two cops walked to the other side of the room to watch, leaving Linda and James alone. Gallier neither looked up nor acknowledged Linda, anxious to be sure James Bergstrom never discovered she'd been the instrument of his capture. As he and Fidelibus watched, the Bergstroms talked. It was easy to sense the frigid cold that accompanied Linda into the room, but Gallier noticed James perceived none of it. It was obvious Bergstrom had no idea how his wife or any other human being besides himself felt.

James reached out for Linda, but she pulled away. Ashley ran to her father. James picked her up and held her in his arms. "What should I tell them?" he asked Linda.

"Everything," she said. "Tell them everything."

Before Linda arrived, James had admitted three attempted sexual assaults and one rape: that of Maggie Heller. Letting him talk to Linda was a risky call. He'd been cooperating well. They didn't know how a meeting with Linda would affect him. Gallier and Fidelibus were both relieved when, after Linda's departure, James talked as freely as before.

As the evening melted into night, Gallier continued to play Bergstrom like a harp, plucking each string precisely far enough to get the desired results. He worked Bergstrom's emotions, tearing him down, then building him up. One by one, accounts of other attacks they'd suspected him of eked

out, detail by detail. Fidelibus clicked away on the typewriter, recording each word of Bergstrom's recounting of
the rape of Jesse Neal, the waitress. As the night wore on,
James appeared tired yet cold and unemotional, describing
in clinical terms what he did to each of the women and how
they reacted. He continually maintained he hadn't really
hurt the women because he hadn't been physically violent
with them. To the two officers it sometimes seemed as if
Bergstrom had thought he'd been on a date with the women.
Though he'd held a gun to their heads or a knife to their
throats, in his mind they were willing participants.

Sometimes when the atmosphere in the room became too
heavy, Gallier sensed Bergstrom straying into his other
world. The HPD sergeant let Bergstrom drift off, his eyes
glazing over. Gallier knew he was recounting one of the
rapes in his mind. "He kept mumbling about some woman
with long red fingernails," Gallier recalled later. "It was like
he was reliving that rape in his mind. We didn't know yet
who she was."

Always Bergstrom returned from his fantasies refreshed
and eager to talk.

Led by Gallier, Bergstrom confessed to the ten cases
they'd most suspected him of, including the attempted rapes
of Andrea Hoggen, Sandy Colyard, and Jenny Karr, and the
rapes of Jesse Neal, the waitress, and—the case that haunted
Gallier the most—Maggie Heller, the Christian woman who'd
cried in his office.

Then Gallier adopted a new tack. He felt certain there
were other rapes out there—including the woman with the
red nails. He needed to know who these women were. He
needed Bergstrom to pick up the momentum of the confession on his own. "Now, James, you're gonna get charged
here tonight. You're not getting out of this," Gallier said.
"It's not going away. You're going to prison."

Bergstrom looked down at his hands.

"You're telling me you didn't hurt anyone. Let me explain
it to you. You see these women for a few minutes. I see them

forever," Gallier said, sternly. "They're afraid to leave their houses or go out at night because an unknown man with a mask attacked them. Think about how they feel."

Bergstrom looked unmoved, almost curious. He appeared as surprised as if Gallier had seriously claimed the moon was fashioned from green cheese.

"At some point, I'm going to be up on a witness stand," Gallier went on. "What will I tell them? That you're an arrogant son of a bitch who doesn't care about anybody? That you didn't think you'd done anything wrong? What will you do when you get out of jail? Do this again? Do you feel any remorse?"

Picking up on Gallier's clue, Bergstrom looked sorrowfully down at his hands, then rubbed his eyes until they were rimmed in red. "Yes, I'm remorseful," Bergstrom said.

"You should do something to let all these women know who you are, James, so they don't have nightmares anymore. So that they can get on with the healing process of their lives. So that you can get on with the healing process of your life."

James Bergstrom looked warily at Gallier. The officer had implied confession might be good for more than his soul. Then he confessed to two cases Gallier had long since written off as not his: the rapes of Cindy McKenzie, the saleswoman with the long red fingernails who'd been attacked as she packed for a routine business trip to Corpus Christi, and of Kimberly Greenmen.

"There was this woman. She had a little girl who was hiding in the kitchen. She must have been about two." Bergstrom began talking about the attack on Greenmen. "I think she'd been paying bills . . ."

By the time Bergstrom finished, it was well after midnight and he'd confessed to four rapes and a string of ten specific attempted rapes. In addition, he talked of other attacks, including two rapes Gallier and Fidelibus couldn't match up with any existing cases. The officers assumed the victims were most likely women who had never reported their assaults.

As the night drew to an end, Gallier and Fidelibus felt certain Bergstrom was undoubtedly responsible for more rapes and attempted rapes than they'd ever know. There had been so many victims that, in the muddle of his fantasy world, James Bergstrom had a difficult time sorting out the different women he'd assaulted. When Gallier asked him how many women he estimated he'd attacked in Houston during the previous two years, unblinkingly Bergstrom guessed as many as thirty. In unspecific terms, he then went on to admit committing one rape in Washington State.

Fidelibus tapped the typewritten sheets of James Bergstrom's confession on the table and handed it to Rusty Gallier. It had come down to one final question: Would James sign it? Gallier looked the pages over. Without a signature, in a courtroom it would be the two officers' word against Bergstrom's. Gallier handed the stack of paper to James and waited.

"We need you to read these and then sign each page," Gallier explained calmly.

"Should I?" Bergstrom asked.

"That's up to you," Gallier said. "I'm not here to give you legal advice. I'm here for your victims. Is it all true?"

"Yeah. It is."

Bergstrom stared at the sheets a moment longer, then paged through them, reading slowly. When he was done he signed each page. Then he handed the stack to Gallier.

"Thanks," Gallier said, smiling. It was the biggest serial rape case he'd ever helped crack. It cleared more cases than any single arrest he'd ever made. The next day Gallier and Fidelibus would videotape Bergstrom's confession for the record, and James Bergstrom would be indicted on fifteen felony counts including four rapes.

Yet none of the officers felt like a hero. Everyone agreed that if there was credit, it belonged to Linda Bergstrom. "We probably would have gotten James eventually," Gallier would say later. "But it may have been a long time. He was cagier than any rapist I'd tracked before. If she hadn't alerted us to him, there could have been a lot more victims before he ever saw the inside of a cell."

Gallier and Fidelibus were exhausted when they checked their prisoner in for the night at the county jail. Sergeant Charles Dunn had clocked thirty-two hours overtime since his landlord had called him Sunday night; he didn't regret an hour of it. Now all that remained was to see that Bergstrom's confessions held up in court. Though they didn't discuss it, each officer was aware of the revolving door of Texas prisons. It was general knowledge that the state's parole board, under court order to stop prison overcrowding, released prisoners serving as little as a month for every year of their sentence. Unless the jury came down hard on Bergstrom, he'd be out in no time. None of them doubted that he'd soon revert to his old ways, free to rape again.

Chapter Forty-Two

When the first newspaper account of Bergstrom's arrest ran in the *Houston Post* on Thursday, April 2, 1992, it appeared Linda might be able to maintain the anonymity she so desired. Under the headline "Officers Hope to ID Suspect as Serial Rapist," Gallier was quoted as saying police had known a serial rapist prowled Houston's southern suburbs since the previous December but that they hadn't pinned Bergstrom as the attacker until he began posing as a water tester in March.

But by the following day, the *Post* carried a new story: one of the wife who had turned in her rapist husband. Though she'd told no one, somehow there'd been a leak. The article quoted residents at Painter's Mill, the Bergstroms' complex, who'd connected their neighbor's arrest with the flyer the apartment's management had circulated after the rape of Maggie Heller.

For days, newspaper and television reporters canvassed Painter's Mill, interviewing neighbors and apartment personnel about James and Linda Bergstrom. Some maintained James seemed a quiet, shy family man with a young daughter and wife, not the type one would imagine as a serial rapist. They pointed out that he had a good-paying job. Others mentioned fighting and shouting they'd heard emanating from the Bergstroms' apartment.

As Linda knew it would, the phone rang in her apartment the afternoon the story broke.

"If it weren't for you, I wouldn't be here," James Bergstrom said, seething from a phone at the Harris County Jail. "You did this to me. You're the one who turned me in."

Chapter Forty-Three

The two camps—prosecution and defense—formed quickly after James Bergstrom's arrest. Chuck Rosenthal, prematurely silver-haired and chronically rumpled but one of the district attorney's most effective assistants, took over for the state. A division chief with seventeen years of experience, Rosenthal, who routinely handled high-profile homicides, just happened to be on intake at the courthouse the day the indictments against Bergstrom were filed. He'd stuck with the case after interviewing the victims. "The most difficult thing in rape cases is establishing a rapport with the victims," Rosenthal would say later. "I didn't want them to think they were being passed around from lawyer to lawyer."

Still it was an uncomfortable case for the prosecutor. Rosenthal had grown up in Texas's valley, near the Mexican border, in a family that didn't discuss such personal matters. "I had a difficult time talking to the women about the specifics of what happened," he'd explain later. "The way I was raised, women didn't talk about that kind of thing unless it's a doctor-patient relationship."

Yet as Rosenthal investigated the case, his first prosecution of a serial rapist, he found it fascinating. "Bergstrom lacked that gene that lets him know other people hurt," he'd say. "The one that it takes to control sexual impulses. There was just something inherently wrong with the guy."

Danny Easterling became Rosenthal's adversary when the court appointed him to take on Bergstrom's case. A tall, lanky redhead who resembles a youngish Red Skelton, the thirty-seven-year-old Easterling had been a defense attorney for eleven years, handling everything from murder cases to traffic tickets. It didn't take long for him to see that this particular client was an attorney's nightmare. "Any competent defense attorney would not have let him give the type of statements and confessions he did," Easterling said later. "He was talking to the police for a week before I was called in."

Ironically, before Rosenthal and Easterling would battle it out in court, there would be another fight, one with Linda at the center. Since the day her story first hit the newspaper, she'd been besieged by requests for interviews by reporters. In fact, the story of the serial rapist turned in by his wife had made headlines off and on all spring.

For Linda, the attention was unwanted. Afraid James Bergstrom would one day want revenge, she would have preferred remaining in the background, allowing Gallier and the other officers to take the credit for her husband's arrest. But once her story broke in the papers and that option was snatched away, she grudgingly decided to raise questions about the nightmare she'd lived. How could police have ignored her for so long? In a Sunday *Houston Chronicle* article, she asked: "Why wouldn't they listen?" Linda appeared on "A Current Affair" questioning why not only police but James's family had failed to come to her aide. *Ladies' Home Journal, People,* and other magazines queued up for interviews. "The Maury Povich Show" scheduled her for a segment, and offers from TV movie producers flooded in.

Then the same criminal justice system that had failed to heed Linda's warnings for more than two years silenced her. Easterling, arguing Linda's interviews would taint the pool of prospective jurors, petitioned the court for a gag order.

State District Judge Carl Walker agreed with Easterling's argument that Linda Bergstrom's First Amendment rights had to bend to her husband's right to a fair trial. Throughout the years of James Bergstrom's beatings and threats, Linda had fought and refused to remain silent. It could only be described as ironic that now that she'd succeeded, the very legal system that had ignored her warnings ultimately succeeded in, at least temporarily, silencing her. She was ordered by the court not to tell her story until her husband's trial was over.

Throughout the summer the legal finagling that surrounds a criminal trial continued. Easterling, as Gallier and the other officers knew he would, immediately filed a motion to suppress James Bergstrom's confession, alleging it was given involuntarily "because there were promises made and inducements." As evidence, Easterling referred to Bergstrom's constant reference to "my problem," and argued that police gave his client the impression that by confessing, he would be given medical care.

On September 11, 1992, three weeks before Bergstrom's scheduled trial date, Rosenthal and Easterling, with his client in tow, stood before Judge Walker to discuss the admissibility of James Bergstrom's confessions. It was a long afternoon. The judge, a balding man with gold-rimmed glasses, frowned from behind his bench as the argument raged. The subject of it all, James Bergstrom, sat silently by in a pale tan jail-issue jumpsuit.

One after the other, the police officers who handled Bergstrom's arrest were called to testify.

"Did you hear Sergeant Gallier read the defendant his rights?" Rosenthal asked Fidelibus.

"Yes, I did," the detective asserted. "Right off the Miranda card."

"Weren't there promises made to Mr. Bergstrom that if he cooperated, y'all would get him help for his problem?" Easterling countered.

"No, sir," Fidelibus said. "Not that I heard."

Dunn gave similar testimony.

"Didn't Mr. Bergstrom tell you, 'I need help'?" Easterling prodded.

"Yes, sir," Dunn said. "And I said I wasn't Monty Hall and I couldn't make him any deals."

Then Rosenthal played the videotaped confession. On the courtroom television screen, as a hushed audience of reporters watched, James Bergstrom, dressed in a blue shirt with rolled-up sleeves and off-white pants, stared at the floor as Rusty Gallier, his back to the camera, read him his Miranda rights.

"Do you understand what I've read you?" Gallier asked.

"Yes," Bergstrom said, mumbling as he would throughout the tape.

"Have you been promised anything to cooperate?"

"No."

Throughout the rest of the hour-long tape, Bergstrom answered Gallier's questions. He admitted how he had circulated through quiet neighborhoods in a sweat suit with a towel thrown over his shoulders. "The ropes or shoestrings were in my sock," he said. "And the ski mask and gun were wrapped up in a towel I threw over my neck. At first I picked the women out randomly. Then I started watching them."

When Gallier inquired about individual cases, Bergstrom acknowledged each and filled in details. At the end Gallier asked, "How many women have you attacked altogether, James?"

"In Houston?"

"Yeah," Gallier said.

"Twenty-five, maybe thirty."

It was damning evidence, the type nearly impossible for a defense attorney to combat.

The next witness was Detective Tonry; the final, Sergeant Rusty Gallier. Both maintained Bergstrom had been given no promises in exchange for his confession.

At the end of the day, Rosenthal was victorious. James Bergstrom was scheduled for trial September 29, and Walker ruled the videotaped confession was admissible.

Negotiations continued as the days counted down to the trial. Rosenthal offered a plea bargain, forty-five years.

Bergstrom refused.

Chapter Forty-Four

The phone rang continually in Linda Bergstrom's apartment in the weeks before the trial. Throughout the night, the answering machine clicked on and off as James obsessively telephoned from the county jail. Usually she'd try to ignore the constant interruptions, but sometimes it wore her down until Linda accepted a call, relayed at a cost of $1.30 each by a jail operator.

"I'm going to get out of here," James would say. "I didn't do anything so awful to them. It's your fault. You turned me in."

"I didn't have a choice," she'd tell him. "You should have gotten help. I tried to get you to see a doctor."

Always she would remind him that the divorce she'd filed for soon after his arrest was final. She was no longer his wife.

"You'll always be my wife," he countered. "Till death do us part, remember? I'm going to get out of here and we'll be a family again."

In desperation, she had her number changed to an unlisted one. Somehow he managed to get it and called again, angry that she'd tried to avoid him. At her request, Southwestern Bell installed a block on her phone to stop his incessant badgering. Then James traded away food to other prisoners in return for their friends and relatives patching him through on three-way calling. Nothing she did seemed to be able to stop him.

At the district attorney's office, the plans for the upcoming trial were taking shape. Bergstrom didn't yet know, but

Rosenthal's plan was to try his best cases, the four actual rapes and the burglary of Sandy Colyard. By grouping them, he reasoned it would be easy for a jury to see that Bergstrom's intention was also to rape Colyard. As backup, he decided to hold in reserve the attempted sexual assaults on Jenny Karr, Andrea Hoggen, Ann Cook, and the others. "I didn't want to confuse the jury by throwing too many cases at them," Rosenthal reasoned. "And I wanted to keep some as a fallback in case I got a bad jury or did a bad job. I wanted more ammunition ready."

Yet he had doubts about his star witnesses' willingness to testify. As the trial neared, a contagious case of cold feet made its way through their ranks. Kim Greenmen, the mother, had left her husband and was living in San Antonio. She'd just started a new job and didn't want to take the time off. Cindy McKenzie, the saleswoman, was afraid if anyone found out about the rape, it could make people view her differently, maybe hurt her career. Maggie Heller, out of the hospital but still having a difficult time coping, wasn't sure she was strong enough. And Jesse Neal had disappeared. Rosenthal couldn't find her. The only one who seemed anxious to testify was Sandy Colyard, and hers wasn't an actual rape case; the charge still stood as burglary.

When the courthouse scuttlebutt brought the prosecutor the information that Easterling had asked for money from the judge to hire an investigator to help in Bergstrom's defense, Rosenthal was even more worried. After checking with his witnesses and finding no one an investigator had approached, he came to the conclusion that Easterling intended to work another angle.

"I knew he was probably hiring some expert witnesses, probably a psychologist," Rosenthal said. "I figured I better find an expert of my own."

The doctor Rosenthal consulted was Michael Jones, Ph.D., a psychologist specializing in adult survivors of abuse. When the prosecutor forwarded a videotape of Bergstrom's confession and a copy of his file, he asked Jones to draw up a profile of Bergstrom for him. "I need to know about this guy," he told him. "Make me a twenty-four-hour expert in rape."

When Jones called Rosenthal back a week later, he began with the impressions he'd gleaned from the taped confession. "This guy really believed he had a minimal impact on his victims," Jones explained. "That's dangerous. In fact, he left deep scars. In his fantasy, he was on a date with these women while he held a gun to their heads. Think of the next time a boyfriend or husband makes love to them. Think of the confusion they'll feel. They're going to have all the symptoms of post-traumatic stress disorder. Two times more likely to commit suicide or experience depression within two years after the attack. Three of four women have a major change in life because of rape: divorce, relationship, their jobs. They can't sleep, have exaggerated responses to problems. It has profound effects.

"As to Bergstrom, he lives in a fantasy world with major distortions and has a tremendous lack of empathy. This guy's going to say he's sorry. He's only sorry he got caught."

"What about treatment?" Rosenthal asked. "What if the defense argues he can be put on probation, monitored and treated?"

"This is such an entrenched problem and he's hurt so many people that he's demonstrated he can't be trusted to be outside prison walls," Jones said. "Some treatment, it could be argued, is better than no treatment. But there's no real evidence that there's a treatment guaranteed to work. It'd be a real roll of the dice."

Rosenthal came away from the conversation with Jones convinced the only treatment for James Bergstrom was a long-term stay in the Texas prison system. "Other people you put in prison, there is at least the anticipation that prison will be such a bad place that it'll factor into whether or not they will commit that crime again," he'd say later. "But I didn't think that with Bergstrom it would matter. I think he's the kind of guy who will eventually give in to his impulses again. It would just be a matter of time."

Then Easterling and Bergstrom threw Rosenthal the kind of pretrial curve ball that could leave a less experienced prosecutor slicing air. The day before their date in the courtroom, Bergstrom changed his plea in all five cases to guilty, but he wanted a jury, not the judge, to sentence him. He planned to beg for forgiveness and throw himself on the mercy of a jury of his peers.

"It scared me when he came in and admitted he was doing wrong and apologized, pleaded 'I'm sorry . . .' I was afraid," Rosenthal recounted later. "Because you don't know what a jury will do. They might be touched enough to give him leniency. You can never predict how remorse will play to a jury."

Chapter Forty-Five

Jury selection in the sentencing trial of James Bergstrom commenced at half past nine on the morning of September 29, 1992. State District Judge Carl Walker opened the proceedings by reading the indictment, four counts of aggravated sexual assault with a deadly weapon and one charge of burglary. Possible penalties ranged from probation to life imprisonment.

Quickly during voir dire, the defense attorney's and prosecutor's opportunity to question prospective jurors, the issues that would dominate this, the sentencing phase of the trial, became finely defined. "Have you or any member of your family ever been the victim of a violent crime?" Danny Easterling asked, attempting to weed out anyone who harbored a personal grudge that could influence the sentence. Then, as an indication of what he would ask jurors to do later, "Would you be open to considering probation as an option in this case if the circumstances indicated it?"

When it was the prosecution's turn, Rosenthal took the opposite approach. "Would you, in the proper case, be able to assess a punishment as severe as life in prison?" he asked each prospective juror. Then, "Have you seen any news reports on this case that would hinder your ability to keep an open mind?"

Three hours later, James Bergstrom had his jury—ten women and two men.

By the time the prosecution mounted its attack that afternoon, Chuck Rosenthal theoretically had everything in place to put James Bergstrom in jail for a very long time. All four rape victims and Sandy Colyard had finally and reluctantly agreed to testify. The day before the trial, an investigator for the DA's office had tracked Jesse Neal to a small town outside Houston. Rosenthal had driven there with Tonry to appeal to her in person. "All I could tell the women was that this was the only way to keep Bergstrom from doing it to someone else," Rosenthal recounted later. "None of them wanted to see him out on the streets again."

As in Washington State, Texas law prohibited Linda Bergstrom from testifying against her ex-husband. She sat silently on one of the massive courtroom benches, surrounded by reporters who noted her every expression. Though she had anticipated this day for years, she felt no exhilaration, rather a deep sadness and an all-consuming fear. "I knew if they didn't put James away for a long time, he'd come after me," she'd say later. "He knew I was the one who put him in jail, and he'd want revenge."

As angry, threatening, and dangerous as James Bergstrom had been with his ski mask on stalking victims, in front of the jury entrusted with deciding his fate, he cultivated the manner of the timid, mild-mannered plant worker his friends at Devoe & Raynolds would have recognized. It was Easterling's job to get as light a sentence as possible for James Bergstrom, and his client's demeanor fit the defense's primary argument, that Bergstrom was ill and needed therapy, not imprisonment, and that if the jury put him away, James Bergstrom would only emerge from a Texas prison an angrier and more brutal predator.

Rosenthal watched Bergstrom's demeanor warily. "I hate to go to trial," he said later. "I do it all the time, but I worry through it every time. You just don't know what a jury is thinking. What is and isn't selling." Bergstrom's conspicuous repentance troubled the prosecutor as he called each of the five women to the stand to testify. It was paramount that the jury understand the damage Bergstrom, this man who now sniveled pathetically before the jury, had dealt each victim.

The prosecution went first.

The first witness on the stand that afternoon was Sandy Colyard, the fourth-grade teacher. She recounted in vivid detail how James Bergstrom, wearing a white hard hat and carrying a clipboard, had knocked on her door on her first day of spring break that March. Then she spoke of her terror when, minutes later, she saw a ski-masked man staring back at her in her bathroom mirror. "He told me to do exactly as he said and I wouldn't get hurt." Colyard grimaced. "He was holding a gun to my head."

"How has this affected you?" Rosenthal asked.

"It was three or four months before I could even sleep at night," Colyard maintained. Anger seething, she focused on Bergstrom, who stared repentantly at the floor, periodically rubbing his eyes until they were rimmed a bright red.

As he would with each victim, when Easterling took the floor, he attempted to minimize Bergstrom's attack on Colyard.

"Could the gun have been a BB gun or something like that?' he asked her.

"I don't know," she said. "It looked real to me."

Next the prosecution called Detective Frank Fidelibus, who recounted Colyard's identification of Bergstrom and the events on the day of his arrest. With Fidelibus, Rosenthal made the point that at least one of James Bergstrom's victims had seen his face and would have been able to identify him whether or not he'd admitted his guilt. That, he hoped, would mitigate the defense's portrait of Bergstrom as the cooperative and eager confessor.

When Easterling took over, he continued to grasp anything that shined a favorable light on his client.

"Isn't it true that Mr. Bergstrom was cooperative?" he asked during cross-examination.

"Yes," Fidelibus answered.

"In fact, he signed the consent to search both his car and apartment, didn't he?"

"Yes, he did."

"What happened to you after Mr. Bergstrom sexually assaulted you?" Rosenthal asked Maggie Heller when she took the stand.

"I spent five weeks in a psychiatric hospital," she said, clutching a handkerchief like a lifeline. "I just couldn't forget what happened. I don't like nighttime now. I'm still affected by it."

"What did he do with the gun?"

"It was cold," Heller said. "I could feel it pressed against my back. I asked him not to hurt me."

"Didn't he loosen the bindings on your hands when you said they were too tight?" Easterling then asked Heller.

"Yes," Heller said. "He did."

"Didn't he say he was sorry?"

"Yes."

"I kept asking him, 'Why are you doing this to me?'" Jesse Neal, the waitress, explained to Rosenthal when asked how the attack had changed her. "Afterward, I just couldn't concentrate on anything. I even lost my job. I just couldn't function. I couldn't tell anybody what happened."

"Didn't he say he was sorry for having to do this to you?" Easterling asked Neal.

"I don't remember," she said, her voice thick with rage and confusion. "Maybe. I don't see why someone has to do something like that."

"I can't be in the house alone anymore," Cindy McKenzie, the saleswoman with the long black hair, said when

Rosenthal asked how the attack had affected her. "Every time I hear a sound I start to cry."

"What did he do with the gun?"

"He put the barrel between my legs," she said, grimacing.

"What did Mr. Bergstrom tell you as he was leaving?" Easterling asked.

"He told me to keep the door locked in the future," McKenzie whispered.

"Where was your daughter while James Bergstrom was sexually assaulting you?" Rosenthal asked Kimberly Greenmen.

"I don't know," she said, staring at Bergstrom throughout her testimony. "She was in the kitchen watching from under a table when he came in."

"Didn't Mr. Bergstrom tell you before he left that your baby was okay?" Easterling asked.

"Yes," she said. "He did."

After Kimberly Greenmen, the prosecution rested.

The defense called its first witness: Irene Bergstrom. Prompted by Easterling, she gave the family history. How she'd met her husband in Greece while he was in the service. How James had been born in a military hospital in Germany, attended parochial school, played basketball and tennis, earned good grades, and never got in any trouble.

"You understand your son was arrested for sexual assaults?" Easterling asked her.

"Yes."

"What was your reaction?"

"I was in shock," James's mother said, her eyes wide at the prospect that her son could have been guilty of such acts. "I couldn't believe it."

"What is your son's attitude like now?"

"He cries a lot. He's sorry."

"What, in your estimation, would be a proper sentence for your son?"

"Something where he would get medical help."

"Would you be willing to assist in that?"

"Yes. That's my firstborn son. It hurts."

Rosenthal asked the harder questions.

"Didn't you know about your son's problems?"

"We didn't know he was raping girls," Irene Bergstrom persisted, her voice rising in alarm. "We asked him, 'Are you doing anything wrong, James?' He said, 'No.'"

When Easterling brought James C. to the stand, James's father looked nervous and tired.

"Mr. Bergstrom, what was your reaction to your son's arrest?"

"A combination of feelings. Crushed, enraged, I felt he'd failed me and the world. That he was kind of a Jekyll-and-Hyde combination, in conflict with the image others had of him. I knew he was mentally upset, somewhat dysfunctional. It seemed to me that he needed some kind of treatment . . . What little portion of goodness there's left in him would be eroded away in prison without treatment."

Next Easterling introduced his first expert witness, Walter Quijano, Ph.D., a former chief psychologist for the Texas Department of Corrections. He talked about the "limited slots" available in the prison program designed to treat sexual offenders and the unlikelihood that James Bergstrom would find adequate treatment within prison walls.

"How would you characterize James Bergstrom?" Easterling asked.

"He has a long-standing deviant sexual history. He first noticed it at a very early age between ten and twelve when he noticed he enjoyed watching television shows that used the combination of force, violence, and nudity or seminudity. He had a young girl he tied down and noticed he enjoyed that. He sexually assaulted her . . . He has a compulsive component. The thought of using force in sex introduces itself, it interjects into his thinking.

"There are a number of clinical impressions. One is pedophilia, a deviant attraction to prepubescent children. This has not reoccurred since the abuse of the girl. The second is voyeurism. The next is sexual sadism. In order to achieve sexual arousal, there is a need to humiliate another person or use force. He falls under the classification of rapists that is the power rapist. That is, the object is to overpower the woman and to have sex. The object is not so much the sex but the overpowering of the woman."

Then, when asked by Easterling, Quijano suggested an alternative treatment in a restrictive setting—the type of program involving electronic monitoring, group and individual therapy, and Depo-Provera, the testosterone-depleting drug sometimes referred to as chemical castration.

"Is it possible that with this type of program, Mr. Bergstrom's problem could be controlled?" Easterling asked.

"It is possible, with much treatment and supervision," Dr. Quijano answered.

Using the information gleaned from his crash course on power rapists, Rosenthal then took over Quijano's questioning.

"I suppose," said Rosenthal, "you're aware of research in the treatment of sexual offenders?"

"Yes."

"In terms of treatment, is there much data?"

"No."

"We really don't understand it well?" the prosecutor pressed.

"No," admitted Quijano. "In fact, there's almost no empirical data."

"Do you know if there's a moderate chance, a good chance, of recovery?"

"In terms of recovery?" Quijano qualified. "If by recovery you mean the disappearance of this impulse, this compulsion, no, that is not probable. Mr. Bergstrom is very ill."

"In terms of the Depo-Provera, isn't it true that testosterone naturally drops with age?" Rosenthal asked. "Most rapists aren't over forty, are they?"

"That's true."

"Wouldn't Mother Nature and Father Time be as effective as Depo-Provera?"

"Yes," said Quijano. "It would."

"Obviously the prison system would be a secure setting for Mr. Bergstrom, wouldn't it?"

"Yes," Quijano admitted. "It would."

The final expert was Dr. Michael Cox, a clinical psychologist at Baylor College of Medicine. As he had with Quijano, Easterling asked Cox to describe James Bergstrom's illness.

"Obviously this is a very serious and tragic disorder," the doctor explained. "It will take many years to feel at all confident that you've begun to turn around this particular disorder. The fantasy of bondage has been around for a long time, and to suppress and manage that fantasy takes a lot of intervention." Then Cox, like Quijano, outlined a program including electronic monitoring and treatment that he judged suitable for James Bergstrom.

When it was his turn to cross-examine, Rosenthal pointed at the jury box. "Dr. Cox," the prosecutor asked, "can you give these people any kind of guarantee Mr. Bergstrom can be rehabilitated?"

"I'm not in the business of selling appliances," Cox said. "I don't give guarantees. I can give probabilities and prognostic statements to the best of my knowledge. That's as far as I can go."

James Bergstrom, the trial's final witness, was next. Seated on the stand, he nervously worked his hands, kneading his palms, often staring up at the ceiling as if to quell tears. He rubbed his eyes, sometimes sobbing quietly, as Easterling took him through a short personal history for the jury. He talked about his years on the Pearland High School varsity basketball team, his refereeing for the YMCA, his tenure on a Trident nuclear sub, his honorable discharge, his stable employment of eleven years at Devoe & Raynolds. Finally he mentioned his "problem."

"It was something that ate away inside me. Something I fought day to day. I hate myself for that, for the problem I have. I need help," he said. Then, to the astonishment of anyone who had listened to the women's terrifying accounts of their rapes, "Thank God, I'm not a violent person who would seriously hurt anyone."

Bergstrom said that he'd been writing a letter of apology to his victims. "I pray every day to God that they and their families won't be forever hurt."

"Are you asking this jury to give you probation?" Easterling concluded.

"Yes," said Bergstrom. "I am."

"Who are you crying for?" Rosenthal asked when he took over questioning."

"I'm crying for everyone involved. It's a very big tragedy for everyone."

"Aren't you crying for yourself? Because you got caught?"

"No, for everyone. The victims, too."

"Mr. Bergstrom," Rosenthal continued. "Tell me again about your problem."

"I have a sexual problem. It's embarrassing. I don't understand why this happens," he answered. "I thank God, I'm not a violent person and I never really hurt anybody."

"You never really hurt anybody?" Rosenthal said, emphasizing Bergstrom's denial of responsibility for his victims' suffering.

"Not physically, no."

"Was this raping a thrill?"

"I don't know if I'd describe it as a thrill. It was something that ate away inside me," Bergstrom said again. "I was very confused about my problem."

"When you talk about 'my problem,' you understand that it's become society's problem?" Rosenthal queried, looking straight into Bergstrom's eyes.

"Yes," he said, deflecting the prosecutor's gaze.

"Mr. Bergstrom, are you telling this jury that if they decide to send you to prison, they'd better do it for a long time, because you'll have the same problem when you get out?"

"That's up to the jury."

Throughout his questioning, Kimberly Greenmen and the other victims watched Bergstrom's every move. Seated with their families, husbands and children, they apprehensively searched the faces of the jurors, wondering how Easterling's well-honed argument for probation was playing.

As Judge Walker dismissed the jury for the day and announced closing arguments would start the following morning, Greenmen's gaze fell again on Bergstrom, the man who had tied her up and raped her on a bright, sunny morning eighteen months earlier. "I wanted him to look at me," she'd say later. "He kept his head down and looked so pathetic. I wanted to ask him, 'Why me?' Why did he have to come into my house? Mess up my life?"

Exhausted from the tension, Linda Bergstrom drove home from court, stopping at the baby-sitter's house to pick up Ashley. Too tired to cook, she detoured through a McDonald's drive-through and bought her daughter a Happy Meal for dinner. That night in her small apartment, the phone rang continuously, as it had so many nights before, with calls from the county jail.

"They got me and they got me good," James said, when she finally accepted a call. "If I hadn't confessed, they never would have gotten me. Those cops lied to me. I thought I'd get treatment. Why didn't you get me a better lawyer? My parents aren't getting me a lawyer either. They say they can't afford it. I didn't hurt those women. I didn't even go all the way with them. I didn't put marks on their bodies, cut them up, or kill them."

"James, you had to be stopped," Linda whispered. "You didn't leave anyone any choice."

"You realize it was you who turned me in," he seethed. "If it wasn't for you, they never would have caught me."

Chapter Forty-Six

When the gavel sounded in Judge Walker's courtroom the following morning, a crowd gathered to hear closing arguments. James Bergstrom's victims and their families occupied the front row. Rosenthal had suggested they come. He wanted them to be highly visible when Danny Easterling, on Bergstrom's behalf, tried to diminish the violence and harm they'd suffered. The Bergstroms sat a few rows back. Often Irene Bergstrom covered her eyes with her hands, as if weary and trying to shut out the sights and sounds of the courtroom. James C. appeared resigned, as if he suspected the day before had not gone well. Perhaps he was considering the awesome responsibility of controlling his oldest son if the jury took Easterling's option and agreed to put James on probation. Surely an electronic monitor would be no match for a man trained in communications on a nuclear submarine.

Detective Frank Fidelibus had also returned. He'd become a part of the case the day he investigated the attack on Sandy Colyard, and he wanted to see it through. He was as worried as Rosenthal that if James Bergstrom somehow managed to escape prison, he would be facing him again someday, another courtroom, more victims.

Linda sat quietly at the far end of the room a few rows ahead of James C. and Irene Bergstrom. She nervously chipped at the remains of her fingernail polish, much of which she'd peeled away during the previous day's testimony.

She thought of Ashley at the sitter's house. She thought of the life she had pieced together for her daughter in the six months since her ex-husband's arrest. There wasn't a lot of money, but they'd managed. She'd disposed of everything in the apartment that reminded her of James, even the bed in which they'd slept. It was a modest beginning, but given a chance, she was sure she could make it work. If he was free again, she felt certain the nightmare would start all over. She knew the divorce wouldn't stop James from coming after her. *He blames me,* she thought.

In a very real sense, everything that had happened in the seven years of her marriage to James Bergstrom had led her to this point. Now it was out of her hands. Whether she would be allowed to start the new life she so desperately desired depended on the verdict of twelve strangers—the ten women and two men on the jury.

"As the judge tells you, you must consider the full range of punishment. That includes probation," Danny Easterling said, as he took the courtroom floor to begin closing arguments. "Let's talk about what you didn't see in the defendant. You didn't see a person who committed aggravated sexual assault and used violent and physical injury. What you didn't see is someone who is not remorseful. Someone who is uncooperative. Someone who didn't confess to four felony crimes that never would have been prosecuted but for his confession. What you didn't see is someone who refused to tell you, 'I need help.'

"This is a case that boils down to the classic decision. It's a tough choice. If you order probation and the judge orders treatment, you're doing something for society. You're doing something for his problem that will never happen again. If you cage him with other men and don't give him a realistic, quality chance at treatment, someday . . . he's going to get out. You never know exactly what type of person he's going to be, [if there's] a reasonable chance that he's going to repeat his criminal behavior and victimize other women, like these ladies.

"Or you take the chance on the man that [he has] got some good in him. A realistic chance at progressive treatment . . . This is a sickness we're dealing with here. The experts told us that . . . If you think Mr. Bergstrom is going to benefit from prison treatment, you're kidding yourselves. You have here the classic case of where do you draw the line? Where do you take the chance? This is a defendant who has enough good in him, and he has enough ability and potential to cure his problems with the proper restrictions. Throw him in a cage with other prisoners and he'll come out a bigger threat, a bitter criminal. Or let's give hope . . . probation with certain restrictions. Warehousing is not the answer."

Then it was assistant DA Chuck Rosenthal's turn: "Let's talk a little about the chronology of this thing. We know that when James Bergstrom was between ten and twelve years old, he started sexually abusing [a little girl] and tying her up and having fantasies about doing that with other women. We know that because the doctor told us the family found out and started locking the girls away. [The parents] didn't tell you that when they got up there and testified.

"James Bergstrom grows up and goes to high school. He marries and goes in the navy. We give him points for that. Then after, he sexually assaults his wife, ties her up, even though she's been a rape victim herself. He starts his window peeping. He ends up in the psychiatric ward in the navy hospital. He gets released and—our good fortune—this guy moves to our town . . .

"He enters these houses. A woman at home paying bills, he ties her up at gunpoint, sexually assaults her while she's terrified for her daughter and herself. Then you're supposed to give him credit for not beating her up? This guy doesn't get any points for not beating people up. He went into their homes. He went into their places of refuge, where they had a right to be safe. He walked into their homes and raped them. It still affects them today. He gave them all life sentences. They can't get rid of it.

"How many rapes would it take before Mr. Easterling agrees this guy needs to go to prison?

"You heard the doctor. He's a pedophile, a power rapist, a voyeur. He is the kind of guy you put in prison. He's compulsive and he's dangerous. He's obviously one of the sickest people you've seen. This guy needs to be locked up for a long, long time. Mr. Easterling told you he's going to get out someday and do it again. So you better make it the maximum. The only way to protect society from people like him is to lock them up and throw away the key. Let Mother Nature and Father Time cure him."

After the jury left the room, James Bergstrom was quickly shuffled out of the courtroom to a holding cell to await the jury's verdict. On the way out, he shot Linda an angry gaze. Instead of the repentant demeanor he'd so carefully cultivated throughout the trial, he now appeared openly defiant and angry.

After he left, the crowd broke into factions. The Bergstroms sat alone, not talking to anyone, even each other. James C. stared down dejectedly at his hands. Frank Fidelibus made his way over to where the victims clustered together. He hadn't talked to Sandy Colyard since shortly after James Bergstrom's arrest. The women were giggling, nervously, and Fidelibus suspected they felt exposed in a room where so many knew the intimate details of what James Bergstrom had done to them.

The minutes, then hours, clicked off the courtroom clock at a maddeningly slow pace. Linda sat alone. Still under a gag order, she couldn't discuss the case with anyone, especially not the reporters scattered throughout the room. It was impossible to concentrate on anything other than what might be going on in the jury room. She couldn't even begin to guess the extent of her ex-husband's retribution if the jury agreed with Danny Easterling and not Chuck Rosenthal. The hell she'd lived could either end or take a new turn in this courtroom.

It was after four P.M.—nearly two hours since the jury began deliberations—when Linda approached her husband's victims. Kimberly Greenmen hadn't returned for sentencing, but Sandy Colyard, Jesse Neal, Cindy McKenzie, and Maggie Heller opened their circle to let Linda in as she approached. "I want y'all to know how sorry I am," she told them. "I wished I could have stopped him sooner. I tried. I'm sorry for what y'all have been through. I was raped once and I know how that felt. I'm sorry. I really wish I could have stopped him sooner."

The buzzer sounded, indicating the jury was returning, and Linda hurried back toward her seat to await the verdict.

"Who's that?" asked one of the women as she walked away.

"That's his wife," whispered another. "The rapist's wife."

Frank Fidelibus, who'd heard the exchange, whispered to the women as Linda walked away. "You've got to understand she was a victim, too," he said. "It wasn't her fault. She did everything she could. In fact, if it wasn't for Linda Bergstrom, her husband would still be free. She's the one who turned him in."

Reassessing Linda Bergstrom, the women hurried to their seats. When Linda glanced back at them, Maggie Heller gave her a friendly smile. It was a thank you.

Moments later, the bailiff escorted James back into the courtroom. Perhaps knowing their decision had already been reached and his remorse was no longer an issue, he glared openly at them as they took their seats. Danny Easterling stood beside him. He had done his best for his client. He'd reminded the jury that they had to consider the full range of punishment, including probation. Now it was out of his hands.

"Have you, members of the jury, reached a decision?" Judge Walker queried.

"Yes, Your Honor, we have."

The bailiff took the sheets of paper, typed charges with a sentence indicated after each, from the jury foreman and handed them to the judge. Linda said a silent prayer, *Please let it end here.*

"In case number 628630 on the first charge of burglary," Walker read in a deep, booming voice that resonated against the brown paneling of the courtroom walls, "we, the jury, sentence James Bergstrom to ten years in the Texas prison system."

Linda's hands were shaking. A ten-year sentence could translate to less than a year in prison. James sought her out in the crowd and glared.

"On the second count, aggravated sexual assault, we, the jury, sentence James Bergstrom to ninety-nine years in the Texas prison system . . ."

Linda slumped against the hard-backed pew, years of tension slipping layer by layer from her shoulders.

"Count three, aggravated sexual assault, ninety-nine years," the judge continued. "Count four, aggravated sexual assault, ninety-nine years . . . Count five, aggravated sexual assault, ninety nine years . . ."

Linda mentally checked off the counts and sentences. Four ninty-nine-year sentences. It would be fifteen years before James Bergstrom could even be considered for parole. That was time enough to raise her daughter and build a new life. Relief flooded through Linda, and she laughed nervously. She could feel James staring at her, his hate boring into her. She smiled back at him, defiant. He could no longer hurt her. She and Ashley would be safe for a very long time.

As Linda walked from the courtroom, she heard Irene Bergstrom sobbing. She looked over and saw James C. sitting stiffly beside his wife, making no effort to comfort her.

Outside the courtroom, in the austere corridor, a pack of reporters clustered around Linda Bergstrom. The bright lights of the television cameras glowed, tape recorders ran, reporters jotted notes on small pads they cupped in their palms.

"Mrs. Bergstrom," one reporter called out. "How do you feel about the sentence?"

"He got what he deserved," she said, smiling wearily.

Then, as reporters shouted questions, Linda Bergstrom turned and walked away. She had Ashley to pick up at the baby-sitters', and she wanted to stop by Colt Hargraves's home to thank him one more time for believing in her when so few others listened. That done, there was so much else to do. By the following morning, when the sun broke through the clouds, she felt certain she would be ready to tackle even more important business, that of living her new life.

Afterword

It's rare to gaze into the eyes of pure evil. It's an impossible experience to forget, one that can haunt a lifetime.

I'd covered crime cases for nearly a decade when, in the fall of 1992, I went to the Harris County Jail to interview James Bergstrom. Linda had urged him to talk with me, to tell his story in the hope that it could help others. "I want people to understand what a serial rapist is like," she'd said. "What goes through his mind." Linda had already filed for a divorce, but James was intent on keeping the marriage together. He'd agreed to talk to me only to please her.

We sat in an office on the jail's second floor. On the floors above us, men and women whiled away long hours in windowless cells, under the glow of fluorescent lights. Some awaited their trials, calling lawyers to plan strategies on the jail pay phones and urging family and friends to send money. Others, those with sentences of months rather than years, counted off the days of their confinements, envisioning walking past the guards and out the maze of doors to freedom. For inmates like James, whose sentences consisted of decades, the jail was a temporary stop before being transported to one of the prisons stretched across Texas, dismal places bordered by cyclone fences and razor wire where inmates had little to do but jockey for favors and try to outwit one another and the guards.

"I don't know why Linda is making me talk to you," James said, glowering at me. We sat only a few feet apart, and I could feel his tension. He was anxious and jumpy. "I don't want my face out there. The guys inside don't like guys like me."

Even within prison there is a hierarchy. Rapists aren't

popular inmates; other criminals scorn them. Those who sexually assault women are held near the lowest level of prison esteem, below murderers and slightly above pedophiles. Although he had yet to disappear behind prison walls, James already claimed he was being bullied.

Despite his misgivings, Bergstrom talked openly with me that day. As Linda had hoped, he told me about growing up, his family life, the seeds of his fascination with control and domination, the building desire he felt stirring in him even as a young man. "I watched television a lot," he said. "And I liked those scenes, like in the old westerns, where the women were tied up and gagged. I liked the idea that I could do that to a woman and have her in my power, and do whatever I wanted to her."

After we discussed his past, he recounted his time in the navy, those months at sea when he planned how he'd live out the urges that were quickly strengthening into obsessions. By the time his sub docked, women were at danger merely driving on the same highway as James Bergstrom, walking down the street, or passing him in a shopping mall. He admitted that his frustrations built, and he'd grown successively more dangerous. At first, he ran away if a woman fought back. In the end, Bergstrom was so bold that he raped one woman while her young child hid nearby. Of course, there were those chilling words to his final victim, the high school cheerleader he threatened to kill.

Yet remarkably, as we talked, it became clear that Bergstrom's fantasies clouded his view of reality. In his eyes, the women wanted him as much as he wanted them. James believed he'd done nothing wrong. Although the women protested and fought back, begging him to leave, he insisted he was merely fulfilling their unspoken desires.

"I saw the way she looked at me," he said about one victim. "She wanted me to do everything I did to her. She wanted more."

When Bergstrom talked with me about his victims, his chest puffed out with bravado. He relished retelling his exploits, his grand successes. That he damaged the lives of his victims and their families didn't impinge on his enjoyment. The only thing James Bergstrom regretted was getting caught.

"Linda knew about my problem. I thought she understood," he said, his face flushed with anger and his fists clenched. "She turned me in. It's her fault that I'm here. It's her fault that I won't get the care that doctor at my trial said I needed for my problem."

"My problem," Bergstrom said, over and over.

Certainly, he had made it Linda's problem as well. "It was personal," she said, recounting how she feared Ashley would ultimately become one of his victims. "I wanted him put away, forever."

As Chuck Rosenthal told the jurors, Bergstrom had also become society's problem. Perhaps he hadn't listened when his own witness, the expert psychologist hired by his lawyer, admitted Bergstrom's "problem" would take many years of therapy and medication, and even then probably not be cured. James Bergstrom free to wander the streets was every woman's nightmare.

When his demeanor wasn't prideful, Bergstrom looked downcast, portraying himself as the victim. He'd had a difficult childhood, he lamented. In school, he hadn't fit in, and he'd been bullied at times. In James Bergstrom's world, everyone else was to blame. He saw only one victim, himself.

Interviews with a psychopath are tricky. At least in the beginning, the interviewer has to rein in disgust, animosity, even fear. Like a police officer hearing a confession, a journalist has to put her feelings aside, to let the murderer or rapist tell his or her tale, without reacting. The wrong expression, a too sharply pointed phrase, and the interview ends prematurely, leaving questions unanswered. Those unanswered questions prevent uncovering the truth, a necessity if one hopes to expose the monster in the shadows and destroy it.

Through my first two interviews with Bergstrom, I sat

back, hiding my disdain, while he expounded on his version of his life and his crimes. Finally, on my third visit to the jail, just a few days before he left for TDCJ, I'd heard all I needed to hear, and I couldn't hold back any longer. I'd brought a card for James to sign, one he asked me to mail to Ashley. As he signed his name inside it, in the same precise hand I'd seen on his navy letters, he talked of Linda, saying that no matter what, she'd always be his wife. "We were married," he said. "The church doesn't recognize divorce."

When I said nothing, he turned again to his victims, losing himself in the memories, so joyous to him, so horrific for his victims. Again he insisted that the women had lusted after him as he'd desired them.

His smug expression sickened me.

"James, that's simply not true. It's all a product of your diseased mind," I said, the mask finally abandoned, my face revealing the contempt I held him in. "Those women hate you. They despise you. You had to threaten them with a knife or a gun before they'd submit to you. And every second with you was a nightmare they'll be troubled by throughout their lives. What you did is absolutely evil, and you have no one to blame for being in prison but yourself."

James stared up at me, and his eyes hardened. For the first time, I saw the man Linda lived with, the angry, fuming, bristling James, a bundle of jagged rage that could strike without notice, a man with so much hate inside him it changed his very appearance. The broad smile turned to a sinister sneer, his jaw clenched, thick veins appeared running down his forehead, and he stared at me with derision.

"This wasn't your little problem, James," I went on, glaring back at him. "There is a monster inside of you. It's a monster you allowed to take over your life, to twist you into something vile."

During our time together he'd talked of God and religion. At one point, James recounted a Bible story, comparing himself to Job, the righteous man tormented by the devil.

"You portray yourself as a martyr," I said. "You're not the victim; you're the perpetrator, the assailant, the embodiment of sin. In the Bible, you are the devil."

The loathing in James Bergstrom's eyes grew more intense, and I saw him raise a clenched fist. The guard moved forward, and Bergstrom lowered his hand. Silently, I stood up to leave. When I turned back, just before walking away, I said, "Those women didn't want you, they loathed you. They are the victims, not you. Until you realize that, you will never change."

As I left, the guard shackled Bergstrom and led him off to be taken back to his cell. Despite my relief at being able to tell Bergstrom who he truly was, I departed feeling ineloquent. There were so many things I wanted to say to him, to open his eyes, to make him confront the fiend he'd become. I'd failed. In truth, I was at best naïve. Years later, I would realize there was nothing I could have said. At some point, cutting through the choppy waters of the Pacific in a nuclear submarine, James Bergstrom had convinced himself he had all the rights and the women he chose as his victims had none.

Fifteen years later, I still look back on my meetings with Bergstrom and shudder. I have never requested a follow-up interview with him. I don't ever again want to look into his eyes and see the seething hatred bottled up inside him.

I have seen Linda again. After years of being afraid of making another commitment, chancing another mistake, she married a police officer and they've built a good life together. They have a home, and Ashley has grown into a bright and beautiful young woman. She's reed thin and into ballet and dance, and doing well in school. In the near future, she'll enter college, with the possibilities of a lifetime ahead of her.

While young, she visited James in prison with his parents. As early as Ashley could understand, Linda began explaining James to her in bits and pieces. By the time Ashley reached middle school, she understood who Bergstrom was.

"I don't have any desire to have a relationship with him," she said. "Ever."

One thing hasn't changed over the decades. Linda still worries about James. He is the darkness that stalks her life. Like me, she fears that one day the prison doors will open and he'll walk out. Perhaps he's spent his time in prison plotting how to get what he wants with less risk next time. "I'm afraid that if he gets out he may kill his next victims," she said. "He won't take the chance that they'll testify and send him back to jail."

The years have passed quickly. To our dismay, James became eligible for parole in March 2007. To keep him inside, Linda, Ashley, and I went on national television and started a protest letter campaign, asking men and women across the nation to write letters to the Texas Department of Criminal Justice voicing their opposition to James being granted parole. It worked, and in July 2007, James's parole was denied. But he'll become eligible again in July 2010, and every two to three years from that point on. The reality is that we will have to be vigilant and continue the fight.

If you'd like to help keep James Bergstrom behind bars, it's a simple process. You don't have to be a Texan to file a protest. All you have to do is write a letter or send an e-mail saying you believe James Bergstrom should not be set free on parole, that he continues to be a danger to society, and that he deserves to spend the rest of his life in prison.

In your letter, include the following information:
Name: James Edward Bergstrom
TDCJ Number: 00659297
SID Number: 04408281
Birth date: 4/6/1963

Your protest can be submitted via e-mail to: *victim.svc@ tdcj.state.tx.us*

Or fax it to: 512-452-0825
Or snail mail to: TDCJ Victims Services
8712 Shoal Creek Boulevard Suite 265
Austin, TX 78757

To those of you who join us in our protest, from Linda, Ashley, and me, and from all the women who would cross paths with James Bergstrom if he were ever set free: Thank you.

Shocking true accounts of murder Texas-style from

KATHRYN CASEY

A DESCENT INTO HELL
THE TRUE STORY OF AN ALTAR BOY, A CHEERLEADER, AND A TWISTED TEXAS MURDER
978-0-06-123087-5

The gripping true story of one of the most brutal slayings in University of Texas history.

DIE, MY LOVE
A TRUE STORY OF REVENGE, MURDER, AND TWO TEXAS SISTERS
978-0-06-084620-6

When college professor Fred Jablin was found dead in his driveway, police immediately turned their attention to his ex-wife—who had lost a bitter custody battle.

SHE WANTED IT ALL
A TRUE STORY OF SEX, MURDER, AND A TEXAS MILLIONAIRE
978-0-06-056764-4

Trophy wife Celeste Beard wasn't satisfied with a luxurious lifestyle and her rich Austin media mogul husband's devotion—so she took his life!

A WARRANT TO KILL
A TRUE STORY OF OBSESSION, LIES AND A KILLER COP
978-0-380-78041-9

Problems had always followed Susan White, but when she remarried and moved to Houston's posh suburbs, she thought the past was behind her—until she met a deputy sheriff named Kent McGowen who would soon become her worst nightmare.